DESIGNING GOVERNANCE STRUCTURES FOR PERFORMANCE AND ACCOUNTABILITY

DEVELOPMENTS IN AUSTRALIA AND GREATER CHINA

DESIGNING GOVERNANCE STRUCTURES FOR PERFORMANCE AND ACCOUNTABILITY

DEVELOPMENTS IN AUSTRALIA AND GREATER CHINA

EDITED BY ANDREW PODGER,
TSAI-TSU SU, JOHN WANNA,
HON S. CHAN AND MEILI NIU

Australian
National
University

PRESS

ANU PRESS

ΛΝΖ SOG Australia & New Zealand School Of Government

Published by ANU Press
The Australian National University
Acton ACT 2601, Australia
Email: anupress@anu.edu.au

Available to download for free at press.anu.edu.au

ISBN (print): 9781760463595
ISBN (online): 9781760463601

WorldCat (print): 1162836373
WorldCat (online): 1162821573

DOI: 10.22459/DGSPA.2020

Cover design and layout by ANU Press

CONTENTS

FIGURES

TABLES

ABBREVIATIONS AND ACRONYMS

ACAT	Aged Care Assessment Team
ACFA	Aged Care Financing Authority (Aus)
ACLEI	Australian Commission for Law Enforcement Integrity
AIHW	Australian Institute of Health and Welfare
ANAO	Australian National Audit Office
AOTC	Australian and Overseas Telecommunications Corporation Limited
APS	Australian Public Service
ASC	Administrative Service Center (PRC)
ATS	administrative trinity system (ROC)
ATSIC	Aboriginal and Torres Strait Islanders Commission (Aus)
BQTS	Bureau of Quality and Technology Supervision (PRC)
CAC Act	*Commonwealth Authorities and Companies Act 1997* (Aus)
CBO	community-based organisations
CEO	chief executive officer
CEPD	Council for Economic Planning and Development (ROC)
CES	Commonwealth Employment Service (Aus)
CFAR	Commonwealth Financial Accountability Review (Aus)
CGC	Commonwealth Grants Commission (Aus)
COAG	Council of Australian Governments

CPB	Central Planning Bureau (ROC)
CPC	Communist Party of China
csQCA	crisp-set QCA
DAS	Department of Administrative Services (Aus)
DCSP	Delivering Community Services in Partnership (Aus)
DEETYA	Department of Education, Employment, Training and Youth Affairs (Aus)
DGBAS	Directorate-General of Budget, Accounting and Statistics (ROC)
DGPA	Directorate-General of Personnel Administration (ROC)
DHS	Department of Human Services (Aus)
DM	deputy mayor
DPP	Democratic Progressive Party (ROC)
DSS	Department of Social Services (Aus)
EPB	Environmental Protection Bureau (PRC)
FDM	first deputy mayor
FMA Act	*Financial Management and Accountability Act 1997* (Aus)
FOI	freedom of information
FSANZ	Food Standards Australia New Zealand
fsQCA	fuzzy-set QCA
GBE	government business enterprise
HDI	human development index
HFE	horizontal fiscal equalisation
HIP	Home Insulation Program (Aus)
IAG	Integrity Agencies Group (Aus)
IMD	Institute for Management Development (Switzerland)
IPAA	Institute of Public Administration Australia
MEP	Ministry of Environment Protection (PRC)
MoG	machinery of government
Moran Review	Review of Australian Government Administration 2010
MPC	Office of the Merit Protection Commissioner (Aus)

NBN	national broadband network (Aus)
NCC	National Communications Commission (ROC)
NDC	National Development Council (ROC)
NDIA	National Disability Insurance Agency (Aus)
NDIS	National Disability Insurance Scheme (Aus)
NDRC	National Development and Reform Commission (PRC)
NFP	not-for-profit
NGO	non-government organisation
NHPA	National Health Performance Authority (Aus)
NPG	new public governance
NPM	new public management
NSC	National Science Council (ROC)
NYBMR	New York Bureau of Municipal Research
OECD	Organisation for Economic Co-operation and Development
OMB	Office of Management and Budget (US)
OTC	Overseas Telecommunications Corporation Limited (Aus)
PA	public administration
PGPA Act	*Public Governance, Performance and Accountability Act 2013* (Aus)
PM&C	Department of Prime Minister and Cabinet (Aus)
PMG	Postmaster-General's Department (Aus)
PRC	People's Republic of China
PS Act	*Public Service Act 1999* (Aus)
PWEC	Party–Government Work Evaluation Commission (ROC)
QCA	qualitative comparative analysis
R&E	research and evaluation (ROC)
RDEC	Research, Development and Evaluation Commission (ROC)
ROC	Republic of China

SEPA	State Environmental Protection Agency (PRC)
SOE	state-owned enterprise
Telstra	Telstra Corporation Limited (Aus)
VAI	vertical administrative institutions
WEF	World Economic Forum
WTO	World Trade Organization

CONTRIBUTORS

Hon S Chan is a professor in the Department of Public Policy, City University of Hong Kong. His research focuses on civil service reforms, cadre personnel management and performance evaluation and management in China. He has published extensively in major journals in the field.

José Chiu-C Chen is Professor and Chair at the Department of Public Management and Policy, Tunghai University, where his teaching and research are focused on non-profit management, personnel administration reform and urban governance. Professor Chen received his PhD from National Chengchi University, Taiwan. He was elected as the president of Taiwan Association for Schools of Public Administration and Affairs (TASPAA) in 2019. He has served as a committee member or consultant to various government agencies, non-profit organisations and social enterprises.

Zitao Chen is a PhD candidate at the School of International and Public Affairs, Shanghai Jiao Tong University. His research interests are in public policy analysis and government performance management.

David Gilchrist is an accountant and economic historian within the University of Western Australia Business School. He undertakes practical, industry-ready research in the area of policy and practice of human services delivery in Australia. Along with his academic work, he has held senior roles in all three sectors of the Australian economy, including as the assistant auditor-general for Western Australia, and has taught at the London School of Economics. The focus of Professor Gilchrist's research is the National Disability Insurance Scheme (NDIS), its pricing and sustainability.

Annwyn Godwin is the inaugural Chief Executive Officer of the Independent Parliamentary Expenses Authority (IPEA). She has held the dual appointments of Australian Public Service Merit Protection Commissioner and Parliamentary Service Merit Protection Commissioner over two terms since 2008. She joined the Australian Public Service in 1990, and has extensive experience in corporate and related fields. Over her career she has served in the senior executive service in a number of agencies and departments including Customs, Immigration and Agriculture. She has also served as Norfolk Island Public Service Commissioner.

Yi-Huah Jiang is the Bauhinia Chair Professor, Institute of Strategic and International Affairs at National Chung Cheng University, Taiwan. He received his BA and MA from National Taiwan University, and PhD in political science from Yale University. Before joining National Chung Cheng University, he was professor in the Department of Public Policy, City University of Hong Kong. He was also a visiting scholar at Cambridge University, Columbia University, Harvard University and Stanford University. Jiang's academic interests lie in political philosophy, democratic theory, national identity, general education and Taiwanese politics.

Helen K Liu is Associate Professor in the Department of Political Science and the Graduate Institute of Public Affairs, National Taiwan University (NTU). Before joining NTU, she worked in the Department of Politics and Public Administration, University of Hong Kong. She has served as an emerging scholar at the Urban Institute, Washington DC; a summer fellow in the RGK Center on Philanthropy, University of Texas at Austin; and a visiting scholar at Peking University. Her research interests are in inter-organisational networks, social service provision, collaborative governance, crowdsourcing adaptation and non-profit management.

Fanrong Meng is Professor at the School of Public Policy and Administration and Executive Director of Research at the Center for Performance Management, Xi'an Jiaotong University. Her teaching and research are focused on performance management in public sectors, environmental governance, science and technology policy and management.

Meili Niu is a professor in the School of Government, Sun Yat-sen University, and the Deputy Director of the Center for Chinese Public Administration Research. Her research focuses on public budgeting and finance. She has over 10 years' experience working as a consultant and adviser to Chinese governments and congresses on budgetary reforms and policy evaluation. She serves on the editorial board of several academic journals, including the *Journal of Public Administration* (Chinese); the *Journal of Public Budgeting, Accounting & Financial Management*, *Perspectives on Public Management & Governance*, and *State and Local Government Review.*

Andrew Podger is Honorary Professor of Public Policy at The Australian National University. He was previously a senior public servant in the Australian Government, with roles including Public Service Commissioner, secretary of the Department of Health and Aged Care, secretary of the Department of Housing and Regional Development and secretary of the Department of Administrative Services. He was also national president of the Institute of Public Administration Australia from 2004 to 2010.

Bennis Wai Yip So is Head and Professor at the Department of Public Administration, National Chengchi University in Taiwan. His recent research interests are in civil service systems in East Asia, and performance management of the public sector. He has published in *Australian Journal of Public Administration*, *Public Management Review*, *China Quarterly*, and *Asia Pacific Journal of Public Administration*.

Tsai-tsu Su is Professor and Director at the Graduate Institute of Public Affairs, National Taiwan University, where her teaching and research are focused on public budgeting, administrative reform and policy analysis. Professor Su received her PhD from Carnegie Mellon University, Pittsburgh, and taught at the State University of New York at Stony Brook before returning to Taiwan. She has served as a committee member or consultant to various government agencies and was the president of the Taiwan Association for Schools of Public Administration and Affairs for two terms.

John Wanna is Emeritus Professor in both the School of Politics and International Relations, College of Arts and Social Sciences, The Australian National University; and the School of Politics and International Relations at Griffith University. He was formerly the Sir John Bunting chair in public administration with the Australia and New Zealand School of Government until 2019.

Mike Woods is Professor of Health Economics at the University of Technology Sydney and a visiting scholar at The Australian National University. His research interests are in health system reform, aged care and economic reform. He was formerly the deputy chairman of the Australian Productivity Commission and was presiding commissioner on more than 20 national inquiries into aspects of economic reform.

Jiannan Wu is Distinguished Professor and Executive Vice Director of the China Institute of Urban Governance at Shanghai Jiao Tong University. He has published extensively in leading Chinese journals and some English-language ones, including *Public Administration, Review of Public Personnel Administration, Public Administration Quarterly,* and *International Public Management Review.* He has served as the vice-president of the National Government Performance Management Research Association of China since 2006, been a member of the Chinese Expert Committee of International Institute of Administrative Sciences (IIAS) since 2010 and treasurer of the Asian Association of Public Administration since 2016. His research interests include performance management, reform and innovation.

Bo Yan is Professor in the School of Public Policy and Administration, Xi'an Jiaotong University. He received his PhD in management from Xi'an Jiaotong University in 2011. He is also a board member of the China-America Association for Public Affairs (CAAPA). His research interests include performance management, accountability and innovation. He has published in a range of journals, including *Australian Journal of Public Administration* and a number of Chinese academic journals.

Pichamon Yeophantong is an Australian Research Council DECRA Fellow and Senior Lecturer in International Relations and Development at the University of New South Wales (Canberra). A political scientist by training, she is an expert on Chinese politics and foreign policy. Pichamon has served as a consultant on regional development issues to the Africa Progress Panel and Overseas Development Institute, among other organisations, and sits on the research committee of Jubilee Australia. Previously, Pichamon was a Global Leaders Fellow at the University of Oxford and Princeton University.

1

DESIGNING GOVERNANCE STRUCTURES FOR PERFORMANCE AND ACCOUNTABILITY

Developments in Australia and greater China

Andrew Podger, Hon S Chan and John Wanna

Introduction

This book – a symposium of papers originating from a workshop[1] at City University, Hong Kong, in June 2017 – examines how governance structures may be designed to promote performance and to ensure accountability. It describes developments in Australia, the People's Republic of China (PRC) and Taiwan.

---

1   The workshop was organised by the Greater China Australia Dialogue on Public Administration, a collaboration amongst scholars across the People's Republic of China (including Hong Kong and Macao), the Republic of China (Taiwan) and Australia. Workshops have been held each year since 2011 involving both scholars and practitioners who are keen to learn more about developments and practices in each other's jurisdictions on issues of common interest.

The book explores in particular the executive arm of government's institutional arrangements for advising on and implementing government policies and programs. It does not aim to explore the basic institutional arrangements of government, though these inevitably shape the structures within the executive. Rather, chapters explore theories of organisational forms and functions in public administration, the 'core' agency structures used in the different jurisdictions, the structures used to deliver public services (including non-government organisational arrangements) and other 'non-core' agency structures such as government business enterprises, regulatory organisations and 'integrity' organisations.

This overview highlights some of the key issues canvassed in the following chapters and the recent developments they describe and analyse. It also fills in the inevitable gaps that exist in the volume's coverage of practice in the three jurisdictions.

The concepts of performance and accountability used in the chapters vary from a narrow focus on administrative delivery with oversight by superior authorities to a much broader appreciation of the impact of both policy and administration against desired outcomes with public reporting and accountability. The concepts are shaped by institutional arrangements, and are also evolving in each jurisdiction over time.

Theories of forms, functions, accountability and performance

As John Wanna argues in Chapter 2, principles for the design of organisational structures are more often honoured in the breach than in the observance, and many contextual factors may influence them. At the same time, structures do help to shape the way that functions are managed and there may be some truth in the adage 'form should follow function'.

Wanna also notes the previous century's increasing emphasis on ensuring bureaucratic structures, such as those described by Max Weber, are democratically accountable upwards, to governing supervisors, and outward to the wider community. More recently a particular emphasis has also been placed on accountability for performance.

The way in which such accountability is achieved is determined in large part by each jurisdiction's political institutional framework. There are considerable differences across the PRC, Taiwan and Australia, perhaps the most significant concerning the relationship between politics and administration. Both Australia and Taiwan have a formal separation of roles while the PRC's party-state system features an integration of politics and administration. Nonetheless, Wanna's discussion of balancing the desire for conformity and the benefits of flexibility, and of balancing political control and 'relative autonomy', has relevance in the PRC as well as Australia and Taiwan, as all three look to improve both accountability and performance, however defined.

These universal issues are addressed in other chapters, including those that explore the increasing use of non-government organisations to deliver public services and the various contractual devices used to ensure a measure of accountability to the public, not just to the executive. The appropriate, or desired, balances vary with the functions involved.

Wanna and Andrew Podger try to map functions to structures with different balances of control and autonomy, not only to describe the differences and relationships but also to suggest some normative framework (notwithstanding the many factors that affect the structures used). Both authors also refer to the influence of informal conventions and practices on the way structures operate, including professional values, norms and cultures, which is a theme also reflected in other chapters.

Podger further draws on developments in institutional and organisational theory and their continuing relevance to public administration structures and processes, particularly with the current interest in behavioural economics and innovation.

High-level structural trends

A common development in the three jurisdictions has been to reduce the number of 'core' departments or agencies over time. In part this was intended to help the political leadership exercise greater control over the whole of government.

Podger refers to Australia's introduction of 'mega-departments' in 1987, which allowed a reduction in the size of the cabinet, with each 'portfolio department' represented in cabinet by its 'portfolio minister'. Non-cabinet ministers and parliamentary secretaries were appointed to support portfolio ministers in defined areas of responsibility. The arrangement continues to operate, supporting a generally effective cabinet coordination process, though it has not proven to be as successful as originally intended in providing ongoing stability in (portfolio) departmental responsibilities (the 2020 arrangements have also blurred lines of accountability between administrative structures and the ministry). Australian governments frequently (too frequently, perhaps) engage in machinery of government changes, often for expedient reasons. Looking back, two recent trends can be detected: a proliferation of agencies occurred around the early 2000s, followed by a rationalisation of agencies from 2013–14 and a reconsolidation of functional agencies under umbrella organisations (e.g. the combination of national security agencies under the Home Affairs ministry).

Yi-Huah Jiang reports in Chapter 4 that Taiwan has had more difficulty in streamlining its overall structure because the Legislative Yuan and not the Executive Yuan establishes the key agencies and determines their functions (in Australia, it is only the prime minister who has the power to determine the Administrative Arrangements Orders that allocate functions and responsibilities to ministerial departments). While modest rationalisation has been achieved, with indicators of some improvements in performance, Jiang identifies a list of lessons to be learned from the attempts at comprehensive structural reform within Taiwan's overall institutional framework, highlighting the various forces constraining reform. He concludes that successful reform may only be possible if Taiwan moves from its unique five arms of government to a more standard three-arms framework (executive, legislature and judiciary), under either a presidential or parliamentary system.

The PRC's institutional framework involves, at least formally, a centralised system controlled by the authoritarian Party leadership and administered by the executive (the State Council). Within this party-state framework, the State Council has modernised its organisational structures through the introduction of umbrella ministries and related agencies. Coordination within the executive arm is undertaken by the General Office of the State Council and core ministries such as the National Development and Reform Commission and the Ministry of Finance, within which the National Budget Office has responsibility for managing an increasingly modern budgetary system. Line ministries and related agencies have a high degree of specialisation and exercise varying degrees of devolved autonomy, which cascades down levels of government with coordination at each level supported by the corresponding arm of the finance ministry (each level also having its own party-state framework of devolved authority).

Non-core agencies and non-government service providers

As Wanna highlights, a key issue in structural design is the balancing of political control and 'relative autonomy'. Podger refers similarly to varying 'degrees of independence'. Arguably, this balancing has been at the forefront of Australian institutional design, although forces of independence and control should be seen as contending discourses.

The Australian experience reflects longstanding organisational pragmatism informed by Western democratic theory, suggesting that administration requires a degree of independence for optimal performance (and to some extent limiting political risk). Whether based on the United Kingdom's 1854 Northcote–Trevelyan Report (Northcote & Trevelyan 1854) or the 1886 Woodrow Wilson lecture on 'The study of administration' (Wilson 1886), most Western democracies have established professional merit-based civil services that are relatively impartial and non-partisan, while nonetheless implementing the policies of the elected government (if at times through the bureaucratic lens of self-interest).

In Australia, successive public service legislation since 1902 has formalised the separation of politics from day-to-day administration and this applies to both core and most non-core agencies. There are, nonetheless, varying degrees of independence according to the formal structures used as well as to informal conventions and practices. The main determinant of independence is whether the organisation function is classified within the 'public service' (low independence), as opposed to being classified in the wider 'public sector' (higher independence) – and a similar set of arrangements exists in neighbouring New Zealand.

The Australian chapters identify the main structures that have evolved within jurisdictions. Apart from the 'core' ministerial departments with limited degrees of independence from political control, these include non-departmental service delivery agencies, statutory regulatory authorities, integrity organisations and government business enterprises. Wanna dissects such a classification into the different dimensions of authority that may be exercised with a degree of autonomy. Podger highlights how the use of different structures and their accountability frameworks have changed over the last 30 years under new public management (NPM) and new public governance (NPG) (such as through contracting out, commercialisation, privatisation and networking). In drawing attention to increasing inconsistencies in recent years, with some functions being subject to increased political control while similar functions have been allowed greater independence, Podger's concern is that such inconsistency may adversely affect performance. He suggests a more coherent and consistent approach so that formal structures and informal processes complement each other in setting the degree of independence appropriate to the particular function.

Mike Woods and David Gilchrist explore in more detail Australia's developments with regard to the delivery of aged care and disability services. Recent innovations in these two areas reflect both institutional theory and neoliberal ideas. Although these contrasting sources of ideas differ in some important respects, they are both premised upon or presuppose a considerable degree of independence from politics, especially through the use of non-government organisations (NGOs) to deliver services as well as greater consumer control over what services are delivered. The reliance on NGOs to deliver services brings with it the need for careful financing arrangements and effective regulation to protect consumers: the new structures that have been established to meet these requirements are more independent of political control in the case of disability services than in the case of aged care services. To date, Australian governments have not relied as much as Singapore's administration on consumer or client satisfaction (or the obverse – complaint systems used to recalibrate service and improve customisation).

David Gilchrist examines developments in the relationship between government and the not-for-profit (NFP) sector in Western Australia (WA). Following an economic audit of the WA public sector in 2009, the then government established a Delivering Community Services in Partnership (DCSP) policy aimed at strengthening the relationship between government and the NFP sector and improving the delivery of community services. A partnership forum was established with a view to supporting a more collaborative approach to policy and practice, to recognise the value of the NFP sector and to identify practical improvements to the way the sector is used. Gilchrist led a series of evaluations of the related initiatives that found further infrastructure investment was needed within government and within the NFP sector, including for training and systems and to streamline contracting processes; they also found there had been insufficient funding of change management to effect the paradigm change intended.

Annwyn Godwin, a former merit protection commissioner in Australia, describes the way her office operated as an example of an 'integrity organisation', and how she was influenced by a number of models of public administration accountability promulgated in Australia since the early 2000s. These models responded to the growth in the number of different agencies and the impact of NPM and NPG. While the panoply of integrity organisations she describes have considerable independence protections in their statutes, she suggests that a more complex balancing of control and autonomy amongst different 'integrity organisations' is emerging, which is in part related to the extent they are expected to pursue enforcement of appropriate behaviour within government or pursue more educative roles. She also sees advantage in integrity organisations working together to optimise their impact.

Yi-Huah Jiang provides a broad overview of Taiwan's institutionalised internal monitoring practices involving its unique five arms of state and, in particular, the key functions of the Examination Yuan and Control Yuan that service and scrutinise the more familiar executive, legislative and judicial branches of government. In Taiwan's extended separation of powers, the Examination Yuan protects Taiwan's politically neutral public service, overseeing the application of the merit principle. In addition, the Control Yuan has administrative policy and oversight functions and is responsible for monitoring the other branches of government encompassing some of the key functions (such as audit and compliance) that, in Australia, are managed by so-called 'integrity organisations'. By its very existence as a separate yuan, the Control Yuan has considerable independence from political control by the executive. The Control Yuan has yet to develop a taste for conducting an assurance measurement of performance of either agencies or programs.

Within the executive, Jiang refers to 'functional institutions' that may broadly be compared to 'core' ministries, 'supportive institutions' that help the Office of the Premier to coordinate and monitor the work of the ministries and 'independent institutions' with a range of regulatory responsibilities. While the last group clearly has substantial independence from political control, the second group's degree of independence from political control is not clear from Jiang's chapter (despite being under the Office of the Premier) and may vary considerably. Jiang is also not convinced by calls for more independence and autonomy, noting the growing importance of collaboration across agencies.

The structures applying in the PRC are not addressed in this volume. Because there is a high degree of integration of politics and administration in mainland China, it is not possible to categorise PRC public sector organisations against a continuum from political control to independence and autonomy. There has been considerable effort in recent years to improve the professional capability of those advising government and making policy decisions and those delivering public services. Reforms over the last few decades indicate the potential to be clearer about organisations' respective accountability arrangements and degrees of independence.

PRC state-owned enterprises (SOEs), for example, have undergone reforms requiring them to be subject to more commercial forms of accountability while allowing them greater management flexibility. Also, social public service institutions such as universities, schools and hospitals focus on service delivery in line with the policies, financing and administrative rules imposed by the core ministries. In some cases, there has been a growing trend to contract NGOs to deliver some services, in parallel with increasing numbers of NGOs in civil society and a relaxation of top-down controls over them.

Nonetheless, under President Xi Jinping, party control across government agencies, including SOEs, and party influence over civil society, have increased significantly (Podger & Chan forthcoming; Song 2018; Shen, Yu and Zhou 2020). This has not detracted from measures to improve 'talent' and professional expertise amongst party cadres and other civil servants (Chen et al. 2015).

In other Chinese-based jurisdictional entities, such as Hong Kong, Taiwan and Singapore, community-based organisations have a much longer involvement in the provision of community support services. In this collection, José Chiu-C Chen and Helen K Liu explore the role of community-based organisations in Hong Kong and Taiwan, highlighting their potential role not only in delivering public services but also in representing their communities and providing space for active deliberation within their communities. Implicit is not only a degree of independence from the vicissitudes of contemporary politics and government policies, but the possibility of contributing to political deliberations consistent with moves towards 'collaborative governance'. Chen and Liu also suggest that the use of these organisations contributes to capacity building in the broader public sector.

Horizontal management and informal processes

Since the 1990s, Australia has joined other Anglophone countries in placing more emphasis on horizontal or whole-of-government approaches to address intractable policy challenges and so-called 'wicked problems'. This is now reflected in public service and financial management and accountability legislation promoting cooperation across and beyond government, even though formal accountability is still based primarily on vertical lines from departments and agencies through ministers to parliament.

This development, and the role of informal processes of collaboration, referred to in the articles by Wanna, Podger and Godwin, is still in its relative infancy. While it is clear that more funding and resources are committed to intractable social and environmental problems, marked improvements in outcomes are not yet evident. For instance, after more than a decade of attempting to 'close the gap' between the wellbeing of Indigenous and non-Indigenous Australians, only two of the targets set were on track according to the 2020 report (DPMC 2020); improvements were reported in some other areas including employment and health but no more than those experienced by non-Indigenous Australians.

The chapters by Fanrong Meng, Zitao Chen and Pichamon Yeophantong and by Bo Yan and Jiannan Wu address the challenges of horizontal management and the role of more informal process in the PRC.

Meng et al. examine why provinces in the PRC nominate to be pilot regions for vertical management of environmental protection. Two sets of conditions are identified, one relating to poorer provinces and the other to richer provinces. In both cases, horizontal competition plays a critical role, but poorer provinces have fewer environmental problems to address and better ecological resources and hence less public pressure and risks from being a pilot. In contrast, richer provinces have greater problems, more public pressure and the resources to deal with the issues, so the risks of not participating may be significant. The vertical management pilots are intended to identify ways to strengthen environmental protection through stronger central controls and greater professional expertise. Political control may well become stronger, but based more firmly on evidence of what works. As the authors caution, how vertical management fits alongside provincial horizontal management is yet to be determined.

Bo and Wu provide a fascinating case study of how a county's small leading group successfully pursued major reform despite doubts about the county's capacity and the possible implications for government employees. Critical to success was the role of the county's first deputy mayor, who led the small group of cadres responsible for the relevant county functions, and his style in managing meetings. The informal processes drew upon Chinese cultural mores to reward or shame participants, as well as acceptance of compromise to make progress. The group demonstrated how horizontal management can succeed in responding to vertical management directions.

Contrasting performance management and accountability in Anglo versus Chinese settings

A number of chapters highlight how different structures and their different balances of political control and independence give rise to different performance accountability arrangements: to whom are they accountable and for what?

Bennis Wai Yip So provides an interesting historical perspective on Taiwan's experience with performance management, contrasting this with the experience of Anglophone countries. He not only traces the long history of performance monitoring in Taiwan (and earlier in mainland China under the Kuomintang), but also how this was originally focused solely on ensuring the proper implementation of policies of the successive heads of government. Taiwan's performance management pathway, therefore, differed considerably from that of Anglophone countries implementing NPM reforms. With democratisation, however, Taiwan has more recently applied aspects of the NPM approach as it shifted first from policy implementation to management, and then to NPM-styled performance evaluation and public accountability.

Conclusions

The context within which reform of institutional structures is debated and pursued in these jurisdictions varies greatly. There are differences in the wider political institutional frameworks, jurisdictional histories, stages of economic development and social contexts. This results in numerous and diverse public policy and management challenges.

There is, however, shared interest in improving accountability and performance in government, and in finding the structures that best support accountability and performance.

In practice, many factors affect the structures used and the balancing involved between political control and administrative independence, and between conformity and flexibility. Nonetheless, some degree of independence and flexibility is conducive to professionalism and performance, and to ensuring outward accountability to organisations' clients and the broader public as well as upwards to organisations' governing supervisors. This is perhaps best illustrated by the growing interest across all jurisdictions in the use of NGOs to deliver some public services.

While typologies of structures and functions differ across these jurisdictions, the chapters in this book suggest that functions could be usefully mapped to different degrees of independence (and different areas of autonomy) to optimise performance and accountability, and hence to different structures. 'Core' functions assisting governments to set policies and determine priorities might best be situated towards the close political control end of the spectrum, while some regulatory functions requiring strict and consistent legal determination, and some government oversight or 'integrity' functions, might be towards the more independent end, with service delivery lying somewhere in between. Government business enterprises also need considerable management flexibility for high performance, but only if they are also subject to firm commercial-oriented accountability.

Such a mapping, however, will never provide more than a general guide, and a myriad of factors must also be taken into account, including experience, reputation and proven performance, and political interest. Informal practices and relationships also always affect the way different structures operate in practice.

In the final short chapter, Andrew Podger presents his reflections on possible lessons, particularly for the PRC. This is drawn not only from the material in the book and the workshop in 2017, but also from his wider observations of public administration practice in China over the last decade. Drawing on his close observation of developments in Australia, he also emphasises that reform of institutional structures is an ongoing challenge and indeed that Australian experience demonstrates serious risks to capability and performance from slowing or backtracking reform. In addition, he notes ways that Australia could learn from China without compromising its firm democratic principles.

References

Chen, L, Chan, H, Jie, G & Jianxing, Y 2015, 'Party management of talent: building a party-led, merit-based talent market in China', *Australian Journal of Public Administration*, vol 74, no 3, pp 298–311.

Department of Prime Minister and Cabinet (DPMC) 2020, *Closing the Gap: Prime Minister's Report 2020*, Commonwealth of Australia, Canberra.

Northcote, SH & Trevelyan, CE 1854, *Report on the Organisation of the Permanent Civil Service*, House of Commons, London.

Podger, A & Chan, H (forthcoming), 'The challenge of comparing public administration in China and Australia: developments and prospects for China', in M De Percy, C Althaus & A Podger (eds), *Public Administration and Politics in Practice: Essays in honour of John Wanna*, ANU Press, Canberra.

Shen, Y, Yu, J & Zhou, J 2020, 'The administration's retreat and the party's advance in the new era of Xi Jinping: The politics of the ruling party, the government and associations in China', *Journal of Chinese Political Science*, vol 25, pp 71–88.

Song, L 2018, 'State-owned enterprise reform in China: past, present and prospects', in R Garnault, L Song & C Fang (eds), *China's 40 Years of Reform and Development 1978–2019*, ANU Press, Canberra, doi.org/10.22459/CYRD.07.2018.19.

Wilson, W 1886, 'The study of administration', *Teaching American History*, accessed 20 Sep 2016, teachingamericanhistory.org/library/document/the-study-of-administration.

2

THEORISING PUBLIC BUREAUCRACIES

Comparing organisational purpose, function and form, while counter-posing political control versus bureaucratic autonomy

John Wanna

Recognisable forms of public bureaucracy and administrative cadre date back millennia and were especially prominent in ancient Egypt, Persia, the Graeco-Roman period and ancient China. These ancient bureaucracies were the earliest forms of state institutions that invented and/or developed some of the basic fundamentals of statecraft such as the creation of writing and record keeping, systems of taxation and tithes, property entitlement, investments in infrastructure, maintenance of public order, security and foreign affairs, as well as monumentalised forms of regime glorification and celebratory displays of power.

Most public bureaucracies from mediaeval to modern times modelled themselves on the two pre-existing forms of hierarchic organisation with which they were familiar and against which they could map themselves – religious and military institutions – with the churches providing more enduring examples of continuity and collective memory. The important lessons drawn from alternative hierarchies came to be regarded as principles geared to the maintenance of authority and organisational capacity (see Weber 1978) – including hierarchic structures and systems of authoritative control, with clear lines of command; the establishment of an administrative class enjoying fixed salaries, tenure of employment, selection on competence or experience and without having a proprietorial interest in the organisation; specialisation and the division of labour, the disaggregation of work duties and tasks giving organisations distinct areas of competence; organisations governed by internal rules and procedures providing stability, predictability and consistency; the assembly of official records and the significance of record keeping in exercising not only administration but also power; and, in later modern forms, the rational-legal determination of decision-making rather than dilettantism or personal whim.

Many of these inherited attributes of public organisation are evident in today's public organisations. Max Weber also noted sociologically that public bureaucracies developed informalities, collective norms and internalised modus operandi. They acted in covert ways, often developed secret languages or codes of communication and sometimes operated concealed budgetary systems (Weber 1978: 992). Public bureaucracies were simultaneously part of the edifice of the nation state but also a 'shadow state' operating from within.

Of course in practice many of these empirically observable 'principles' (which were transformed into generic normative guidance) were often more honoured in the breach than in the observance (see Gouldner 1954). Hierarchic control could be undermined by distance or powerful rival actors. Clear lines of command could be contravened, violated or convoluted. Offices were sometimes sold to willing aspirants, or given to kith and kin, and bribery and corruption prevailed. Staff often developed a virtual proprietorial interest in the organisations in which they served. Competency was aspirational not guaranteed. Decisions could be based on emotion or ad hoc grounds and justified by administrative fiat. Records were often incomplete or corrupted and available only to the initiated. And internal rules could be arbitrary or fickle and variable in application. The perennial dilemma in bureaucratic modes of organisation is if bureaucrats are conditioned to following orders, rules and procedures throughout their tenured careers, who provides the leadership qualities at the pinnacle of the pyramid that is essential for the bureaucracy to function? This is sometimes called the 'Weberian paradox' (Beetham 1974).

Prior to the early 20th century (and in Weber's seminal writings), these largely inherited principles essentially related to the organisational design of bureaucracies and the administrative tasks at hand – favouring insular structures; the inculcation of inward-looking perspectives; the imperatives of operational transactions (competence and efficiency), with some notions of standardisation, equity of conditions and treatment; and service-wide endeavour. There was little appreciation of the need for such bureaucratic structures to demonstrate democratic accountabilities, or for these organisations to be publicly accountable both upward to their governing superiors (legitimate authorising officers) and outward to the wider community. Providing the ruler or ruling class was more or less satisfied with the administrative capabilities of their administrative echelons then all was well. Bureaucrats were not themselves held accountable for errors or maladministration, with political executives nominally answerable for their supportive administrative organs to the legislature and/or monarch, the media and general public.

Greater interest in the overall accountability of the bureaucracy began to develop in the late 19th century, initially addressing issues of legality, judicial and financial probity, administrative due process, legislative scrutiny of administrative spending and the independent assurance of resource usage (with audit acts and auditors-general who were increasingly made independent from the executive), followed by expanding notions of answerability to the legislature of ministers or other important office holders. In the United States the accountablity of Congress to the electorate played an important role in demanding accountability from federal office holders from the president down (both in their appointment and execution of their roles). Various regulatory functions administered oversight through such things as the *Pendleton Civil Service Reform Act 1883*, which insisted on propriety; the Wilsonian emphasis on roles and competencies; and the enforcement of greater transparency through the *Freedom of Information Act 1966*.

In parliamentary jurisdictions, with a reliance on conventions of 'responsible government', regular explanations to parliament over policy decisions, public service performance, maladministration or mishaps became the norm, especially as disciplined party dominance increased the tenure of governments. Waves of interest in expanding and codifying accountabilities increased in the post–World War II years, so that the imperatives of accountability and transparency now play a more significant part in organisational structures, cultures and dynamics (Shergold 2004; Mulgan 2003).

Contemporary public organisations have to continually balance their organisational form and performance with their need for reputational standing and multidimensional legitimacy (in the eyes of the public, political supervisors, peer groups, stakeholder groups and experts in the field). They have to deal with many eventualities that will affect their organisational form and shape – e.g. planning and research, budgeting and resourcing, administrative or policy design, regulatory mandates and enforcement, coordination and communication as well as a panoply of accountability requirements. It is also imperative that public agencies retain legitimacy in the eyes of their stakeholders, and maintain public trust and confidence (a phenomenon most keenly observed when agencies lose this credibility). These factors influence organisational design and adaptation and shape the possibilities or scope for relative autonomy. In an alternative conceptualisation, Carpenter (2001) enunciated these qualities or necessary conditions as organisational differentiation from political influences, organisational capacities often uniquely framed, and reputational credibility.

Various authors have identified some of the (contestable) principles or rationales for organisational design, usually with some *post hocery* and a degree of backward mapping. They prompt the awkward question of how much intentional design was purposefully commissioned from the beginning and how much was subject to incremental adaptation (see Podger 2013). Many of these principles focus on the range and extent of their activities, the types of complexity public bodies have to handle, their client bases and service imperatives, and the degree of political dependency/independence warranted by the function. Historically, the main organising principles for public bodies were tied to purpose, place or location, processes undertaken, or the persons served (Gulick 1937).

More recently, scholars have added the principle of consolidation to the notion of a prime function or purpose by joining like-with-like functions to amalgamate units and create better economies of scale (Pollitt 2013; see also Davis et al. 1999 who review machinery of government changes over 50 years). Others have argued that organisational form tends to be shaped by what successive governments regard as the most important areas of public policy that they want represented at the cabinet table. Since the 1980s, many governments have hived off specialist delivery agencies from departments (executive agencies) in the belief that as relatively autonomous business units or cost centres they will perform better both for the government and clients (James 2003; Halligan & Wills 2008).

But other realpolitik factors also played a part in contouring bureaucratic forms. Sometimes governments wished to make symbolic statements about priorities, or they resorted to making machinery of government changes to paper over administrative shortcomings or policy crises. In addition, weak ministers or perceptions of ministerial overload could lead to agencies being divided or broken up, and restructuring might be triggered by dissatisfaction with the quality of policy advice or service delivery. These surreptitious rationales were rarely admitted openly by governments for fear of inciting scepticism or even ridicule.

To what extent does purpose and function determine organisational form in public bureaucracies?

To ascertain whether an agency's purpose and functions determine its organisational form (as normative theory suggests they ought), we need first to ask generically how far public organisations are able to customise their structure and form. This is not a simple question because many overlapping and contending requirements simultaneously apply to any public organisation, including constitutional and/or statutory obligations, administrative policies and procedures, centrally specified instructions, guidelines and memorandums. Organisations also face pressure to adapt their presence to their responsibilities, which are often closely geared to the nature of their interactions with clients or constituents (e.g. social service departments have community-based branches, educational departments operate community-level schools and training facilities, agricultural departments typically operate regional structures to be close to their clients or to provide research and testing facilities). Hence, governments and their organisation components must balance the requirements imposed from top-down imperatives and bottom-up pressures to service their clientele.

Accordingly, organisational form is shaped primarily by twin forces. On the one hand, there are pressures for *conformity*, imposing commonality, consistency and standardised application aimed at making organisations similar, routinised and comparable. Similar management structures, budgetary and corporate planning requirements, staffing profiles and remunerations, and reporting obligations are generally imposed either by parliaments or by core executive agencies operating in the name of the legislature. Often the specific rationales for these conformist requirements are not spelled out in detail, nor are agencies necessarily aware of them. They are often imposed by decree out of a compulsion for political control and/or to comply with standardised operating procedures and accountability criteria.

Many agencies find conformist pressures to be constraining and frustrating – even claustrophobic – and often counterproductive, adding little to the ability of the agency to address its responsibilities. Some conformist requirements distract, undermine or erode the capacity of the agency to conduct its business or meet its expected performance levels. These impediments include onerous reporting requirements or regimes unrelated to their core business.

Traditionally, conformity was promulgated centrally as a means of exerting control over the fragmented organisational structure of government, particularly in the era when most public services were delivered 'in-house' by public servants and government employees. Centrally imposed edicts gave governments and core executives a semblance of control and orderly systems of administration (see, for example, the Australian Public Service and Merit Protection Commission 2001). They enabled central agencies to observe the behaviour and practices of their departments and agencies, and imposed a blend of public accountabilities and executive accountabilities over administrative units (with much of the latter being internally imposed).

More importantly, consistent reporting was expected to provide the centre with comparable data about compliance to procedural requirements and performance. Regular tinkering with central edicts was often a reflection of frustration at not getting sufficient information from decentralised units or a fear that the utility and effectiveness of routine requirements would decline over time as agencies became used to them. Sometimes the demands from the centre increased and expanded, at other times arbitrary changes were made with the intention of keeping line agencies on their toes.

More recently, and especially alongside the adoption of new public management (NPM) and new public governance (NPG), central agencies examined the efficacy of traditional central controls to discern whether they were anachronistic or counterproductive. A raft of 'dysfunctional' central impositions and controls were abolished or reduced in significance and annoyance. Centrally imposed control over employee numbers and grades was gradually removed, budgetary flexibilities were introduced, managers were given greater freedoms and managerial discretion to achieve objectives, and onerous procurement mandates were relaxed; in most cases, these 'impeding' central controls were replaced by a raft of results-oriented central requirements. So, although agencies were given greater operational freedoms (Pollitt & Bouckaert 2004), they were nevertheless subjected to a more centralised set of guidelines on processes and reporting (e.g. budgets, staff management, community engagement, annual reporting, performance reporting).

In theory, this meant that agencies had greater latitude to reshape their organisational structures and delivery arms (Osborne 2010). In practice, many agencies used their new freedoms to divest themselves of lower grade staff (clerical workers and assistants) and inflate the size of their middle-level executive and, particularly, the numbers appointed to the most senior levels (e.g. senior executive service). Arguably, many agencies across the Western world became inordinately top-heavy compared to 20 or 30 years ago, with a panoply (or public exhibition) of executives designated to monitor every conceivable functionality. As self-administering organisations, universities were particularly susceptible to this inflation of executive positions (Coaldrake & Stedman 2013; Marginson & Considine 2000). Going forward, we may see the reimposition of staffing controls or quotas for senior executives.

A further interesting aspect of modern public administration in the NPG era (or 'new political governance' era, see Aucoin 2012) is that agency executives can ask whether their current bureaucratic form is suited to purpose and aligned to their core businesses. Agency heads could not realistically ask (or do anything about) this question in bygone eras, but there are now possibilities for customisation if agency heads are prepared to explore them. The experimentation with 'executive agency' models provides some heuristic examples for emulation, but also offers some cautions and warnings about the dangers of 'roguish' behaviour.

Empirically, there is now scope for scholars to gauge how far have agency heads have gone in exercising their ability to shape their agencies. It is worthy of more detailed research to explore the extent that agency executives (and to some extent their presiding ministers) have proactively exploited their new latitude.

Dimensions of independence – balancing 'control' and 'relative autonomy'

It is common to conceptualise the balance between 'political control' and 'organisational autonomy' as a spectrum ranging from no independence/autonomy through to full independence/autonomy (see O'Faircheallaigh et al. 1999; Wanna 2008). Similar exercises in classifying a desired degree of political control versus autonomy have been undertaken for statutory bodies (see Uhrig 2003; Wettenhall 2005; Edwards et al. 2012[1]). See table below.

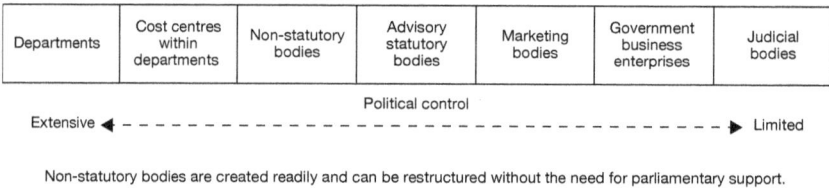

Departments	Cost centres within departments	Non-statutory bodies	Advisory statutory bodies	Marketing bodies	Government business enterprises	Judicial bodies

Political control

Extensive ◀ – ▶ Limited

Non-statutory bodies are created readily and can be restructured without the need for parliamentary support.

Figure 2.1. Spectrum of political control over public sector organisations
Source. O'Faircheallaigh et al. (1999)

Public agencies range from ministries and departments that are close to executive government and under direct political control, to judicial bodies and integrity commissions that enjoy a relative degree of independence for their operations and decision-making (but not necessarily over the appointment and/or dismissal of senior staff, which may still be politically determined). Different traditions of governance are also important here (see *Public Administration*, special issue, vol 81, no 1, 2003) as, under Westminster parliaments, ministers and departments tend to possess little intrinsic autonomy, whereas, in many European parliamentary democracies with *Rechtsstaat* traditions, ministries retain considerable autonomy within their portfolio responsibilities. North American

---

1   See especially Chapter 2, 'The rise of corporate and public governance'.

jurisdictions tend to be more programmatically driven (and include the imposition of sunset clauses) where agencies effectively 'house' programs and may gain a degree of autonomy through the particular provisions of specific programs.

Being convenient and close to government, the departmental form has not waned in popularity, although their number, size and range of responsibilities has been altered regularly (through machinery of government changes, which perform essentially the same function in the public sector as mergers and demergers do in business). Departments possess the important advantages of being politically flexible, sensitive to ministerial preferences/priorities and able to work confidentially on sensitive topics out of the public gaze. The extent of political control can range from dirigisme and overt directives over bureaucratic directions, priorities and agendas, to a latent semblance of figureheading positional power or an amorphous 'authorising environment' where things may be done 'in the minister's name' (see Moore 1995). Some (but by no means all) departments are beholden to (or captured by) professional standards and cultures that can serve to enhance their independence (e.g. departments of health or social services, or environment or transport).

New Zealand and the United Kingdom typically have a large number of ministerial departments (30+) often with multiple ministers within a portfolio or multiple ministries reporting to a minister. Some jurisdictions, like New Zealand, distinguish 'departments' from 'ministries', with departments largely having combined policy and administrative roles and ministries being largely administrative or service delivery units (but now the terms seem interchangeable and ministries include the portfolios of environment, defence and civil defence, economic development, education, foreign affairs and trade, and social development). This segregation (which seems to outsiders somewhat artificial or idiosyncratic) may hark back to the wartime separation of the New Zealand War Cabinet from the War Administration during World War II, with the former charged with decision-making and the latter 'with responsibility for all matters connected with the war'.

Generally, departmental organisations (and ministries) are subject to ministerial direction and control, but some have won or been allowed a degree of discretion in selected areas of their activities (e.g. operational matters, choosing their style of management, initiating research, funding specific activities). Government-wide statutes may also provide departments with the capacity to make quasi-autonomous decisions (i.e. not involving ministerial direction), as with compliance to public service acts, freedom of information (FOI) acts, and the requirements of accountability acts governing financial administration, audit, secrecy and integrity. Together these acts provide statutory protections (and requirements) for departmental executives that underscore the public accountability of them as public organisations. Ministers generally have no involvement in the appointment of departmental staff, and this is primarily a form of protection for ministers against accusations of favouritism or nepotism.

Statutory bodies (such as advisory boards, regulatory bodies, health boards, research institutes, sporting administrators) generally have a higher degree of autonomy but are still subject to overall direction from the government – the so-called 'strategic control' variously exercised over such authorities. Often with the establishment of statutory authorities, the main objective is to depoliticise a particular function and to prevent ministers from either meddling or being blamed for unpopular decisions (i.e. to avoid political control or political accountability).

The range of specialist functions that governments may wish to keep at arms' length from political interference not only include regulatory, judicial and integrity bodies, but also railways, utilities, cultural entities, universities and some independent bodies serving as funding providers (e.g. grant administering bodies in research or artistic excellence). But, as Warhurst (1980) argued some decades ago, governments have a myriad of ways of influencing nominally independent statutory bodies by making ministerial changes to board representation, adjusting budgets, altering the empowering act of the body, making them subject to other legislation, using departmental oversight, and even having a 'quiet word' with a minister or ministerial staffer. Judicial and integrity commissions have been given the most autonomy, but are still subject to budgetary review and financial controls, politicised appointment processes and the odd rebuke or criticism from ministers.

Specialist agencies, in particular, tend to develop and protect their level of autonomy through professional norms, codes of practice and inculcated trainings. Professional norms and practices are important to bureaucratic independence not only because disciplinary training and culture creates particular values and mindsets, but because external professional requirements can dictate behaviour, predetermine decisions and stipulate what can and can't be done. Examples include accounting standards, health requirements, educational pedagogies, engineering compliances, legal precepts and codes, and cultural conventions.

The professions have also created powerful associational interest groups that speak for them and can shape accepted practices and regulatory policies. Comprised of quasi-independent specialists and technicians, these professional associations can dictate how their members behave and decree what decisions are deemed appropriate. They have external credibility and authority. Tensions between governments and their architects, accountants, medical practitioners, engineers and educators are legendary in many jurisdictions. Often the heads of public organisations with large professional workforces are themselves members of the same profession and share the same world views as their staff, perhaps making them compliant with professional demands.

Bureaucratic independence or autonomy is never absolute in the public sector; rather, 'relative autonomy' is a more likely condition to which agencies can aspire or can acquire. So, what forms of departmental 'relative autonomy' might be identified? The following is a list of possibilities where degrees of autonomy might be practised:

- structural separation from the political sphere and executive control
- the ability to make policy decisions and determine the agency's priorities and agendas
- the ability to initiate research independently and, perhaps, publish the product of this research
- budgetary freedom to deploy resources within a departmental expenses account and, where appropriate, retain a portion of external revenue generated as a result of its activities
- the ability to determine the location and physical presence of the agency, including selecting properties, buying or leasing facilities, co-locating or decentralising
- the ability to establish a staffing profile; make appointments; recruit, promote and train staff; and the ability to investigate internal practices and cultures
- the ability to hire and fire external consultants and other advisory actors

- the ability of senior management to communicate directly with the public, parliament and the media; for instance, by speaking publicly on policy and administrative topics within their portfolio, making submissions to or public appearances at inquiries, and clarifying misunderstandings in the public realm
- the ability to report their activities, performances and finances as they see fit, subject to some legislative or executive guidance for wholly public bodies.

Agencies are unlikely to enjoy all these possible dimensions of 'relative autonomy' simultaneously. Some 'freedoms' come with additional constraints imposed. For instance, greater latitude in operational policy matters or administrative discretion may come at the cost of greater reporting requirements or performance expectations. Other 'freedoms' may be held but exercised with caution or a degree of self-censorship. Examples might include agencies with the capacity to initiate research and publish findings that selectively publish only those reports that do not embarrass the government or sit within the government's comfort zone.

To illustrate this point, the Australian Treasury retains the ability to initiate its own research on economic matters and routinely does so, and has on occasions attempted to keep such research confidential. For example, it chose to release a stringent critique of government overspending at the time of the change of government in 2007 (from Liberal under Prime Minister John Howard to Labor under Kevin Rudd), rather than at the time when the excessive spending was occurring under Howard (Laurie & McDonald 2008). It also collated research on housing affordability (which was becoming prohibitively expensive for sections of the community) and chose not to release such information so as not to embarrass the government of the day, even resisting FOI requests seeking the information's release. The chart below depicts various dimensions of bureaucratic autonomy, mapped against different types of structural organisation.

Table 2.1. Dimensions and degrees of organisational autonomy versus political control in public administration

Dimension	Agencies (central and line)	Special authorities (statutory bodies)	Integrity bodies, AG, judiciary, independent commissions	Public enterprises and commercial units	NGO networked bodies linked with government
Separation from political control, govt directives • own wishes	• low/moderate • close ministerial control relationship subject to ministerial powers qualified by degree of ministerial autonomy vis-à-vis government	• moderate • operate under government/ statutory requirement, often enjoy functional autonomy; subject to ministerial directives	• high; variously independent of government for decision-making	• semi-independent from government, but often required to contribute • can be subject to 'guidance'	• independent of government, but have complex dependencies • balance own autonomy with access and relationship building
Ability to make own policy decisions • determining own priorities	• low–moderate range and requires government approval • ministers can direct and enjoy discretion and implementation freedoms	• moderate, not much outside remit • operationally independent • more subtle ministerial influence	• high but only within remit • no ministerial involvement	• moderate • more subtle ministerial influences	• governments likely to set agendas and funding • NGOs subject to contracts, but more operational autonomy
Research and analytical abilities, own planning capacities • set own research priorities, forecasting abilities	• some potential, but have often been cut back • have considerable policy and operational expertise	• some have virtually none; others high and significant • usually latitude is specified in statutory provisions	• largely autonomous • research base around cases, complaints, reviews within their remits	• not significant outside technical and commercial considerations	• variable, but increasingly are developing analytical capacities to bargain with government

Dimension	Agencies (central and line)	Special authorities (statutory bodies)	Integrity bodies, AG, judiciary, independent commissions	Public enterprises and commercial units	NGO networked bodies linked with government
Budgetary and financial autonomy • set own budget • allocate own budget • determine own locations/sites	• limited capacity to set own budget • constraints on use of resources • discretion-limiting	• Limited capacity to set budget but likely to be able to shape internal allocations	• receive fixed budgets • additional funding associated with additional functions, offices or scale	• usually self-determined, but often levy paid back to govt (dividend) • governed by financing logics not budget dependencies	• not dependent for own organisational resourcing, but increasingly dependent for government contractual work
Ability to make own staffing appointments	• limited to internal staff appointments • set own employment numbers/profile subject to central directives (APSC) • agency heads appointed separately by government	• political appointments to boards, then latitude to appoint below • may exert influence in senior appointments still subject to central directives	• various degrees of political involvement on senior appointments, then latitude below	• more commercially driven • enjoy latitude to appoint staff and consultants	• autonomy to make own appointments and partnerships
Personnel and human resource management • including industrial bargaining, setting wages and conditions	• ability to recruit, promote and dismiss staff • rules govern senior staff appointments • constrained ability to set remunerations	• ability to recruit, promote and dismiss staff • rules govern senior staff appointments • constrained ability to set remunerations	• ability to recruit, promote and dismiss staff • constrained ability to set remunerations	• able to set remuneration and conditions for staff and consultants	• ability to set remunerations but often largely voluntary/honorary

Dimension	Agencies (central and line)	Special authorities (statutory bodies)	Integrity bodies, AG, judiciary, independent commissions	Public enterprises and commercial units	NGO networked bodies linked with government
Communication abilities • able to issue own press releases, statements	• limited outside officially required documentation • dissemination of public interest information	• have ability to issue communications often informative or promotional not political	• autonomous; able to engage in public debate • can prosecute issues of public importance	• autonomous • usually restricted to commercial matters affecting them or their environment	• autonomous but tends not to critique government (bans sometimes); usually conduct special pleading for own sector
Reporting and accountabilities • formal requirements versus own capacities • monitoring and oversight functions	• routine, standardised; don't widely report unless seeking wider input • accountable through minister • reports must comply with parliamentary guidelines	• official requirements, but free to make other report and publications • accountable through board and director • reports must comply with parliamentary guidelines	• self-accountable and peer credibility • often do not explain/ justify decisions/ actions made or taken • some subject to parliamentary oversight	• routine corporate law requirements, maybe material included in some government reports • accountable through shareholding entities (which can include govt ministers)	• own requirements, minimal incorporated entity reporting • accountable to own board

Source. The author

Exercising autonomy through operational and informal structures

In practice there are myriad supporting operational factors underlying and sustaining these freedoms, including program design and implementation, budget submissions and the ability to redeploy financial resources, collaborative engagement with other public bodies, stakeholder and network relationships (including the capacity to negotiate through veto points), public relations and media management, and audit and performance review. In terms of implementation and operational capacities, agencies possess a bounded but proximate autonomy to make decisions because they are closest to the action and have discretionary latitudes. Moreover, not everything within an agency's mandate is open to transparent oversight, so it often has wiggle room for increased discretion.

In addition to public organisations being allowed (or managing to achieve) certain degrees of formal independence and relative autonomy, they can also exercise autonomy through informal cultures and structures. These informal structures typically increase where authorising environments are distant or latent, mandates are contested or unclear, boundary issues are malleable or in dispute, and external changes punctuate routines. Informality may also increase to the extent that the agency has a determined leadership and management skills championing certain policy or administrative options (and conversely may be found in agencies characterised by corruption or maladministration). And, as already mentioned, professional cultures can enhance the scope for agency discretion and local autonomy.

Looking outwards, agencies can engage in building professional networks and stakeholder alliances as latent supportive constituencies and active players protecting the agency's mission. Turning to supportive networks can be important in politically charged circumstances, where agencies enjoying credibility with stakeholder/interest groups are able to withstand pressures from the political executive and perhaps gain backing for alternative proposals.

Earned autonomy

'Earned autonomy' is not a measure of autonomy from ministers, but rather a performance and budgetary concept that is invoked to grant a certain degree of latitude to agencies considered by government executives and central agencies to be performing well. This is a concessionary measure granted by central agencies to high performing or competently managed agencies (even according to reputational recognition) to enable them to direct their administrative efforts to their core business (and divest themselves of onerous but often less meaningful accountability reporting). Success provides them with circumscribed freedoms. Even so, no agency is totally free to determine its own budget.

Agencies with earned autonomy may enjoy more freedom to deploy their resource envelopes and may also be granted privileges including enjoying less onerous forms of formal accountability, such as reduced budgetary scrutiny. Service-wide requirements (e.g. right to information, equity, financial compliance and so on) continue to apply to these agencies, however, and they must still achieve meaningful results and convince the traditional layers of oversight of their above-average performance.

Earned autonomy is often closely associated with the influence of public choice methodologies in NPM/NPG jurisdictions that favour specialisation. Agencies using principal–agent theory to organise their activities tend to rely on contractual management rather than autarkic provision. Providing contracts deliver value for money and desired outcomes, these agencies may be less onerously reviewed by central agencies or the relevant legislatures. Simply relying on principal–agent models, however, is no 'cure-all' and no guarantee of heightened performance, and often has severe limitations not to mention associated perversities.

Notions of constitutional bureaucracy

Ideas about the constitutional role of the bureaucracy became popular after the Gomery Inquiry into accountability in the Canadian federal government under Prime Minister Jean Chrétien in 2004–06, and they have found some support in other Westminster jurisdictions including in the United Kingdom, Australia, New Zealand and Singapore. The key argument maintains that the bureaucracy is the bedrock of the modern state, with wide and important constitutional responsibilities concerning stewardship of the state and, possibly, the longer term public interest. Such notions of the public service enjoying a privileged constitutional status within the state apparatus (which formally it doesn't, but the idea can be traced back to the United Kingdom's Northcote–Trevelyan Report of 1854) are based on traditional (nostalgic) custodian ideas of the public service constituting an ongoing permanent institution of state that is distinct from the comings and goings of daily politics but governed by an array of externalised legislation and guidelines subject to ministerial control.

This contested and controversial set of ideas is not least disputed by the political executive (in the United Kingdom, Canada and Australia). Those promoting this view argue that the bureaucracy ought to play a stewardship role – serving the interests of the government of the day, while also monitoring and protecting the integrity of public administration, including guarding against improper requests or misconduct from ministers or their staff. Gomery even recommended that departmental heads write formally and inform parliament if they suspect their minister of improper behaviour – a recommendation rejected by subsequent Canadian governments (see Wanna 2006).

Following criticisms of the utilitarian nature of NPM in Australia, the notion that public agencies and departmental heads should have the responsibility to exercise stewardship has been written into the revised amendments to the *Public Service Act 1999*. However, 'stewardship' is not defined or given specific parameters – it is not clear whether it means responsibility for good administration, stewardship over the maintenance and augmentation of organisational capacities, or a broader custodian role acting in the public interest. The latter interpretation was particularly argued by Louis Sossin (2006) in his submission to the Gomery Commission in which he laid out the 'constitutional argument for bureaucratic independence and its implication for the accountability of the public service'. Expressions of constitutional bureaucracy can include cases where senior public officials claim to be serving the Crown foremost, rather than the minister or the government of the day. Some police commissioners (and perhaps some senior military officers) in Westminster systems have typically been the type of functionaries who have claimed independence from government and higher loyalty to the monarch (e.g. the Salisbury affair in South Australia, see Cockburn 1979).

Independence has limits

No form of bureaucratic independence, whether awarded or acquired, is limitless. Independence comes with the responsibility to exercise it appropriately, astutely and justifiably – and, as Moore (1995) reminds us, has to be protected, prosecuted and renegotiated vis-à-vis the changing political environment and circumstances. Even the judiciary, which enjoys high degrees of independence, faces political and public criticism of its sentencing and bail decisions. In Australia, mainstream media criticism has been directed at the Australian Human Rights Commission for overstepping its mandate and especially its former head, Professor Gillian Triggs, for politicising the commission (see Wanna 2015). Similarly, the Productivity Commission, a fiercely independent adviser on economic and social policy has intentionally self-censored its independence by preferring only to take formal references from government (the Treasurer), rather than independently initiate research and investigations (which it theoretically can do). It has (perhaps sensibly) chosen to provide independent hard-headed advice *to* government and be respected for the quality of that advice, rather than be independent *of* government. Other integrity-type bodies and independent commissions often face similar dilemmas (such as auditors-general, parliamentary budget offices and information commissioners).

Conclusions

On balance, a degree of 'relative autonomy' is probably a 'good thing' to aim for and offers encouragement to lift performance and aspirations to improve capabilities for the public good. It has the potential to expand the horizons of public executives and their management teams, underscoring the value of public service and good public administration. But it is not without risks and potentially negative aspects (open to bureaucratic capture, goal displacement, covert operations). The Latin phrase *quis custodiet ipsos custodes* readily comes to mind (who guards the guards themselves). Done well, relative autonomy requires strong oversight from governing boards or corporate management teams within the agencies concerned (including from community representatives, experienced former ministers and stakeholder representatives).

When they choose to act, ministers retain the authority to curtail autonomy, amend an agency's mandate or priorities, restructure agencies, increase oversight, change management personnel, and merge functions or disassemble them. Ministers or cabinets are not likely to do this on a whim, but changing political preferences and priorities, or performance concerns may push them in that direction.

Importantly, as a final point, it is worth remembering that bureaucratic independence versus political control is not just an 'either/or' condition, or a zero-sum game. Other dimensions of organisational capacities remain significant and readily observable. For example, agencies may aspire to be high performers in terms of integrity, performance and the quality of client service without necessarily changing the degree of overall political control or level of independence. 'Relative autonomy' is an important concept to explore as we go forward in public administration but it is no silver bullet to defeat malfeasance or maladroit administration.

References

Aucoin, P 2012, '"New political governance" in Westminster systems: impartial public administration and management performance at risk', *Governance*, vol 25, no 2, pp 177–99, doi.org/10.1111/j.1468-0491.2012.01569.x.

Australian Public Service and Merit Protection Commission 2001, *Serving the Nation: 100 Years of Public Service*, Canberra.

Beetham, D 1974, *Max Weber and the Theory of Modern Politics*, Allen & Unwin, London.

Carpenter, D 2001, *The Forging of Bureaucratic Autonomy: Reputations, Networks and Policy Innovation in Executive Agencies*, Princeton University Press.

Coaldrake, P & Stedman, L 2013, *Raising the Stakes: Gambling with the Future of Universities*, UQP, St Lucia.

Cockburn, S 1979, *The Salisbury Affair*, Sun Books, Melbourne.

Davis, G, Weller, P, Craswell, E & Eggins, S 1999, 'What drives machinery of government change? Australia, Canada and the United Kingdom, 1950–1997', *Public Administration*, vol 77, no 1, pp 7–50, doi.org/10.1111/1467-9299.00142.

Edwards, M, Halligan, J, Horrigan, B and Nicoll, B 2012, *Public Sector Governance in Australia*, ANU E Press, Canberra, doi.org/10.22459/PSGA.07.2012.

Gomery, J 2005/6, *Commission of Inquiry into the Sponsorship Program and Advertising Activities*, Phases I and II reports, Canadian Government, Ottawa.

Gouldner, A 1954, *Patterns of Industrial Bureaucracy*, Free Press, Glencoe.

Gulick, L 1937, 'Notes on the theory of organization', in L Gulick & L Urwick (eds), *Papers on the Science of Administration*, Columbia University, New York.

Halligan, J & Wills, J 2008, *The Centrelink Experiment: Innovation in Service Delivery*, ANU E Press, Canberra, doi.org/10.22459/CE.12.2008.

James, O 2003, *The Executive Agency Revolution in Whitehall: Public Interest Versus Bureau-Shaping Perspectives*, Palgrave Macmillan, London, doi.org/10.1057/9781403943989_2.

Laurie, K & McDonald, J 2008, 'A perspective on trends in Australian Government spending', *Economic Round-up*, Treasury Paper, Canberra.

Marginson, S & Considine, M 2000, *The Enterprise University: Power, Governance and Reinvention in Australia*, Cambridge University Press.

Moore, M 1995, *Creating Public Value*, Harvard University Press, Cambridge, Mass.

Mulgan, R 2003, *Holding Power to Account*, Palgrave Macmillan, London, doi.org/10.1057/9781403943835.

O'Faircheallaigh, C, Wanna, J & Weller, P 1999, *Public Sector Management in Australia: New Challenges, New Directions*, 2nd edn, Macmillan, Melbourne.

Osborne, S 2010, *The New Public Governance? Emerging Perspectives on the Theory and Practice of Public Governance*, London, Routledge, doi.org/10.4324/9780203861684.

Podger, A 2013, 'Organisational structures and public sector performance', conference paper, UNDP Seminar on Social Public Service Reforms, Beijing, Sep 2013.

Pollitt, C 2013, 'Thirty years of public management reforms: has there been a pattern?', in J Bickerton & G Peters (eds), *Governing: Essays in Honour of Donald Savoie*, MacGill, Montreal.

Pollitt, C & Bouckaert, G 2004, *Public Management Reform: A Comparative Analysis*, 2nd edn, Oxford University Press.

Shergold, P 2004, 'Lackeys, careerists, political stooges: personal reflections on the current state of public service leadership', *Australian Journal of Public Administration*, vol 63, no 4, pp 3–13, doi.org/10.1111/j.1467-8500.2004.00396.x.

Sossin, L 2006, *Defining Boundaries: The Constitutional Argument for Bureaucratic Independence and its Implications for the Accountability of the Public Service*, research paper, Gomery Commission of Inquiry, Canadian Government, Ottawa.

Uhrig, J 2003, *Review of Corporate Governance of Statutory Authorities and Office Holders*, Commonwealth of Australia, Canberra.

Wanna, J 2006, 'Insisting on traditional ministerial responsibility and the constitutional independence of the public service: the Gomery Inquiry and the Canadian sponsorship scandal', *Australian Journal of Public Administration*, vol 65, no 3, pp 15–21, doi.org/10.1111/j.1467-8500.2006.00490a.x.

—— 2008, 'Independence and responsiveness: re-tying the Gordian knot', *Australian Journal of Public Administration*, vol 67, no 3, pp 340–44, doi.org/10.1111/j.1467-8500.2008.00591.x.

—— 2015, 'Triggs in uncharted waters: the Human Rights Commissioner has overestimated the independence her office confers', *ANU Reporter*, special edition, ANU, Canberra.

Warhurst, J 1980, 'Exercising control over statutory authorities: a study in government technique', in P Weller & D Jaensch (eds), *Responsible Government in Australia*, Drummond, Richmond, Victoria, doi.org/10.1080/00323268008401765.

Weber, M 1978 (1922), *Economy and Society: An Outline of Interpretive Sociology*, vol 2, University of California Press, Berkeley.

Wettenhall, R 2005, 'Parliamentary oversight of statutory authorities: a post-Uhrig perspective', *Australian Parliamentary Affairs*, vol 20, no 2, pp 39–63.

3

HOW INDEPENDENT SHOULD ADMINISTRATION BE FROM POLITICS?

Theory and practice in public sector institutional design in Australia[1]

Andrew Podger

Introduction

Government administration in Australia is separate from politics, but the degree of independence varies. Broadly, the main functions of Australian government administration, such as policy advising, service delivery, industry regulation and oversight of government, can be mapped to its main organisational structures: ministerial departments, service delivery agencies, statutory authorities and government business enterprises (GBEs). Over recent decades, particularly as governments have focused on performance – including by using market-type mechanisms to improve efficiency and networks across and beyond government to

---

1   This article builds upon presentations made by the author to a United Nations Development Programme workshop held in Beijing in 2013 (not published), and earlier to a 2011 workshop at The Australian National University hosted by the HC Coombs Policy Forum on 'Accountability structures for citizen-centred public services' (Podger 2011). In 2019, the author drew on the material in this article in major submissions to the Independent Review of the Australian Public Service (Thodey Review).

improve effectiveness – the mix of structures has changed and their accountability frameworks have adjusted. The mapping of functions to structures remains complex – rather like 'signposting the zoo', as a former New Zealand colleague suggested – in part because of continuing debates over the appropriate degree of the administration's independence from politics for different government activities.

This chapter proposes a framework of formal and informal structures and processes that might guide future governance arrangements for different functions in the Australian public sector, with a view both to promote organisational performance and to ensure appropriate accountability to the public.

First, the chapter provides some background on institutional theory as well as political and organisational theory and practice, and their relevance to public sector organisational structures in Australia. This suggests that, while there is no single or static optimal governance structure, generally, 'form follows function' and public sector structures are shaped by judgements about the balance between political control and organisational independence appropriate for the functions involved.

The main organisational structures now used in Australia for different types of functions – and their governance arrangements – are then described, including how the legal framework has evolved over the last three decades in response to new public management (NPM), new public governance (NPG) and subsequent reforms. Examples are given of developments in structural arrangements for the different types of organisations as these reforms have been introduced and reviewed. This highlights some of the contemporary challenges Australia faces, including to develop a consistent approach towards balancing political control and bureaucratic autonomy, and to identify structures most appropriate to providing citizen-centred services.

The chapter finishes with a possible framework of both formal rules and informal processes that would support greater consistency and coherence, and that might enhance the performance of organisations with different functions and ensure their appropriate public accountability. The framework draws on both the theoretical discussion and the history of Australian practice, as well as the contemporary challenge to provide services that are responsive to the needs and preferences of citizens and their families and communities.

Theoretical considerations

Institutions[2]

Institutions set the 'rules of the game'; that is, the way in which people organise regular interactions (Ostrom 2005). There are often multiple layers of institutions and each layer is shaped by and, in turn, influences the others (for example, in the public sector, the layers comprise constitutions, laws, policies and policy processes, and administration). They may involve formal rules, laws and structures, and also informal processes, conventions and practices. Preferably these are self-reinforcing and mirror beliefs and cultures, but they may sometimes be in conflict with them.

Institutions help to reduce uncertainty, setting constraints and coordinating the views and actions of those involved. Accordingly, they can foster efficiency. At the same time, however, there may be costs involved with institutional weaknesses and failures.

Institutions change and evolve, affected by social, environmental and technological developments. They themselves also affect societies and polities: they are political actors in their own right (March & Olsen 1984). An 'agency perspective' focuses on how individuals shape the system; while a 'structuralist perspective' focuses on how institutions react to exogenous changes and, in turn, establish a new cohesive social structure that shapes people's behaviours.

Political institutions

Institutions are particularly important to the study of politics and public administration as they have an impact that goes beyond how people interact to the way they make choices (Ostrom 2005). They shape the opportunities that people have, as citizens, to be heard, to participate in decision-making and to access public services (Lowndes & Roberts 2013). Informal institutional rules can be as powerful as the formal ones, for example, in setting a professional public service ethos.

---

2   This brief summary draws heavily on the literature review in Talbot-Jones (2018).

McIntyre argues that the 'power concentration paradox' creates dangers in political frameworks that disperse control of decision-making too far, as well as those that unify decision-making too firmly at the centre (McIntyre 2003). A balance is required to ensure that the political system can respond flexibly, decisively and in a timely way to changing circumstances, while also limiting the scope for capricious or arbitrary behaviour.

Advanced democracies have 'a thick web of social and economic regulatory institutions' (to use McIntyre's phrase), which generally avoid the extremities of centralised and fragmented power. This web includes the judiciary, the legislature (often bicameral), a free press, a multi-level government structure, multiple parties, a range of semi-independent authorities (separate from the political executive), and non-state actors that monitor and contest policy and performance.

The question explored here is whether, within this 'thick web', and particularly within the bureaucratic arm of the executive, there is sufficiently explicit understanding of the *degree of independence* appropriate to different functions in order to achieve the optimal balance.

Australia's political institutions

Australia's public sector organisational structures operate in the context of a market economy and a strong civil society, and within a parliamentary democracy and a federal intergovernmental framework.

- **Market economy:** government activity is generally limited to addressing market failures or delivering public goods, ensuring a fair distribution of income and material wellbeing, and setting a stable social and economic framework within which individuals and businesses can go about their daily lives and business with confidence.
- **Civil society:** government activity complements a strong civil society by supporting extensive networks of non-government organisations (NGOs) providing community services and representing and advocating for various society interests.
- **Parliamentary democracy:** the executive government comprises the party with majority command over the elected parliament (or at least the lower house), is accountable to the parliament and is subject to the law. The judiciary is independent of the executive and the legislature. There is a clear separation between politics and administration

within the executive, in which services are managed by professional, non-partisan public servants in line with the policies and programs set by the elected government.

- **Federalism:** Australia's provincial governments (states and territories) are sovereign or semi-sovereign authorities and are responsible for the delivery of most public services (schools, public transport, hospitals, police).

Within this essentially liberal-democratic framework, public sector organisations within the executive arm of government are:

- *accountable to* the parliament (and hence to the public) through the system of ministerial accountability, with each organisation reporting to a minister and each minister being held accountable to the parliament
- *accountable for* their performance in utilising public resources efficiently, effectively, economically and ethically in accordance with the law and the organisation's purposes as set by the elected government and/or the parliament.

The ways in which this accountability operates vary with the functions involved and the requirements set by the parliament. The separation of politics from administration gives administrators a degree of independence to ensure that their decisions are impartial, non-partisan and according to the law while remaining in line with the lawful directions of ministers and the policies of the elected government. This degree of independence varies, with some organisations having statutory powers provided by the legislature that constrain ministerial directions. The nature of the 'performance' for which agencies are held accountable also varies depending on the functions being performed.

The balance between political control and organisational independence is also affected by informal conventions and practices. The degree of bureaucratic autonomy, regulated through formal rules and structures or informal conventions and practices, may be affected by such factors as the importance that the legislature or the public place on impartiality, the reputation of the organisation for its expertise or pursuit of the national good, and the strength of its relationships with the public or with powerful stakeholders (Carpenter 2001). These factors or considerations demonstrate that the organisational structures within government are determined not only by the formal frameworks but also by the behaviours of the organisations themselves and associated informal arrangements, and that the formal frameworks set by the legislature may be fashioned by the past and expected future behaviour of the bureaucrats involved.

In line with NPM reforms, accountability arrangements over the last four decades have shifted from an emphasis on conformance with rules and processes to an emphasis on performance for results. Organisations' governance arrangements have also evolved with a shift to devolution of management authority, the use of markets for the delivery of services and an associated change in functions within government to purchasing and regulating rather than delivering services (Keating 2004). There has also been a 'thickening' of the relationship between politics and administration in recent decades (Light 1998) with increased resources for partisan support of ministers and a more general 'professionalisation' of politics.

More recent NPG and post-NPG reforms have modified NPM's emphasis on vertical accountability to promote horizontal or whole-of-government coordination and wider networking with civil society (e.g. Rhodes 1997; Osborne 2010; Pollitt & Bouckaert 2011), and take advantage of new technology. The use of third parties to deliver public services has been extended to encourage greater collaboration focused on 'citizen-centred' services that are responsive to individual needs and preferences. Associated with these developments is more 'downwards and outwards' accountability direct to citizens complementing the formal 'upwards' accountability through ministers to the parliament, with administrators and their non-government partners expected to achieve 'public value' (O'Flynn 2007). This idea of 'public value' is not without its critics, who are uneasy about constraining the role of elected politicians in Australia's parliamentary system of government (Rhodes & Wanna 2007).

These developments, as indicated further below, have affected governance arrangements for organisations with different functions, in some cases allowing greater independence within defined performance expectations, and in others imposing closer political control. Similarly, there are instances in which structures have been merged to achieve greater coordination and other instances where organisations have placed greater reliance on data linkages and other more informal networking processes. A key question is whether these developments warrant some adjustment to either the formal rules or the informal conventions and practices that give effect to the degree of independence of different administrative functions.

Organisational theory and practice

Organisational theory has evolved over the last century from Frederick Taylor's 'scientific management' (Taylor 1947), emphasising formal structures with clear authority, firm rules and distinct jobs based on skills; Max Weber's 'bureaucracy' (Weber 1978), delivering products and services efficiently and consistently on a large scale; to the identification of 'organic' as distinct from 'mechanistic' functions (Gulick & Urwick 1937), and the importance of behavioural factors (e.g. Maslow 1954; Simon 1957; McGregor 1960; Likert 1961; Herzberg 1968) and informal, non-hierarchical arrangements that support individual performance, productivity and innovation.

Australian practice in government broadly followed these theoretical developments, first with the use of semi-independent authorities to develop and manage the railways and various utilities and the emphasis in the public service on merit-based appointments, firm establishments and defined jobs (Public Service and Merit Protection Commission 2001; Australian Public Service Commission (APSC) 2003); and then, much later, the increasing employment of economists and other social science graduates and the shift away from detailed job classifications in the 1980s, when technological development drove radical changes.

More recent organisational theory emphasises both formal and informal structures and processes, the nature and mix varying with different organisational functions and circumstances. Mintzberg, for example, describes five types of structures that are suited to different organisational purposes and situations (Mintzberg 1979). Evidence of continued technological change places further emphasis on 'flexibility' and 'agility' to promote and respond to innovation, though it is not always clear what this specifically requires in terms of formal and informal structures and processes other than the greater use of ad hoc project teams, new start-up organisations and capacity to quickly reorganise and integrate horizontally rather than control vertically. There remain, however, functions that are more suited to stable structures with firm controls, including in professional fields reliant on high levels of training and associated professional regulation as well as businesses with ongoing products and services requiring stable divisions led by middle managers under central oversight.

Current Australian public sector management rhetoric focuses on 'innovation' and 'agility' (Parkinson 2016; Independent Review of the APS 2019), but the implications for organisational structures are yet to be explained. Moreover, Weberian bureaucratic attributes such as consistency and impartiality remain core values in the public sector notwithstanding the importance of embracing and responding to change (Podger 2016). It may therefore be likely that organisational structures within the public sector will continue to change with the functions being performed, and to involve mixtures of formal and informal rules and processes.

Australia's main public sector organisational structures and their legal framework

The main public sector functions in Australia are:

- provision of policy advice to ministers
- purchasing of public services
- delivery of public services
- regulation of industries and services
- provision of expert research and statistics
- oversight of various aspects of government activity
- commercial delivery of services where there is market failure, such as where there is a natural monopoly.

Very broadly, these functions can be mapped to Australia's main organisational structures:

- departments undertaking policy advising and purchasing of services and which work directly to ministers who are elected politicians
- service delivery agencies or executive agencies, operating within the policies set by ministers and funded by government, sometimes on a purchaser/provider basis through ministerial departments, with a focus on effective and efficient management and on meeting the needs of clients

- statutory authorities the functions of which are set out in legislation and that operate with considerable independence of ministers, often undertaking regulatory functions or specialist research or oversight of government activities (the last group is sometimes referred to as 'integrity' organisations)
- GBEs operating primarily commercially with limited reliance on government resources.

These distinctions are not always clear. For example, some service delivery agencies have their own legislation and are therefore statutory authorities, and services are frequently delivered by departments rather than non-departmental organisations; other structures fall between these major types (e.g. museums and specialist service providers that rely mostly on government revenue but operate in a quasi-commercial manner); and organisational arrangements within some larger agencies handle particular functions somewhat differently to the agencies' primary functions (e.g. independent statutory committees and semi-independent bodies working within ministerial departments responsible for regulatory functions, and bureaus within departments conducting semi-independent research). There are also various types amongst these main structures (e.g. GBEs that are corporations or companies, and companies that are limited by shares or guarantees). Department of Finance reports since the early 2000s have identified this complex array of organisations (e.g. Department of Finance and Administration 2005a; Department of Finance 2020).

At the national government level, public service and financial management law is the primary legislation setting out the formal rules for governance and accountability. Both have been substantially reformed since the early 1980s (APSC 2003) and the most recent changes came into force in 2013 and 2014 (Podger 2018).

Public service legislation

The new Parliament of the Commonwealth of Australia passed legislation for its public service shortly after federation in 1901. The *Public Service Act 1902* covered all employees of the fledgling Commonwealth Government, with a central employer and a rules-based approach to establishing a firm 'merit-based' career public service to implement the decisions of the elected government and its ministers. While the legislation was replaced in 1922, this approach continued until the 1970s (Minns 2004).

Starting in the late 1970s, the central employer (the Public Service Board) began to allow more flexibility by delegating powers to the agencies it oversaw. This began with establishments (internal agency structures and numbers and levels of positions) and moved on to recruitment and promotion and, in the 1980s, aspects of pay and conditions. In 1987, the Public Service Board was abolished and replaced by the smaller and less powerful Australian Public Service Commission, with more employment powers devolving to agencies. Much of the oversight of agencies shifted to the finance department through its budget processes, which reinforced the move to performance management based on outputs and outcomes.

The *Public Service Act 1999* (PS Act) confirmed agency heads as the employers of staff. All employees must uphold legislated public service values including impartiality and being 'apolitical' (non-partisan) and accountable, and the merit principle. These attributes imply a degree of independence from ministers notwithstanding the requirement to be responsive to the elected government and subject to lawful directions by ministers. The PS Act also strengthened the accountability of agency heads for agency management and performance.

Most publicly funded government organisations are now subject to the PS Act. Those outside its regulation include GBEs, bodies with military-style employment (police and defence force) and bodies with distinct workforces and significant independence of government (e.g. the Australian Broadcasting Corporation and the Commonwealth Scientific and Industrial Research Organisation). Just over half of all Commonwealth public sector employees are currently covered by the PS Act and the rest are employed under their organisations' authority or other legislation.

The legislation was reviewed following the Moran Review (Review of Australian Government Administration 2010), and an amended PS Act came into force in July 2013. The amendments addressed some problems arising from the degree of devolution introduced during the reforms (which had gone further than devolution in any other country) and promoted more collaboration across government. They also strengthened the role of the public service commissioner and made departmental secretaries responsible for the 'stewardship' of their agencies, addressing ongoing capability as well as current performance.

Importantly, these changes strengthened the formal distinction in Australia between politics and administration, increasing the degree of independence of the public service in terms of its apolitical, impartial and professional character, whether the public servants work in ministerial departments or service delivery agencies or statutory authorities. This shift is partly in response to strong trends in the opposite direction in recent years via informal practices through, for example, the growing number and influence of political advisers outside the public service working for ministers (Podger 2013a); those informal practices remain significant.

Financial management legislation

Until 1997, financial management and accountability was governed by the *Audit Act 1901*, which was also passed by the new Commonwealth Parliament shortly after federation. The legislation and its associated regulations and directions set out detailed processes for authorising expenditure of public moneys appropriated by parliament, giving the Treasury (and, after 1977 when Treasury was split, the Department of Finance) considerable powers over the financial management of all government agencies.

Throughout the 1980s in particular, Finance increasingly delegated its powers, especially in the case of agencies that were not so dependent on government revenues (by allowing these to retain and spend the moneys they raised), as it shifted its attention to performance in terms of results rather than proper use of inputs (Management Advisory Board and Management Improvement Advisory Committee 1992). Separate controls over allocations for salaries, consultancies, travel, training and office consumables were replaced by controls over aggregate 'running costs' and performance measures and targets were introduced. Those not reliant on government revenues were relieved of all detailed controls and required to report only on such measures as returns on assets and the delivery of community service obligations (see below regarding GBEs).

This devolutionary process and the distinction between types of agencies culminated in new legislation passed in 1997, the *Financial Management and Accountability Act* (FMA Act) and the *Commonwealth Authorities and Companies Act* (CAC Act). Broadly, the FMA Act applied to agencies that were financially dependent on general revenue and came under direct control by ministers: it gave their chief executives considerable authority for financial management of appropriated moneys so long as this was done efficiently, effectively and ethically, and there was open accountability for performance of the agency through the chief executive to the minister and the parliament. The CAC Act applied to agencies operating on a more commercial basis and those with some statutory independence from ministers: it provided further devolution of authority and, for commercial bodies, accountability arrangements akin to those applying to private firms under corporations law.

Both Acts were principles-based rather than prescriptive and, for the most part, proved successful in giving effect to NPM's emphasis on devolved authority in exchange for much tighter accountability for results.

The legislation's bifurcation led, however, to some problems due to inconsistency in the allocation of agencies to one Act or the other, and difficulties arising from the application of commercial rules to non-commercial statutory authorities; there was also concern about the lack of a single set of principles applying to all agencies. A 2003 review of statutory offices and officeholders (Uhrig 2003) attempted to convey firmer guidance on when agencies should have boards or just chief executives but did not address the legislation. The Department of Finance subsequently issued guidance on the appropriate structures for different government functions, drawing on the Uhrig Report and advising on the suitability of financial management law to individual organisations and whether they should be under the PS Act or not. The guidance clearly favoured ministerial departments as the default option (Department of Finance and Administration 2005b).

Criticism of the Uhrig Report (and to a lesser extent the Finance guidance) was widespread (Wettenhall 2004–05; Gourlay 2004; Halligan & Horrigan 2005), mainly for its failure to appreciate the complexity of public sector management and the range of structures that are appropriate for different functions, and for imposing a firmly private sector approach.

Commencing around 2010, the Department of Finance conducted the Commonwealth Financial Accountability Review (CFAR) (Department of Finance and Deregulation 2012). This broader review was the trigger for new legislation, the *Public Governance, Performance and Accountability Act 2013*, which replaced both the FMA and CAC Acts. It provides a more coherent whole-of-government approach to performance management and accountability and expands the previous legislation's principles approach while simultaneously recognising the appropriateness of a wider range of agency types. It uses a more practical bifurcation of agencies, essentially on the basis of the extent of reliance on government revenues, with 'Commonwealth entities' being those more reliant and 'Commonwealth companies' being those operating commercially (and subject to corporations law). The classification of different Commonwealth organisations remains complex, however, as is evident in the Department of Finance's *Australian Government Organisations Register* (Department of Finance 2016a) and its most recent 'flipchart' (Department of Finance 2020).

The Department of Finance has updated its 2005 advice on the most appropriate structure for different government activities. The assessment template (Department of Finance 2016b) guides reviews of existing organisations as well as proposed new organisations through a series of 'gateways':

1. whether the Commonwealth has the constitutional power to undertake the activity
2. whether the government is best placed to undertake the activity, in whole or part, compared to an external body
3. whether the activity can be conducted by an existing Commonwealth body, in whole or in part.

The guidance seeks information to substantiate whether the activity requires statutory independence or should operate commercially, and also requires cost–benefit analysis of viable options for a body's governance structure. This seems likely to continue the 2005 guidance that favoured ministerial departments or, at least, large organisations with economies of scale (or the use of shared corporate services with other organisations). The template does not, however, include specific views on the appropriateness of certain structures for certain functions, but simply requires reviews to present arguments. The Department of Finance nonetheless presumably assesses the arguments presented and advises ministers, and the chances are that it gives more weight in its decision-making to the cost–benefit analysis and ministerial control than to other factors.

Examples of structural developments and reforms

Ministerial departments

Departments provide the closest support to ministers through policy advice, assisting with the preparation of legislation required to implement government policy and ensuring that the government's policies and programs are properly managed. In many cases, particularly at provincial government level where the emphasis is more on service delivery than high-level policy, departments often directly manage the government's programs. As indicated below, Australia has not moved as far as some other countries down the NPM path of separating policy advice (in departments) from service delivery (in executive agencies), though it has always had some services managed in non-departmental organisations.

The prime minister has the authority to determine the allocation of responsibilities between ministers and departments via the Administrative Arrangements Orders. This power to change departmental responsibilities and structures is exercised frequently in Australia and presents considerable flexibility in the overall structure of government, with the corollary of administrative disruption. Factors in the allocation of functions include not only promoting improvements in performance via better linking of related functions and adjusting to new priorities and circumstances, but also political considerations such as balancing the governing party's geographic and factional interests.

A significant development in Australia was the introduction of 'super departments' overseen by a portfolio minister with support from assistant ministers. This approach began at the Commonwealth level in 1987 and has been replicated by most provincial governments. The two main advantages have been to give departments sufficient breadth of responsibility to manage effectively their public service and financial powers and to support better policy coordination by having every portfolio (and its department) represented in the cabinet by its senior portfolio minister without allowing cabinet to become unmanageably large, and by each portfolio minister having one or more junior ministers to ensure sufficient political attention to the range of issues for which he or she had responsibility. A further advantage claimed at the time was that the new arrangement would ensure more stability over departmental structures and responsibilities through the combinations of functions with strong long-term connections.

Key respects of the 1987 restructuring have been sustained for the last 30 years. The concept of portfolio ministers and portfolio secretaries (the public service heads of the portfolio ministers' departments) has continued and to a degree strengthened. On the other hand, after a few years of greater stability, the precise responsibilities of portfolios began again to change frequently, particularly following changes in prime ministers. While key long-term linkages were mostly retained, on occasion they were not and, in some cases, the arrangements were not consistent with the original portfolio structure principles (particularly the December 2019 arrangements, which blurred lines of accountability to the ministry and cabinet (Podger 2019)). Nonetheless, the Australian Government continues to have no more than 20 departments (currently 13), though there are currently 23 ministers in the cabinet. Some provincial governments operate with fewer departments and portfolio ministers.

The Health portfolio provides an example. The Minister for Health is currently assisted by three junior ministers with specific responsibilities for aged care, senior Australians, youth, sport and regional health (one of the junior ministers also has responsibilities in a different portfolio). Their responsibilities are set in part by the prime minister and in part at the discretion of the portfolio minister. The Australian Department of Health is responsible for advising these ministers and the government on all aspects of national policy on health, aged care and sport – this includes health financing issues and intergovernmental agreements and detailed matters such as the listing of medicines for the Pharmaceutical Benefits Scheme and of medical services for the Medical Benefits Schedule.

The department also manages significant regulation functions such as the safety and efficacy of therapeutic goods, and manages some service delivery programs including residential and home-based aged care services programs (purchasing these services from non-government providers), Indigenous health programs (again mainly purchased from non-government providers) and public health programs. These various functions of the department often utilise external expertise through statutory committees, and sometimes have their own organisation within the department (such as the Therapeutic Goods Administration).

While the department has retained responsibility for managing many regulations and service delivery programs, the portfolio includes a number of separate agencies undertaking various regulatory, research and service delivery functions. The departmental secretary is also known as the 'portfolio secretary' and has responsibility, for example, for budget coordination across the portfolio, policy advice across the portfolio and advising on appointments to the other portfolio agencies.

Non-departmental service delivery agencies

There is provision in the PS Act for 'executive agencies' to be established separate from departments but without their own legislation. In practice, Australia has generally made little use of this structural option, though it was for a time promoted in other countries pursuing NPM reforms (e.g. New Zealand and the United Kingdom via Prime Minister Margaret Thatcher's 'next steps'), separating policy from administration under purchaser–provider arrangements that imposed firm performance regimes on the executive agencies. More frequently, Australia has used agencies with their own statutes to deliver certain government-funded services independently of ministerial departments. Longstanding arrangements include the Australian Taxation Office, for which independence from politics is seen to be particularly important. There are in fact more than 100 statutory authorities at the Commonwealth level, and similarly large numbers at the provincial level. This subsection considers those whose main function is to deliver government-funded services while those with a regulatory, integrity or research role are included in the following two subsections, and those that are primarily commercial are discussed in the subsection on GBEs.

As mentioned above, many service delivery programs continue to be managed by ministerial departments. Nonetheless, a reform trajectory can be identified in a number of areas of service delivery: from wholly departmental management of policy and service delivery to their separation between departments and non-departmental agencies, to a further separation of purchasing, usually by a ministerial department; from providing by non-departmental agencies, to competitive tender with government providers (now commercialised) and non-government providers, which some cases has evolved into ongoing collaborative partnerships with NGOs; and, finally, to privatisation of government providers. This trajectory was by no means the standard approach, but it can still be seen as an undercurrent in many contemporary political and academic debates about the future of such human services as health, schools and disability support.

Perhaps the most radical example of this trajectory is employment services. Unemployment benefits were paid by the Commonwealth Department of Social Services (DSS) from the 1940s and were managed, along with other pensions, benefits and allowances, via a network of DSS offices. In the late 1940s, the government sought to more actively assist jobseekers and introduced employment services to link unemployed people to employers seeking workers. This was managed by a new legislated corporation, the Commonwealth Employment Service (CES), working under the Minister for Labour and National Service and in conjunction with his department. The nationwide network of CES offices registered job vacancies and drew them to the attention of jobseekers, even arranging job interviews and advising on selections in some cases. Responses by jobseekers in receipt of benefits were used for the purposes of the benefit work test managed by DSS. CES offices were often located close to the DSS offices.

In 1997, DSS was split and its service delivery role transferred to a new statutory authority, later named Centrelink (Halligan & Wills 2008). Centrelink was also given the responsibilities of the former CES along with responsibility for the delivery of some other human services (e.g. housing assistance). DSS and the Department of Education, Employment, Training and Youth Affairs (DEETYA) each retained policy responsibility for their respective functions, as did other departments affected by the split (e.g. housing). The initiative reflected the NPM interest in improving efficiency by separating policy from administration, but with the added element of establishing a 'one-stop-shop' and allowing rationalisation of offices across the country.

Around this time, DEETYA experimented with contracting private sector organisations to help longer term unemployed people gain sustained employment, through training and rehabilitation services. This involved not just separating policy from administration but also separating purchasing from providing. In 1998 this experiment was translated into a much wider tender process for employment services with payments based on successful employment outcomes. Initially, the Job Network involved both private sector providers (including for-profit and not-for-profit organisations) and an in-house provider, Employment National, created out of the former CES component of Centrelink. In a later tender process, however, the government provider was not successful and was subsequently wound up. Job Network (now called Job Services Australia) remains today a system of non-government providers paid by the Department of Employment via competitive tender with payments based on successful outcomes (Jarvie & Mercer 2017).

While this is an example of a classic NPM trajectory, more recent developments with other human services demonstrate some reversal of direction. The creation of Centrelink in 1997 proved to be highly successful (Halligan & Wills 2008) and, in 2004, the then government decided to press further the idea of integrated human services by establishing a small Department of Human Services (DHS) overseeing Centrelink and several other service delivery agencies (including the Health Insurance Commission responsible for most Medicare entitlements and the Child Support Agency responsible for ensuring maintenance payments for children in families whose parents have separated). DHS was given responsibility for service delivery policy as distinct from service delivery (which remained with Centrelink and the other service delivery agencies) while the development of functional policies on social security and Medicare remained with the respective line departments and their ministers. DHS's responsibility involved ensuring information systems were linked and further rationalisation of offices, and encouraging experimentation with greater collaboration with clients and external organisations (the 'citizen-centred services' agenda, see Bridge 2012).

In 2008, the then Labor government took this approach in a new direction by incorporating the separate agencies within the ministerial department (DHS) and forcing much greater integration and stronger ministerial involvement. Legislation to formalise this arrangement was passed in 2011. Critics feared this would in time reduce the focus on clients and professional service delivery as the department spent more time 'looking upwards' rather than 'downwards and outwards', and might dilute the vital links between functional policies and their administration (Podger 2013b). Recent criticism of the department's handling of clients provides evidence in support of these concerns (Parliament of Australia Community Services Reference Committee 2017).

In December 2019, the government announced the abolition of DHS and the intention to replace it with a new executive agency attached to the Department of Social Services, a partial move back towards having service delivery separate from a ministerial department (Prime Minister 2019).

Another example of changing directions concerns Indigenous programs. In the 1980s, a statutory authority, the Aboriginal and Torres Strait Islanders Commission (ATSIC), was established with a unique governance structure including a board of elected representatives of Indigenous communities. Continuing problems with this governance arrangement, including over the chief executive's dual accountability to the board and the minister, led to its abolition in 2005, with responsibility for its programs being transferred to a ministerial department (initially the Department of Immigration and Multicultural and Indigenous Affairs). In 2013, this responsibility was transferred to the Department of Prime Minister and Cabinet (PM&C), ostensibly to demonstrate the priority being given to Indigenous wellbeing. Critics, however, have expressed concern that the department has no service delivery experience and that a separate agency would ensure a stronger focus on clients and communities (National Congress of Australia's First Peoples 2016).

Notwithstanding the partial reversal of the trend towards separating policy from administration, interest in greater autonomy in other service delivery fields including health, education and disability services has increased. The state of Victoria introduced a purchaser–provider split for hospital services in 1995 using a system of 'casemix' funding related to hospital outputs based on episodes of care (developed previously by the national Department of Health). Public hospitals were no longer part of the department but operated as independent corporations with their own executive boards. While other states have been slow to follow this example (which delivered substantial efficiency gains as hospitals, working with professional independence from their parent departments, focused more carefully on costs and the management of their patients), national governments have increasingly pressured them to do so.

In 2010, a new intergovernmental agreement (Council of Australian Governments (COAG) 2010) imposed a nationwide purchaser–provider split based on casemix funding that has given all public hospitals (or networks of hospitals) greater autonomy in exchange for more disciplined funding and performance reporting. Regional primary health organisations were also established (Department of Health and Ageing 2010) with autonomy based on community and professional governance arrangements, with their role being to help with the planning and coordination of primary care services (which are mostly provided by doctors working in private practice but funded via Medicare). Under the Liberal governments of Tony Abbott and Malcolm Turnbull, these organisations have been reorganised as primary health networks with even greater independence from the Health Department but subject to performance oversight (Dutton 2014).

A report on school education (Gonski 2011) was largely endorsed by both sides of politics, particularly in regard to needs-based funding and proposals for greater school autonomy subject to community participation and improved performance management.

The National Disability Insurance Agency (NDIA) is a statutory authority sitting within the Social Services portfolio but separate from the relevant ministerial department (the DSS). It is currently introducing a new disability insurance scheme across Australia involving decentralised service delivery tailored to the needs and preferences of individuals and their families, and with most service provision by NGOs. The NDIA has a board that includes people with strong professional and community experience in the field.

These examples demonstrate that, notwithstanding the reforms of the last 30 years, there remains a range of different approaches to service delivery structures in Australia. Arguably, separate and more independent government or non-government service delivery organisations are better positioned to be responsive to citizens' needs and preferences than ministerial departments, though they need to share information to promote good policies and deliver coordinated services.

Statutory regulatory organisations

Australia frequently utilises statutory authorities to manage regulations that are sensitive and require an emphasis on procedural fairness without political consideration and/or require specialist expertise. Ministerial departments may also manage regulations (as mentioned above) and, when they do, they must act impartially and properly under public service and administrative law. The perception of independence is, however, generally greater when a separate statutory authority manages the regulation or other activity. Such independence is often reinforced by greater security of tenure for the agency head.

In most cases, these organisations are funded by government revenues (and/or levies on the industries involved) and they are subject to the same financial management regime as departments; their staff are also usually employed under the PS Act and are therefore required to uphold public service values and obey the code of conduct. They are also subject to administrative laws that require open and fair decision-making.

The NPM reforms that have reduced the government's role in direct service provision and increased its role in purchasing have also led to an increase in the extent of regulation and to some increase in the number of statutory authorities. In the health area, for example, the new system of casemix purchasing of hospital services led to the establishment of a new authority (the Independent Hospital Pricing Authority) to set the 'efficient price' for these services and also to a new performance monitoring authority (the National Health Performance Authority). Subsequent concerns about the number of new regulatory agencies and their cost led to the abolition of some and the transfer of their responsibilities to other existing organisations in line with the Department of Finance's assessment template (most often the transfer has been back into ministerial departments).

Another field where regulation activity has undergone significant change is in ensuring the efficient operation of the market. On the one hand, this has involved a degree of 'deregulation' as government intervention in the market (such as promoting cooperatives of producers or protecting small producers) has been reduced, and on the other hand it has involved new regulatory activity to promote competition and stop collusion or other anti-competitive practices, and to ensure transparency and proper governance of private companies. This regulation is conducted mostly by new or strengthened statutory authorities such as the Australian Competition and Consumer Commission and the Australian Securities and Investment Commission, which operate in the Treasury portfolio but independently of the department and the minister (the Treasurer).

Integrity organisations

The statutory authority model is also standard for 'integrity organisations' such as the auditor-general's office (Australian National Audit Office), the electoral commissioner, independent commissions against corruption, ombudsman's offices, public service commissions and the bureau of statistics. In some cases the integrity officer heading the agency is referred to as an 'officer of the parliament' to convey his or her independence from the executive arm of government and the organisation's closer attachment to the legislature; some have close links with the judiciary.

The strengthening of administrative law and emphasis on human rights over recent decades has resulted in an increase to the number of these authorities. They include such bodies as the Office of the Australian Information Commissioner and the Australian Human Rights Commission.

Their independence from ministers is based on their role in overseeing aspects of executive government, protecting the integrity of the democratic process or providing authoritative data for the operations of government and the market. The degree of independence is set out in their respective legislation. There is some debate as to which organisations sit within this category as some must operate within the executive and independently of it (e.g. public service commissions).

Government business enterprises

A broad trajectory of reform of the governance of public enterprises is identifiable over the last 40 years or more, from management within departments to separate agencies or statutory authorities to commercialised businesses and, in some cases, to privatised businesses. That said, Australia has long used government-owned authorities and companies to undertake some activities, such as infrastructure or utilities services, reflecting in part Australia's limited private capital and the historical lack of capacity for competition for such services (Wettenhall 1996, 1998).

These organisations interacted with ministers before reform, though not generally in regard to the professional delivery of services, and, in their case, the reform trajectory has been truncated so that social objectives ('community service objectives') have been more clearly identified and funded directly from the budget or via transparent discounts from profit targets and dividend payments; ministerial oversight has increasingly been limited to these and to broad direction akin to that of major shareholders; and, subsequently, consideration has been given to partial or full privatisation with community service obligations funded directly through government programs.

Postal and telecommunications services perhaps present the most significant example of Australia's GBE reforms. For most of the last century, the biggest national government organisation was the Postmaster-General's Department (PMG). Established from former provincial organisations shortly after federation in 1901, it employed well over half of all Commonwealth public servants from 1901 until 1975. While structurally a ministerial department, the PMG was responsible for administering the *Post and Telegraph Act 1901*, which set out the powers and responsibilities of the minister (the postmaster-general) and the head of the department (the director-general). It required substantial government-funded infrastructure to provide postal and telegraphic services that were seen to be natural monopolies and that should be available to all Australians (an important social objective). Employees were public servants under the PS Act, and the department was subject to standard, centralised financial management controls.

In 1975, the PMG was split with the establishment of two statutory corporations (Australian Postal Corporation – later known as Australia Post – and the Australian Telecommunications Corporation – later known as Telecom) separate from the ministerial department (initially still called the PMG but later the Department of Communications). Policy remained with the minister and policy advice with the department, but administration was left to the two statutory corporations, which were expected to operate in a more commercial way while still reporting to the minister. The corporations were each governed by a board appointed by the government and with a chief executive officer (CEO) (initially also appointed by the government but later by the board). Staff were no longer employed under the PS Act but directly by the corporations. The corporations were still subject to the Audit Act but with considerable delegation of authority from the Treasury. The extent of ministerial and Treasury oversight was, however, the cause of ongoing tension for the next decade.

In the 1980s, as the NPM agenda emerged more clearly, a new set of guidelines for statutory authorities and GBEs was issued by the then Minister for Finance (Walsh 1987). The 'Walsh guidelines' articulated more clearly the respective roles of ministers and the GBE's boards and management. Ministers would not only appoint the board but also set each GBE's commercial performance target (e.g. its rate of return on assets), approve the board's strategic plan, agree on the disbursement of profits (usually requiring dividend payments to government) and major new investments or divestments, and identify 'community service obligations' (e.g. a standard price for all domestic letters, access to a telephone line at a capped price).

The board and management would have responsibility for operational matters, including employment, allocation of resources and contracting, but would report publicly to ministers and the parliament on their commercial performance and in respect of community service obligations. These guidelines broadly reflected corporations law requirements in the private sector, with the role of ministers being akin to that of shareholders and the role of the board akin to that of a private sector board. They were given effect through the delegations and oversight approach of the Department of Finance. Australia Post and Telecom were amongst the first to be subject to these Walsh guidelines.

The 1997 financial management legislation, with its distinction between FMA Act bodies and CAC Act bodies, consolidated existing practice for Australia Post and Telecom as set out in the Walsh guidelines, placing them under the new CAC Act.

The late 1980s and early 1990s saw a transfer of Telecom's regulatory role to an independent regulator and the opening of the telecommunications market to competition. Following a review of structural arrangements in 1990 among the then three carriers (the Overseas Telecommunications Corporation Limited (OTC) and a government-owned satellite company, Aussat, having also been established), Telecom was merged with the OTC to form the Australian and Overseas Telecommunications Corporation Limited (AOTC), which was subsequently renamed Telstra Corporation Limited (Telstra) in 1993. Aussat was sold along with the right to operate a second fixed-line carrier in competition with Telstra.

It was against this background – and the prospect of the opening of Australia's telecommunications market to full competition in July 1997 – that the then Labor government decided to partly privatise Telstra while retaining majority public ownership. Almost half (49.6%) of the shares in Telstra were subsequently issued to the public in two tranches: the first in 1997 (33%) and the second in 1999 (16.6%). The partial privatisation was criticised by advocates of public ownership and those of a more market-based approach, the latter arguing either for full privatisation or the separation of the copper wire network (arguably still a natural monopoly at the time) from the provision of services over the network, which might be fully privatised and open to competition.

A new conservative government subsequently decided on full privatisation. Additional shares in the company were issued to the public in 2006 with the residual 17 per cent government shareholding transferred to a government investment company (the Future Fund) that was established to fund liabilities accumulated by unfunded government employee superannuation funds.

The reform trajectory was more recently interrupted by the Labor government's decision in 2008 to create a national broadband network (NBN). The government's policy was for 93 per cent of premises to have access to the NBN through fibre optic cable and the remaining 7 per cent of premises to be connected to the NBN through fixed wireless and satellite technologies. The government established NBN Co Ltd, a wholly government-owned company, to roll out this network. This company's role is restricted to infrastructure provision and the supply of wholesale services; it is not allowed to offer retail services over the network.

NBN Co Ltd has subsequently entered into a multi-billion-dollar contract with Telstra to participate in the rollout. These developments have been accompanied by new regulatory arrangements that limit competition developing in the broadband market, a move designed to enhance the financial viability of NBN Co Ltd. The Labor government's stated intention nonetheless was to eventually fully privatise NBN Co Ltd.

The Abbott (conservative) government, elected in 2013, revisited these arrangements with a view to reducing construction costs and the rollout timetable through the use of fibre-to-the-node technologies rather than fibre-to-the-premises connections. Its policy includes removal of regulatory impediments to the construction and operation of non-NBN access networks, though it is locked in for now to the existing contractual arrangements between Telstra and NBN. The commitment to the full privatisation of NBN Co Ltd once construction of the NBN is completed remains.

Australia Post remains a fully government-owned corporation. In responding to market forces and new technology, however, it has moved far from its origins. Most of its physical service outlets are now franchised through local supermarkets and newsagents; its offices offer a wide range of services beyond traditional postal services (including as one-stop-shop access points for government services in many rural areas); it is responding to the emergence of a private delivery industry as internet purchasing has expanded; and it does much of its business online.

Despite this transformation, it still has community service obligations to meet, particularly with regard to the price of stamps for domestic letters and ensuring access to postal services around the country. The advance of the internet and increasing competition from private parcel delivery companies raises the serious possibility of privatising Australia Post, although neither side of politics has agreed to take that step.

This general trajectory, in full or in part, can be seen in other national commercial-type services such as Qantas (originally a private company, but nationalised in the 1940s for national development purposes, commercialised, partially privatised and finally fully privatised) and in many provincial government utilities such as power companies (some fully privatised, others only commercialised). The approach was made more systematic after 1995 when COAG established an intergovernmental agreement on competition policy (COAG 1995) requiring all jurisdictions to review systematically where government action, whether by regulation or government provision, might restrict competition.

Internal government services

In parallel with the GBE reform trajectory, Australia has experienced an interesting sequence of reforms to its management of internal government services such as government property and asset services, government cars, construction and employees' and welfare recipients' health tests.

Many of these services were owned and managed by a ministerial department (mostly the Department of Administrative Services (DAS) at the Commonwealth level). During the 1980s and 1990s these arrangements went through amendments to improve efficiency (Tanzer 1992). Broadly, these steps were:

- First, agencies using the services were required to pay user charges (rents for property, hire charges for cars, etc). Agencies received partial supplementation to their budgets in recognition of these additional charges and budgetary funding to the DAS was withdrawn. The imposition of the charges encouraged agencies to review how much of each service they really needed.
- Second, agencies were allowed to negotiate better deals with alternative providers of services. Many shifted to private rental properties, for example, or contracted with private hire car firms and used private publishing services.

- Third, the DAS was permitted, within limits, to offer its services beyond its government agency clients.

- Fourth, as a consequence of the second and third developments, DAS conducted an internal restructuring, establishing each of its service delivery functions as a 'business' with an advisory board to help set its commercial strategy and with accrual accounting introduced to help assess its commercial performance. These 'businesses' were legally under the control of the department's secretary and his minister, but an effort was made to change the culture from a bureaucratic one to a customer-focused one.

- Fifth, some of the businesses were incorporated as government-owned companies (e.g. the car business became AusFleet), and some others were wound up (e.g. Australian Construction Services). Assets were sold (e.g. inner city properties) during this process, to the considerable advantage of the government, which was seeking to reduce its debts at the time.

- Finally, a number of the businesses were privatised (e.g. AusFleet) and remaining policy oversight was shifted to the Department of Finance.

The overall effect was to achieve efficiencies and budget savings, while also ensuring that government agencies could tailor required services to support their business rather than be forced to accept a one-size-fits-all arrangement.

Intergovernmental bodies

Australia's federal system of government has led to the creation of some intergovernmental organisations aimed at supporting cooperation and coordination amongst governments and allowing, in some cases, shared responsibility for particular functions.

Key intergovernmental forums were informal for many years and functioned without dedicated staff operating in a separate organisational structure. These included the Premiers' Conference (regular meetings of first ministers) and the Loan Council (meetings of treasurers that set ceilings on each government's borrowings). Both these forums were chaired by the Commonwealth and, as its revenue-raising capacity surpassed that of provincial governments, the Commonwealth was increasingly able to control agendas and influence decisions.

The Commonwealth's dominant role in revenue raising also facilitated what became an important principle in the federation: horizontal fiscal equalisation (HFE). This involves ensuring provincial governments have equal capacity to deliver services to their populations, with a distribution of Commonwealth revenues to make up for variations in revenue-raising capacity and costs of delivery. The intergovernmental Commonwealth Grants Commission (CGC) was established in the 1930s to advise governments on the distribution of revenues needed to give effect to HFE, with decisions then taken by the Premiers' Conference. The CGC is legally a Commonwealth statutory authority, but it is led by a board of commissioners with members nominated by the Commonwealth and the states. As a highly professional, technocratic organisation, its advice is rarely ignored.

Over the last 40 years or more, the Commonwealth has broadened its policy interests and used its financial powers to influence many provincial government programs including in such service delivery areas as hospitals, schools, housing and community services. This increased sharing of responsibilities has required the development of greater capacity for coordination and cooperation. COAG replaced the Premiers' Conference from the early 1990s and brought a wide range of supporting ministerial councils that had emerged over previous decades within its general purview. Some of these ministerial councils developed small full-time secretariats attached to a relevant state or Commonwealth department that supported both the ministerial council and the advisory committee of relevant departmental secretaries.

COAG itself is supported by staff in PM&C. An intergovernmental agreement was reached in 2008 to clarify roles and responsibilities within a new financial framework aimed at improving performance across jurisdictions in areas of national importance. The agreement included the establishment of an independent COAG Reform Council with dedicated staff resources to monitor and evaluate jurisdictional performance (O'Loughlin 2013). Under the Abbott government, however, this council was abolished as a budget savings measure, leaving PM&C solely responsible once again for supporting COAG.[3]

---

3   As this book was in production, the Prime Minister announced that the 'National Cabinet', which had operated to oversee the cross-jurisdictional response to the COVID-19 pandemic, would continue into the future replacing COAG as the central forum for inter-governmental relations.

Other bodies have emerged over the last 30 years to support or manage shared responsibilities. For example, the Australian Institute of Health and Welfare (AIHW) was established in 1987 as a Commonwealth statutory authority but with a board that includes state nominees and people with experience in nominated fields such as health, housing and community welfare. The AIHW is a statistical and research body that uses administrative data from all jurisdictions to report publicly on the state of Australia's overall health and welfare and on the activities of all governments in these fields. The Great Barrier Reef Marine Park Authority is also a Commonwealth statutory authority but managed through shared powers with the State of Queensland. In managing this World Heritage park it has been given some powers over environmental management of the neighbouring Queensland coastal area. The shared approach began in 1975 with initial Commonwealth legislation and was subsequently reinforced through an intergovernmental agreement and the establishment of the Authority, which has a board including representatives of Queensland.

In some areas, the intergovernmental arrangements involve New Zealand as well as Australian jurisdictions. New Zealand is an active observer at COAG and all its ministerial councils and, in some cases, it has agreed to be bound by decisions taken. A particular example is in the field of food safety. Food Standards Australia New Zealand (FSANZ) is formally a statutory authority under the Commonwealth of Australia but the legislation sets out a joint governance arrangement across the two countries. FSANZ is responsible for the food standards code for both countries and this is enforced in each country by regulations managed locally (in Australia, mainly by provincial and local governments). Policies that guide the food standards set by FSANZ are determined through the Legislative and Governance Forum on Food Regulation, which is effectively a ministerial council comprising health and agriculture ministers from the Commonwealth of Australia, New Zealand and the Australian state and territory governments.

A possible, more coherent framework of formal and informal governance rules and processes for Australian Government organisations

Despite NPM and related reforms over the last 30 years, and more recent attempts to provide a coherent legislative framework for the governance of public sector activities in Australia that promotes organisational performance and ensures public accountability, Australia still has an eclectic mix of structures and governance arrangements and, notwithstanding the Department of Finance's assessment template, lacks firm policy on optimal future arrangements. Australia is hardly alone in this respect: the colourful term 'signposting the zoo' to describe attempts at coherence about when to use which structure originated in New Zealand.

As indicated by institutional, political and organisational theory, governance arrangements are always likely to involve a mix of formal rules and informal conventions and practices, and the degree of bureaucratic autonomy is determined as much by political judgements as by the particular functions to be performed.

That said, there are a number of factors that should influence those political judgements and the formal governance structures imposed to promote performance and ensure public accountability. These reflect the fact that there are several and, at times, competing principles behind the management of public sector activities, whether in Australia or elsewhere, such as:

- 'The public interest': public policies and programs should reflect the collective interests and preferences of the people, whether they be determined through formal democratic processes (such as Australia's parliamentary system and the role of elected ministers in determining policies in the public interest) or other forms of public engagement and consultation.

- Fairness and justice in decision-making: within the policy frameworks set by the government in the public interest, administrative decisions should be made impartially and professionally, strictly according to the law, and without influence from personal connections or political or social affiliations.

- Performance: public resources utilised for the delivery of government services should be applied effectively to meet the government's policy objectives, and used as efficiently as possible.
- Public accountability: decisions should be made transparently and decision-makers should be held accountable to the public whether through democratic processes or other public review arrangements.

While all these principles are important, the balance between them may vary with the function being performed. Judgements about the appropriate formal structure in the Australian political context might be influenced primarily by:

- the degree to which the function relies upon government revenues rather than user charges
- the importance of responsiveness to the government's political direction in the public interest as compared to the importance of independent decision-making for reasons of fairness or justice or professional expertise
- the importance of a focus on meeting the needs of clients compared to the importance of responsiveness to the government's political direction.

NPM, NPG and more recent developments, which are driven in part by technological changes and associated changes in community expectations, have added to the array of structural options (including the use of third parties) as well as further dimensions (or principles) of good public sector management. The latter include in particular:

- the ability of citizens and communities to directly influence services
- the capacity for collaboration across public services to meet the needs and preferences of citizens and communities.

The lack of coherence in current Australian structural arrangements is not just a theoretical concern. It may also contribute to weaknesses in public sector capabilities and performance, as revealed in recent reviews and debates (e.g. APSC 2014; Shergold 2015; Banks 2008 and 2018; Independent Review of the APS 2019), such as in longer term strategic policy advising, implementation of new policy measures and management of risk.

Table 3.1 sets out guidance on how well different formal structures in the Australian framework address competing principles, and hence their suitability for different functions.

Table 3.1. Possible mapping of formal structures to different key principles

COMPETING PRINCIPLES	STRUCTURAL OPTIONS							
	Ministerial department		Executive agency	Statutory authority	Government company	Specially created non-government company	Third party under contract	Third party in partnership
	Fully part of department	Separate office in department						
Importance of democratic/ministerial oversight and control	S	S	M/S	W/M	W	W	W/M	W
Independence of administration	W	W/M	M	S	S	S	M	S
Ability of citizens/communities to influence services	W	W/M	M	M	M/S	M/S	M	S
Capacity for collaboration	M/S	W	M/S	M/S	W	M	W/M	M/S
Importance of specialty/niche service	W	M	M/S	S	S	S	S	S
Linking policy and administration	S	S	M	W/M	W	W	W/M	W/M
Relevance of commercial principles for efficiency	W	W/M	W/M	W/M	S	M/S	M/S	M/S

W = weak support for the principle; M = medium support for the principle; S = strong support

Source. Author's presentation

Informal processes and arrangements may be used to complement the formal structure chosen to address perceived weaknesses and to reinforce strengths. Table 3.2 illustrates the sorts of (mostly) informal arrangements that may be used.

Table 3.2. Possible complementary and more informal processes

1. Democratic/ministerial oversight and control may be strengthened by:
   a. ministerial approval of strategic directions
   b. ministerial 'statements of expectations' about the way in which an independent agency should administer its responsibilities
   c. agreements between ministerial departments and agencies

2. Administration may be made more independent by:
   a. statutory obligations including in-program legislation
   b. delegated authority
   c. decision-making and reporting frameworks and processes (including public reporting and the use of advisory committees and boards)

3. Citizens/communities' capacity to influence may be strengthened by:
   a. advisory committees and other consultative arrangements
   b. reduced legislative prescriptions
   c. delegated authority
   d. budget flexibility, funds pooling
   e. appropriate agency culture, 'public service motivation', staff continuity, career paths

4. Capacity for collaboration may be strengthened by:
   a. shared information and shared corporate services
   b. linked data
   c. inter-agency committees with appropriate political authority
   d. regional or local cross-agency forums
   e. pooled budgets

5. Expertise in particular fields may be strengthened by:
   a. identified specialist units and advisers in departments
   b. public reporting
   c. staff continuity, particular career paths
   d. partnerships and staff interchange with external specialist organisations

6. Links between policy and administration may be strengthened by:
   a. regular committee processes, joint task forces
   b. protocols about reporting experience and initiating policy proposals
   c. purchaser/provider agreements with the policy departments

7. More 'commercial' approaches to program management may be strengthened by:
   a. separate decision-making and reporting processes for identified programs
   b. appropriate financial incentives and budgetary flexibility.

Source. Author's presentation

Some inconsistency is apparent in the current complex Australian approach, which favours greater use of NGOs to deliver public services (these are sometimes also purchased by an independent statutory authority (e.g. NDIA)) and the greater use of purchaser–provider arrangements (e.g. in health), and simultaneously to favour returning service delivery functions to ministerial departments (e.g. Centrelink, Indigenous affairs). Greater consistency might be gained, along with improved client services, if Australia returned to making more use of non-departmental agencies to deliver a range of services.[4] As with the contracted non-government service delivery arrangements, care is needed to ensure that complementary formal and informal processes provide adequate linkages between policy and administration.

In part, the apparent inconsistency may be related to wider changes that are underway in Australian public administration. Firmer political control over administration has been evident now for some time, including through ministerial appointments of partisan support staff, and the desire for such control may sometimes override other considerations. At the same time, governments that need to negotiate with other parties to have legislation passed may agree to demands for more independent administration of certain functions despite the appearance of inconsistency.

Conclusion

Australia has long used a wide range of organisational structures for different government functions. The structures and processes in tables 3.1 and 3.2 are relevant to Australia's particular context of parliamentary democracy, market economy and a federal government framework. They involve a mix of formal rules and informal processes and practices, drawing on organisational as well as political theories. The appropriate mix of formal structure and informal processes reflects political judgements, the reputation of the agencies involved and public attitudes to the functions being performed.

The story of gradual reform over the last 30 or 40 years reveals a process designed to improve government efficiency and effectiveness in a world of increasing global competition driven by new technology. Structural reform has been a significant component of Australia's reform experience.

---

4   Perhaps the 2020 replacement of DHS with Services Australia represents a step in this direction.

Recent action has attempted to present a more coherent financial and personnel framework that could help to identify the appropriate structures for different functions and their accountability processes. There remain, however, significant inconsistencies in current practices and more could be done to clarify which structures are most suited to which functions, and what informal arrangements might best complement the formal rules. This is most evident with respect to service delivery.

It seems likely that the next stage of reform will focus on further increasing the responsiveness of government-funded services to the needs and preferences of individuals and different communities. Support for the use of non-government agencies to deliver services is based on their independence and flexibility to respond to individual circumstances, yet there are simultaneous moves to bring some government service delivery back under closer political control within ministerial departments. The challenge is to find the structures and processes most suited to responsive service delivery while also ensuring appropriate accountability to the government and the wider Australian community.

References

Australian Public Service Commission (APSC) 2003, *Australian Experience of Public Sector Reform*, Commonwealth of Australia, Canberra.

—— 2014, *State of the Service Report 2014*, Commonwealth of Australia, Canberra.

Banks, G 2008, 'Evidence-based policy-making: what is it? How do we get it?', ANZSOG/ANU Public Lecture Series, Canberra, doi.org/10.22459/CRAPP. 05.2009.10.

—— 2018, 'Whatever happened to "evidence-based policy making"?', Alf Rattigan Lecture 2018, Australia and New Zealand School of Government, www.anzsog. edu.au/resource-library/news-media/alf-rattigan-lecture-whatever-happened-to-evidence-based-policy-making.

Bridge, C 2012, 'Citizen centric service in the Australian Department of Human Services: the department's experience in engaging the community in co-design of government service delivery and developments in e-government services', *Australian Journal of Public Administration*, vol 71, no 2, pp 167–77, doi.org/ 10.1111/j.1467-8500.2012.00763.x.

Carpenter, DP 2001, *The Forging of Bureaucratic Autonomy: Reputations, Networks and Policy Innovation in Executive Agencies*, Princeton University Press.

Coombs, HC 1976, *Final Report of the Royal Commission into Australian Government Administration*, AGPS, Canberra.

Council of Australian Governments (COAG) 1995, *Competition Principles Agreement*, COAG, Canberra.

—— 2010, 'COAG Meeting Communique, 19–20 April 2010', COAG, Canberra.

Department of Finance 2016a, *Australian Government Organisations Register*, Canberra.

—— 2016b, *Commonwealth Governance Structures Policy Assessment Template – Review of New or Existing Body*, Canberra.

—— 2020, *Flipchart of Commonwealth entities and companies*, www.finance.gov. au/government/managing-commonwealth-resources/structure-australian-government-public-sector/pgpa-act-flipchart-list.

Department of Finance and Administration 2005a, *Commonwealth Entities and Companies Flipchart*, Commonwealth of Australia, Canberra.

—— 2005b, *Governance Arrangements for Australian Government Bodies, August 2005*, Financial Management Reference Material no 2, Commonwealth of Australia, Canberra.

Department of Finance and Deregulation 2012, *Shaping the Focus: A Framework for Improving Commonwealth Performance*, Commonwealth Financial Accountability Review Position Paper, Australia.

Department of Health and Ageing 2010, *A National Health and Hospitals Network for Australia's Future*, Commonwealth of Australia, Canberra.

Dutton, P 2014, 'Primary health networks to drive better primary health care', press release, 15 Oct, Canberra.

Gonski, D 2011, *Review of Funding for Schools: Final Report*, Australian Department of Education, Employment and Workplace Relations, Canberra.

Gourlay, PD 2004, 'Recommendations not worth the wait: the Uhrig Report', *Canberra Times Public Sector Informant*, Sep.

—— 2017, 'The folly of Home Affairs super ministry revamp', *The Public Sector Informant, Canberra Times*, 1 Aug.

Gulick, L & Urwick, L (eds) 1937, *Papers on the Science of Administration*, Columbia University, New York.

Halligan, J & Horrigan, B 2005, *Reforming Corporate Governance in the Australian Federal Public Sector: From Uhrig to Implementation*, Issues Paper Series no 2, University of Canberra.

Halligan, J & Wills, J 2008, *The Centrelink Experiment: Innovation in Service Delivery*, ANU Press, Canberra, doi.org/10.22459/CE.12.2008.

Herzberg, F 1968, 'One more time: how do you motivate employees?', *Harvard Business Review*, Jan–Feb, pp 53–62.

Independent Review of the Australian Public Service 2019, *Our Public Service Our Future*, Final report (also known as the Thodey Report), Department of Prime Minister and Cabinet, Canberra.

Jarvie, W & Mercer, T 2017, 'Australia's employment services 1998–2012: using performance monitoring and evaluation to improve value for money', in A Podger et al. (eds), *Value for Money*, ANU Press, Canberra, doi.org/10.22459/VM.01.2018.13.

Keating, M 2004, *Who Rules? How Government Retains Control in a Privatised Economy*, Federation Press, Annandale, NSW.

Light, PC 1998, *The Tides of Reform: Making Government Work, 1945–1995*, Yale University Press, New Haven and London.

Likert, R 1961, *New Patterns of Management*, McGraw-Hill.

Lowndes, V & Roberts, M 2013, *Why Institutions Matter: The New Institutionalism in Political Science*, Palgrave MacMillan, doi.org/10.1007/978-1-137-32913-4.

Management Advisory Board and Management Improvement Advisory Committee Task Force on Management Improvement 1992, *The Australian Public Service Reformed: An Evaluation of a Decade of Management Reform*, Australian Government Publishing Service, Canberra.

March, JG & Olsen, JP 1984, 'The new institutionalism: organisational factors in political life', *American Political Science Review*, vol 78, no 3, pp 734–49, doi.org/10.2307/1961840.

Maslow, AH 1954, *Motivation and Personality*, Harper and Row.

McGregor, D 1960, *The Human Side of Enterprise*, McGraw-Hill, New York.

McIntyre, A 2003, *The Power of Institutions: Political Architecture and Governance*, Cornell University Press, Ithaca and London.

Minns, B 2004, *A History in Three Acts: Evolution of the Public Service Act 1999*, Occasional Paper no 3, Commonwealth of Australia, Canberra.

Mintzberg, H 1979, *The Structuring of Organizations*, Prentice-Hall Inc, Englewood Cliffs, New Jersey.

National Congress of Australia's First Peoples 2016, *#redfern statement*, also issued by Reconciliation Australia, www.reconciliation.org.au/election-2016-the-redfern-statement/.

O'Flynn, J 2007, 'From new public management to public value: paradigmatic change and managerial implications', *Australian Journal of Public Administration*, vol 66, no 3, pp 353–66, doi.org/10.1111/j.1467-8500.2007.00545.x.

O'Loughlin, MA 2013, 'Accountability and reforms to Australia's federal financial relations', *Australian Journal of Public Administration*, vol 72, no 3, pp 376–81, doi.org/10.1111/1467-8500.12035.

Osborne, S 2010, 'Introduction', in S Osborne (ed), *The New Public Governance? Emerging Perspectives on the Theory and Practice of Public Governance*, London, Routledge, doi.org/10.4324/9780203861684.

Ostrom, E 2005, 'Understanding the diversity of structured human interactions', in E Ostrom, *Understanding Institutional Diversity*, Princeton University Press.

Parkinson, M 2016, 'IPAA annual address to the Public Service', Australian Department of Prime Minister and Cabinet, Canberra, 6 Dec.

Parliament of Australia Community Services Reference Committee 2017, *Report: Design, Scope, Cost-Benefit Analysis, Contracts Awarded and Implementation Associated with the Better Management of the Social Security System Initiative*, Canberra, 21 Jun.

Podger, A 2011, 'Accountability structures for citizen-centred public services: workshop summary', HC Coombs Policy Forum, The Australian National University, Canberra.

—— 2013a, 'Mostly welcome, but are the politicians fully aware of what they have done? The *Public Service Amendment Act 2013*', *Australian Journal of Public Administration*, vol 72, no 2, pp 77–81, doi.org/10.1111/1467-8500.12015.

—— 2013b, 'A wish-list for a better government', *Canberra Times Public Sector Informant*, Jul.

—— 2016, 'Innovation in the public sector: beyond the rhetoric to a genuine "learning culture"', in J Wanna, H-A Lee & S Yates (eds), *Managing under Austerity, Delivering under Pressure*, ANU Press, Canberra. doi.org/10.22459/MUADUP.10.2015.07.

—— 2018, 'Making accountability for results really work?', in A Podger et al. (eds), *Value for Money*, ANU Press, Canberra. doi.org/10.22459/VM.01.2018.06.

—— 2019, 'The Thodey Report has an excessive amount of rhetoric and is not an easy read. And there's Morrison's response. Where to from here?', *The Mandarin*, 19 Dec.

Pollitt, C & Bouckaert, G 2011, *Public Management Reform: A Comparative Analysis: New Public Management, Governance, and the Neo-Weberian State*, 3rd edn, Oxford University Press.

Prime Minister 2019, *New Structure of Government Departments*, Media Release, 5 Dec, Canberra.

Public Service and Merit Protection Commission 2001, *Serving the Nation: 100 Years of Public Service*, Canberra.

Review of Australian Government Administration 2010, *Ahead of the Game: Blueprint for the Reform of Australian Government Administration*, Australian Department of Prime Minister and Cabinet, Canberra.

Rhodes, RAW 1997, *Understanding Governance: Policy Networks, Governance, Reflexivity, and Accountability*, Open University Press, Buckingham, Philadelphia.

Rhodes, RAW & Wanna, J 2007, 'The limits to public value, or rescuing responsible government from the platonic guardians', *Australian Journal of Public Administration*, vol 66, no 4, pp 406–21, doi.org/10.1111/j.1467-8500.2007.00553.x.

Shergold, P 2015, *Learning from Failure: Why Large Government Policy Initiatives Have Gone So Badly Wrong in the Past and How the Chances of Success in the Future can be Improved*, Australian Public Service Commission, Canberra.

Simon, HA 1957, *Administrative Behaviour*, 2nd edn, MacMillan.

Talbot-Jones, J 2018, 'Institutions matter: an introduction to the role of institutions in public policy', in M Fabian & R Breunig (eds), *Hybrid Public Policy Innovations: Contemporary Policy Beyond Ideology*, Routledge, New York and London, doi.org/10.4324/9781351245944-3.

Tanzer, N 1992, 'How commercialisation has helped in the efficient delivery of services by the Department of Administrative Services to the Australian Public Service', seminar paper, 'Reforming the public service – lessons from recent experience', Centre of Australian Public Sector Management seminar, Griffith University, Brisbane, 3–4 Jul.

Taylor, FW 1947 (1911), *Scientific Management*, Harper and Row.

Uhrig, J 2003, *Review of Corporate Governance of Statutory Authorities and Office Holders*, Commonwealth of Australia, Canberra.

Walsh, P 1987, *Policy Guidelines for Commonwealth Statutory Authorities and Government Business Enterprises*, Parliamentary Papers, AGPS, Canberra.

Weber, M 1978 (1922), *Economy and Society: An Outline of Interpretive Sociology*, University of California Press, Berkeley.

Wettenhall, R 1996, 'Public enterprise management in Australia: a pioneer among developing countries', in A Farazmand (ed), *Public Enterprise Management: International Case Studies*, Greenwood Press, Westport, Connecticut.

—— 1998, 'The rising popularity of the government-owned company in Australia: problems and issues', *Public Administration and Development*, vol 18, pp 243–55, doi.org/10.1002/(SICI)1099-162X(199808)18:3%3C243::AID-PAD14%3E3.3.CO;2-1.

—— 2004–05, 'Statutory authorities, the Uhrig Report, and the trouble with internal inquiries', *Public Administration Today*, no 2, pp 62–76.

4

GOVERNANCE STRUCTURE, ORGANISATIONAL REFORM AND ADMINISTRATIVE EFFICIENCY

Lessons from Taiwan

Yi-Huah Jiang

The efficiency of government has long been one of the major concerns of public officers, entrepreneurs, non-government organisations (NGOs) and scholars of public administration. The public services that government provides to citizens – ranging from education, health care, transportation, affordable housing, to job opportunity and social security – involve substantial public expenditure. It is therefore reasonable for the general public to demand that the government is efficient and effective.

To improve government efficiency, scholars have attempted to analyse the parameters of public performance and examine the relationship between public expenditure and citizen satisfaction with government services (Hauner & Kyobe 2008; Morgeson 2014). Government reforms in different countries and regions have been carefully studied with regard to their similarities and differences (Pollitt & Bouckaert 2011; Christensen, Dong & Painter 2008; Meyer-Sahling & Yesilkagit 2011; Cepiku & Meneguzzo 2011). One of the issues that has not been thoroughly explored, however, is the relationship between governance structure and administrative efficiency. The structure of government – namely, how government agencies and departments are organised to manage their functions – is critical to public sector performance. The attempts made by many countries to reform their organisations is a testament to the importance of finding the best governance structure to realise the mission of serving the people efficiently and cost-effectively.

This chapter explores the relationship between government structure and administrative efficiency by examining the case of organisational reform in Taiwan since 2008. It begins with a brief introduction to the structure of the Taiwanese Government and some background to the organisational reform that began in 2008. This is followed by a detailed analysis of the reform scheme and what has been accomplished so far. As the structure of government is still undergoing adjustment, it is only possible to evaluate its initial achievements and to identify the limitations it faces. The chapter provides this assessment and some lessons to be learned from the experience to date on the political and administrative sides. This is followed by some thoughts on factors beyond organisational reform that affect government efficiency and that deserve further investigation, including the influence on Taiwan of the constitution, regime and intergovernmental relations. The chapter concludes that Taiwan needs to consider constitutional change, not just organisational reform, if it is to achieve necessary efficiency in government administration.

Taiwan's governance structure and its problems

The central government of Taiwan is constructed according to the Constitution of the Republic of China (ROC), which follows its founding father Dr Sun Yat-sen's idea of a 'five-power constitution'. Instead of the more popular approach of 'three-power' checks and balances between the executive, the legislative and the judiciary, Dr Sun's constitutional framework consists of five branches of government power: the Executive Yuan, Legislative Yuan, Judicial Yuan, Examination Yuan and Control Yuan.

The Executive Yuan is the highest administrative institution of the country. Its leader, the premier, is appointed by the president of ROC and is responsible for the planning and implementation of all public policy except national security policy, which falls within the jurisdiction of the president. The premier nominates ministers and high-ranking political officers to the president for appointment. The premier and his or her ministers hold weekly meetings to discuss and decide the bills to be submitted to the legislature for deliberation, the major policies of the country, and the government budget necessary for their implementation.

The Legislative Yuan is the legislative body of Taiwan. As the only representative chamber in the unicameral system, the Legislative Yuan is generally regarded as the parliament of the country. Of the 113 seats in the Legislative Yuan, 73 are elected from single-member districts, 34 are elected based on the proportion of nationwide votes received by participating political parties, and six seats are reserved for the indigenous people of Taiwan.

The Judicial Yuan is the highest judiciary institution of Taiwan and comprises the president and vice-president of the Judicial Yuan and 15 Justices from the Council of Grand Justices. They are nominated and appointed by the president of ROC, with the consent of the Legislative Yuan. The Council of Grand Justices is responsible for the interpretation of the ROC Constitution and its laws.

The Examination Yuan is in charge of all national examinations and management of civil service personnel. In this capacity, it independently governs the qualification screening, protection, death benefits and retirement of civil servants. The Examination Yuan consists of a president, vice-president, two ministers and 19 council members, who are nominated and appointed by the president of ROC, with the consent of the Legislative Yuan. In effect, it protects the professional non-partisan civil service that, in other countries, lies within the executive arm of government, keeping it separate from politics.

The Control Yuan is an investigatory agency that monitors the other branches of government. It is composed of a president, vice-president and 29 council members, who are nominated and appointed by the president of ROC, with the consent of the Legislative Yuan. Council members can investigate and impeach high-level officers, including the president of the country. Its unique institutional design is based on the traditional Chinese Censorate. The Control Yuan is sometimes compared to the Court of Auditors of the European Union, the Government Accountability Office of the United States and the Australian National Audit Office, but it also encompasses other oversight (or 'integrity') functions, such as those performed in other countries by ombudsmen.

The president of ROC is the highest leader of the country. He or she not only selects the premier and ministers of the Executive Yuan, but also nominates all the presidents, vice-presidents, grand justices and council members of the Judicial Yuan, the Examination Yuan and the Control Yuan. The president is directly elected by the people through general elections, and is in charge of national security; that is, national defence, foreign affairs and cross–Taiwan Strait policy. Although the president does not chair cabinet meetings (which are convened by the premier), he or she is free to hold meetings with the premier and ministers. The president's decision on important matters of public policy is usually final.

When people talk about 'government' in Taiwan, they might refer to the five-branch government led by the president, or the executive branch only. Officially, the five yuans are parts of the central government, but the Legislative Yuan is not conventionally regarded as such. For the purpose of simplicity and consistency, the term 'government' is used to refer to the Executive Yuan in the rest of this chapter unless explained otherwise. Discussion of governance structure, organisational reform and administrative efficiency refers to what happens in the Executive Yuan because that is where the central administration is located.

Originally the ROC Government consisted of 10 institutions under the Executive Yuan, including eight ministries (such as Interior, Foreign Affairs, National Defence and Finance) and two commissions (Mongolian and Tibetan Affairs and Overseas Chinese Affairs). As time passed, more institutions were created to manage the new responsibilities commensurate with the country's socioeconomic development. By 2006, the number of institutions under the Executive Yuan reached a record high of 37, including eight ministries and 29 commissions or councils (Chu 2012; Hsiao 2012).

Most of the 37 institutions are **functional institutions** that provide specific public services to the people, such as the Interior, Foreign Affairs, National Defence, Finance, Education, Justice, Economic Affairs, Transportation, Health, Labor Affairs, Agriculture and Environmental Protection. Some other institutions are **supportive institutions** and support the Office of the Premier to monitor and coordinate the work of various ministries, such as the Central Personnel Administration; Commission for Research, Development and Evaluation; Council for Economic Development; Government Information Office; and Office for Budget, Accounting and Statistics. In addition to these two categories, there are **independent institutions** that perform their duties independently and without political considerations, including the Central Bank, Central Election Commission, Fair Trade Commission, Financial Supervisory Commission and National Communication Commission. Fixed-term appointments guarantee the impartiality of the members of these independent institutions.

The increase in the number of institutions over the years is an example of the government's desire to respond to the emerging needs and expectations of the people. If an institution does not exist to meet a specific demand, the easiest response is to create a new institution to deal with it. The negative impact of organisational proliferation is, however, too obvious to neglect. The following shortcomings have been discussed repeatedly in the past decades (Yeh 2002; Shih 2005; Hsiao 2012).

1. **Size:** it is generally held that, to maintain effective communication and administration, an organisation should have fewer than 20 subordinate organisations. A central government with 37 ministries and councils is certainly beyond a reasonable span of control. It is difficult for the premier to communicate with all the ministers in an efficient way, let alone make quick decisions when emergencies occur. A higher transaction cost results from negotiation with more than one ministry.

2. **Confusion:** according to its original design, there is a clear distinction between the ministry and the commission or council in the Executive Yuan. The ministry is an agency responsible for a specific domain of public services, such as national defence, foreign affairs, economic development, finance, education, justice and transportation. The commission or council is an agency designed for cross-area negotiation and cooperation, such as the National Development Council or the National Science Council. Yet many newly established institutions do not follow this rule, which has confused the respective functions of ministries and commissions. For instance, in principle, a ministry should take care of labour affairs, but it has instead become the business of a council. The same is true for agriculture, cultural affairs and public health.

3. **Overlap:** as the number of public service institutions increase, it is inevitable that the function of one institution will overlap that of another from time to time. For example, the Council for Hakka Affairs regards itself as responsible for the promotion of

Hakka culture (such as music and dance). Yet the Council for Cultural Affairs also sees Hakka culture as part of the national culture within its remit. It is difficult, therefore, to apportion responsibility for those cultural activities that have some Hakka element but are not entirely Hakka. Overlap and conflict with regard to sport education and athlete training also occurs between the Ministry of Education and the Council for Sports Affairs, and between the Ministry of Economic Affairs and the Council for Youth with regard to the development of youth enterprise and youth employment.

4. **Lack of flexibility:** Taiwan's institutional framework is 'hard' rather than 'soft' because of strict regulations relating to the number, functions and personnel of the institutions. The Acts concerning those institutions can only be amended with the approval of the Legislative Yuan. Especially for tier-three agencies (namely, the subordinate institutions of the ministries and councils, such as the Immigration Agency of the Interior Ministry or the Customs Administration of the Finance Ministry), all the directors must be permanent civil servants and cannot be recruited from the civil society. The advantage of this system is a more stable and consistent public service. Its disadvantage is the lack of flexibility, innovation and responsiveness in administration. To alleviate the problem, the government may open some key positions to talented people who are not permanent civil servants, such as the director of the Tourism Bureau.

5. **Non-responsiveness:** the government is accountable to the people, and ministries should also be responsive to the demands of the times. In a fast-changing society and with the onset of globalisation, many new issues and challenges need to be addressed by the government so that the people can enjoy a secure and comfortable life. Salient concerns include environmental change, cross-border crime, the prevention of epidemics, cyber security, global terrorism, a low birth rate, an ageing society, and enhancement of new high-tech industries. These are issues that previous government agencies have not seriously addressed and they must be responded to with more effective reorganisation or restructuring of government.

6. **Inefficiency:** efficiency and effectiveness are always the top priority of government performance; however, this is difficult to achieve in a government with 37 tier-two institutions and more than 100 tier-three agencies. To be sure, size is only one reason for governmental inefficiency in Taiwan. The procedure to initiate, deliberate and

decide a public policy is as critical as the number of institutions or agencies that the policy involves. Decision-making procedures would be improved by simplifying the steps for policy innovation, and creating a more transparent administrative environment in which transaction costs are significantly reduced.

It is for these reasons that the demand for organisational reform is increasingly urgent. Streamlining government and making it more efficient and responsive to the expectations of the people is so widely agreed among politicians, bureaucrats, scholars and NGOs that, no matter which party is to lead the country, organisational reform is expected to occur quickly.

The scheme of the 2008 organisational reform

The earliest proposal for organisational reform was expressed in 1987, when the Executive Yuan set up an ad hoc committee to streamline the government. Progress was slow due to a lack of determination and opposition expressed from the institutions or agencies that were to be merged. Versions of the restructure have also changed over the years, reflecting the ideas of different administrations. The major achievement before 2008 was to pass the Basic Code Governing Central Administrative Agencies Organizations, which prescribed that the number of tier-two institutions should be limited to 22, including 13 ministries, four councils and five independent institutions. This code does not, however, specify what these ministries and councils should be. That difficult question needs to be solved in an amendment of the *Organizational Act of the Executive Yuan 2010*.

In 2008, with the inauguration of President Ma Ying-jeou, the process of organisational reform was reinvigorated. A new ad hoc committee was established in the Executive Yuan, chaired by the vice-premier. The Commission for Research, Development and Evaluation was in charge of the task of developing a new scheme and coordinating all 37 ministries and councils to complete the reorganisation. The scheme was announced publicly in 2009 with the stated mission to 'create a streamlined, flexible and efficient government'. Echoing the demands from academia, the business sector and civil society, the major goals of the reorganisation were set out as (Jiang 2013; Song & Hu 2013; Hsiao 2012; Song & Hsieh 2009):

1. to reduce the number of ministries and councils from 37 to 29 by merging and restructuring

2. to clearly distinguish the respective nature of ministries, councils and independent agencies

3. to define the function of each ministry to avoid overlapping of business or oversight of government services

4. to strengthen the capability of the Executive Yuan by increasing the number of ministries without portfolio and restructuring the offices inside the Executive Yuan

5. to reduce the number of tier-three institutions from 100 to 70

6. to allow some tier-three institutions to have heads who are not permanent civil servants so as to introduce innovation and breakthrough to government activities

7. to restructure government agencies so that emerging challenges can be adequately addressed

8. to dramatically simplify administrative procedures and improve administrative efficiency

9. to control the total number of central government civil servants with quotas for various types of personnel

10. to create a new form of governance (the administrative corporation) that carries out specific public duties but has more flexibility in personnel and financial management

11. to make the policy decision-making process more transparent to the general public

12. to promote e-government so that the people will have easier access to government.

Details of how the major institutions were to be merged and restructured under the organisational reform are set out below and an overview of the organisations before and after the merging plan provides a rough idea as to what is happening under the organisational reform (See Table 4.1).

Table 4.1. List of institutions before and after the reform

Institution before the reform	Transition	Institution after the reform
Ministry of the Interior		Ministry of the Interior
Ministry of Foreign Affairs		Ministry of Foreign Affairs
Ministry of National Defense		Ministry of National Defense
Ministry of Finance		Ministry of Finance
Ministry of Education		Ministry of Education
Ministry of Justice		Ministry of Justice
Ministry of Economic Affairs		Ministry of Economic and Energy Affairs
Ministry of Transportation		Ministry of Transportation and Construction
Mongolian and Tibetan Affairs Commission	Merged into Council of Mainland Affairs	
Overseas Compatriot Affairs Commission		Overseas Chinese Affairs Council
Council for Cultural Affairs		Ministry of Culture
Council of Labor Affairs		Ministry of Labor
Veterans Affairs Commission		Veteran Affairs Council
National Youth Commission	Merged into Ministry of Education	
Atomic Energy Council	Merged into the Premier's Office	
Mainland Affairs Council		Mainland Affairs Council
National Science Council		Ministry of Science and Technology
Research, Development and Evaluation Commission	Merged into National Development Council	
Department of Health		Ministry of Health and Welfare
Environmental Protection Administration		Ministry of Environment and Nature Resources
Government Information Office	Merged into the Premier's Office	
Consumer Protection Commission	Merged into the Premier's Office	
Public Construction Commission	Merged into Ministry of Transportation and Construction	
Council of Agriculture		Ministry of Agriculture
Council for Economic Planning and Development		National Development Council
Council of Indigenous Peoples		Council of Indigenous Peoples

Institution before the reform	Transition	Institution after the reform
Council for Hakka Affairs		Council for Hakka Affairs
National Palace Museum		National Palace Museum
Sports Affaires Council	Merged into Ministry of Education	
Coast Guard Administration		Ocean Affairs Council
Central Bank		Central Bank
Financial Supervisory Commission		Financial Supervisory Commission
Directorate-General of Budget, Accounting and Statistics		Directorate-General of Budget, Accounting and Statistics
Central Personnel Administration		Directorate-General of Personnel Administration
Fair Trade Commission		Fair Trade Commission
Central Election Commission		Central Election Commission
National Communications Commission		National Communications Commission

Source. The author

While the scheme announced in 2009 has not yet been fully implemented, it remains the basis for the restructuring underway. Under the scheme, six new ministries were to be created. To enhance the government's capacity to protect the environment and to manage natural resources, the Environmental Protection Administration was to become the Ministry of Environment and Natural Resources. To integrate the capability to assist the least advantaged through social welfare and medicare, the Department of Health was to merge with the agencies of social welfare and become the Ministry of Health and Welfare. To promote cultural innovation and cultural industry, the Council for Cultural Affairs was to incorporate international cultural exchange and be upgraded as the Ministry of Culture. To show the government's determination to help workers and farmers, the Council of Labor Affairs and the Council of Agriculture would be expanded and transformed into the Ministry of Labor and the Ministry of Agriculture respectively. Finally, to facilitate the development of future industry, the National Science Council would become the Ministry of Science and Technology.

To streamline the government and reduce the problem of overlapping responsibilities, the following institutions would be merged with relevant ministries: Coast Guard Administration; Commission for Research, Development and Evaluation; Consumer Protection Commission;

Council for Atomic Energy; Government Information Office; Mongolian and Tibetan Affairs Commission; National Youth Commission; Public Construction Commission; and Sports Affairs Council. With the merger of nine institutions, and the creation of the Ocean Affairs Council, the total number of tier-two institutions would be reduced from 37 to 29.

All the other institutions of the Executive Yuan would remain more or less the same, although some would change their name to reflect a new mission following the incorporation of other institutions. For instance, the Ministry of Transportation would become the Ministry of Transportation and Construction because it has taken over the responsibilities of the former Public Construction Commission.

The organisational reforms involve a profound and comprehensive restructuring of the central government in Taiwan. As the legislature must amend more than 100 Acts, it was hard to estimate how much time it would take to complete the reform. The Commission for Research, Development and Evaluation hoped for the project to be completed by the end of 2011, but that proved wishful thinking. Until now, four of the new proposed ministries have been created, but another three are still struggling in the messy negotiation process of the Legislative Yuan. Among the nine institutions to be merged, six have disappeared, but three remain. With the coming to power of President Tsai Ing-wen in 2016, the momentum for organisational reform has declined because the new government is less enthusiastic about promoting administrative efficiency through institutional streamlining.

Assessment of organisational reform in Taiwan

Although organisational reform is not yet complete, it is possible to estimate the initial impact of the scheme by comparing the pre- and post-reform efficiency of the Taiwan Government.

According to the World Competitiveness Rankings published by the Institute for Management Development (IMD), Taiwan's performance improved dramatically after the organisational reform scheme was passed by the Legislative Yuan in 2010. Before the reform scheme was launched (2007), Taiwan was ranked 18th out of all the evaluated countries. It then jumped to 13th with the beginning of the reform (2009), but dropped to 23rd in 2009 because of the global financial crisis. Following the passage of the Organizational Act of the Executive Yuan, several new ministries were created between 2010 and 2014, while others were merged. Taiwan's ranking rose to somewhere between 8th and 13th, which is a substantial upgrade compared with the previous years.

The World Competitiveness Rankings is composed of four major factors (economic performance, government efficiency, business efficiency and infrastructure). Government efficiency is most relevant here and Taiwan's ranking for this factor shows significant improvement since 2010, even better than its performance in world competitiveness as a whole. The same pattern appears when probing into the sub-factor of institutional framework, which may be directly related to organisational reform. Taiwan's performance reached a record high during 2010–13, but has gradually declined since, probably because the reform process was held up in the legislature (see Table 4.2 and Figure 4.1).

Table 4.2. Taiwan's performance in the IMD rankings

	2007	2008	2009	2010	2011	2012	2013	2014	2015	2016	2017
World competitiveness	18	13	23	8	6	7	11	13	11	14	14
Government efficiency	20	16	18	6	10	5	8	12	9	9	10
Institutional framework	29	23	20	14	13	15	16	20	19	16	15

Source. IMD (2007–17)

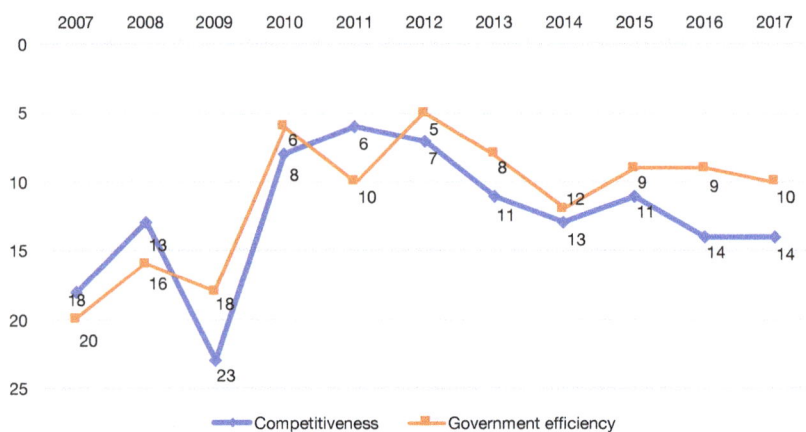

Figure 4.1. Taiwan's competitiveness and government efficiency in the IMF rankings

Source. IMD (2007–17)

The Global Competitiveness Report published by another international NGO, the World Economic Forum (WEF), reveals a similar pattern for Taiwan's performance during these years (see Table 4.3).

Table 4.3. Taiwan's performance in the WEF rankings

	2007	2008	2009	2010	2011	2012	2013	2014	2015	2016	2017
Competitiveness	14	17	12	13	13	13	12	14	15	14	15

Source. WEF (2007–17)

These rankings make it clear that Taiwan's government efficiency significantly improved after the implementation of organisational reform, especially following the mergers and restructuring that were carried out in 2010–13. Some caution is warranted, however, about the correlation between organisational reform and government efficiency because the latter encompasses several indicators, and organisational streamlining is only one of them. A more systematic and thorough study is yet to be done.

In addition to this evidence suggesting the reform has contributed to improvements in Taiwan's government efficiency, there are other important lessons to be learned from Taiwan's organisational reform experience so far. These lessons reflect the reality and subtleties of a concrete reform that inevitably has positive and negative impacts. They are based on the author's observations and thoughts and draw on his practical experience in government as well as his current academic perspective.

To begin with, opposition from the institutions to be merged is always a major obstacle of organisational reform. Some institutions vehemently resist the change because they do not want to be incorporated into other institutions. Some institutions engage passively and reluctantly in the reform process and try to postpone the merger. A sense of dignity, institutional loyalty, memory of the past and anxiety about the uncertain future are all reasonable grounds for individuals to resist or hesitate. The leaders of these institutions may also publicly and privately lobby the legislature against the merger plan. Some compromises often need to be made in order for the project to proceed.

Second, the effect of institutional mergers is not always as positive as the proponents envisage. In some cases, the incorporating institutions do not appreciate the value of the incorporated agencies and, therefore, the integration turns out to be less organic than intended. Organisational dysfunction frequently results when two or three institutions merge but do not really become one body. It takes time for them to find a way to work together. The vision and mentality of the leader of the enlarged institution is critical. If he or she can take the opportunity to set a new vision for all the agencies under his or her control, the ministry can create a brand-new image, owned by all parts of the organisation, and deliver a new message to the people as to what public service it provides. Otherwise, the merger may turn out to be no more than a reduction of institution numbers.

Third, the political cost of institutional merging is yet another price of organisational reform. The merged institutions have pre-existing 'constituencies' – service recipients and NGOs that need their subsidy or support. When the service is transferred to another institution, the constituency may well complain or even protest in the belief that their interests are under threat. For instance, athletes and sports associations are not happy about the incorporation of the Sports Affairs Council into the Ministry of Education because it means downgrading the former to a tier-three agency. Similarly, many consumers and consumer associations are reluctant to see that the Consumer Protection Commission will disappear, although another institution will continue to perform the function of consumer protection. When angry 'constituents' express their dissatisfaction and bitterness in elections, the current government pays a political price.

Fourth, a purpose of organisational reform is to introduce flexibility by prescribing that only the tier-one institution (the Executive Yuan) and tier-two institutions (ministries and councils) need to be enacted by the legislature. The organisational code for tier-three institutions (agency and bureau) would not need legislative amendment and this will allow the government to reform subordinate institutions more easily to cope with a changing social environment. The Legislative Yuan, however, does not agree and insists that the organisational Acts concerning all three levels of institution must be passed and amended by the legislature. As a result, there are still many bills held up in the legislature, and no hope that they will be passed soon. The legislature itself is one of the reasons for government inefficiency.

Fifth, the reform's mission to reduce the quota of government employees has resulted in many institutions finding it difficult to provide the quality public services that the people expect. One important feature of modern democracy is that people expect more from government, and that politicians promise more to voters. It is a dilemma for government to provide more services with reduced manpower. Of course, solving this dilemma is at the centre of government efficiency – getting more things done more quickly with less cost. But there is a limitation to this golden rule. When the size of government is streamlined to an extent beyond reasonable capability, the necessary public services simply cannot be delivered.

Sixth, multiple institutional design is a good idea in itself because it can make the governance structure more flexible, creative and efficient. That is the reason why Taiwan has not only conventional ministries and agencies, but also independent institutions and administrative corporations. It is important, however, to use the most appropriate type of institution for the function involved. As independent institutions, the Central Election Commission and the Central Bank are good examples of impartial policymaking and implementation. The function of the National Communications Commission (NCC), however, fails many people's expectation. NCC is responsible for supervision of mass media competition and promotion of the communications industry. The weight that it places on scandal prevention in its regulatory role, unfortunately, makes NCC a nightmare for the telecommunication industry to approach in looking for support. A possible solution is to separate the two major functions of NCC so that another institution takes responsibility for industrial development.

Seventh, a government institution's autonomy is important in shouldering the responsibility of specific public service delivery or administrative regulation. Yet, in an age when most businesses are cross-boundary in nature (such as e-commerce, international worker immigration and climate change), inter-organisational negotiation and cooperation is even more important than institutional autonomy. The role of a minister without a portfolio has been created to mediate differences among institutions and make coordinated decisions involving cooperation across agencies to address complex issues on behalf of the premier, so that important public policy will not be too narrowly conceived or too favourable to any particular interest group. To have a more efficient and effective government, the task of inter-departmental negotiation is an essential responsibility requiring efficient processes.

Eighth, the job of streamlining administrative procedures is no less important than that of streamlining government. If procedures are hampered by unnecessary checks and balances, government becomes a major source of private sector frustration and resentment. Especially when organisational restructuring is too difficult to be accomplished, the only way to help the government move forward is to revise and simplify administrative procedures.

There are many lessons to be learned from Taiwan's experience of organisational reform so far. The ones outlined above may be of relevance to any other government considering comprehensive reform. Although the background, motivation and problems to be solved will differ from one country to another, the underlying challenges and obstacles are likely similar, whether they be overlapping of government functions, proliferation of institutions, opposition expressed by merged organisations, or the political cost to be paid for a serious reform. If political practitioners and academics who envision government reform could pay attention to as much experience as possible from preceding cases, the chance of success would be greater.

Thoughts beyond the organisational reform

This chapter has focused on factors that are directly related to Taiwan's program of organisational reform that began in 2008. The enhancement of government efficiency, nevertheless, is not merely a question of institutional restructuring. Some broader institutional factors are no less important for the improvement of government efficiency. In this section, two specific elements are explored as having a profound impact on government performance in Taiwan: the constitutional framework and central–local relations.

Taiwan's constitutional framework establishes a semi-presidential political system. After election by the people via general election, the president is the leader of the country. The Executive Yuan, however, is led by the premier, who is appointed by the president and is not an elected politician. According to the ROC Constitution, ministers are selected by the premier, to whom they are responsible. The president has direct control only over the ministers of National Defense, Foreign Affairs and Mainland Affairs. The Executive Yuan is accountable to the Legislative Yuan and the premier and ministers must regularly answer questions from the legislature regarding policy and budget. A system in which the leader of the country (the president) and the leader of the government (the premier) are two different people is also known as a 'dual-head' system (Elgie, Moestrup & Wu 2011; Wu 2016).

Semi-presidentialism differs from a parliamentary system in that its popularly elected head of state is more than a ceremonial figurehead. It differs from a presidential system in that the cabinet, which is led by the premier, is responsible to the legislature, which may force the cabinet to resign through a motion of no confidence. Many countries have adopted semi-presidentialism as their political system, including France, Russia, Portugal and Poland. The system's merits rest in the political stability achieved by protecting the fixed-term president from harsh criticism by the legislature or the people, and in the opportunity to change unwelcome policies by asking the premier (but not the president) to resign. The system's shortcoming is frequent confusion of accountability as to who (the president or the premier?) should take responsibility for policy failures. The possibility of government inefficiency also arises because the cabinet is accountable to the president (who unofficially decides the position of ministers) and the legislature at the same time (Shen & Wu 2017).

The disadvantage of semi-presidentialism is manifest in Taiwan where the problem of government inefficiency is increasingly evident. Government efficiency is not merely a matter of how public officers plan and execute policy quickly. It also relates to the formation and effective and transparent communication of policy between the executive and the legislature. Semi-presidentialism creates a complex network of responsibility for public officers. Ministers and high-level officers must have the support or endorsement of the president and the premier before announcing policies. When the opinions of the president and the premier differ, the officers must revise their plans to accommodate the two leaders, which can be an exhausting, frustrating and time-consuming process.

After the administration makes a decision, policy is further scrutinised and revised in the legislature. If the opinion of the legislature differs from the opinions of the president and the minister, negotiations begin again until a consensus can be reached among the three stakeholders. The quality of Taiwan's legislature, unfortunately, is very poor. It takes limited responsibility for its role in determining informed policy and efficient government. Rather than focus on the content of a bill or policy, it more often seeks the attention of the mass media by presenting irrelevant and populist questions. In the past few decades the government budget has, without exception, been passed only after the budget year has long started.

Nor does the legislature follow its own rules and procedures, and endless negotiation replaces the rule of the majority. Numerous bills are blocked in subcommittees and the plenary committee year after year, as is exemplified by the delays in enacting the bills regarding organisational reform. Other important bills, such as those concerning food safety, epidemic prevention, assistance to the disabled or a free trade zone, have been victims of legislative dysfunction and inefficiency. Government efficiency is the task of the 'whole government', including the president and the legislature. To address efficiency without considering Taiwan's constitutional framework and its operation will never lead to the right answer.

The problem of the relationship between the central and the local government is another important aspect affecting government efficiency (Shen, Liu & Zeng 2016). To effectively implement policy, the central government must make reasonable decisions that are well executed at the local level. Cooperation between the central and the local government, therefore, is critical to the success of public policy. In the case of food safety, several scandals over recent years have involved tainted milk powder, toxic starch, plasticisers in prepared foods and adulterated cooking oil. These crises highlighted the shortcomings of the food safety management system, from manufacturing processes to product inspections. To cope with this problem, the Executive Yuan held a series of inter-departmental meetings between the Ministry of Health and Welfare, the Council of Agriculture, the Environmental Protection Administration, the Ministry of Economic Affairs, the Ministry of Justice, and several other agencies. As a consequence, the central government established a farm-to-table production traceability system to monitor agricultural products throughout their production, manufacture, distribution and sales. It also amended laws to prescribe heavier punishments and higher fines for violation of the regulations. Because the central government cannot reach every corner of the country, it is up to the local government (especially health and the police departments) to carry out the examinations and inspections.

It is difficult for the general public to appreciate which part of government work is done by the central government or the local government. Whenever a food scandal happens, people tend to criticise the central government when, in fact, it may be a failure of local government. It is pointless to argue who is to blame during a food safety crisis; people long for a safe and happy life. When a government cannot guarantee the safety of food or water, the responsibility of a particular tier of government is immaterial; it is the lack of efficiency or effectiveness that is readily apparent to the community.

Cooperation between central and local governments is essential to government efficiency. In a complex world, only multiple coordination and cooperation within the government, with some sharing of responsibilities but clear and distinct roles by the different players, can provide efficient and satisfactory public service. It is a lesson that we cannot learn from the limited perspective of organisational reform.

Conclusion

This chapter explores the overall governance structure of Taiwan (the Republic of China) and the scheme of organisational reform that was launched in 2008. Such a reform is necessary for Taiwan to improve its administrative efficiency, and some gains have been made, though not yet as many as proponents of reform had hoped. The reform process has been a valuable effort, even if the government has paid a high political cost. It is hard to imagine, however, how an oversized and increasingly ossified government can handle the pressing challenges of globalisation without adjusting its organisation and functions. The pity is that, with the inauguration of a new government in 2016, the incomplete reform process lost momentum and there seems little likelihood of progress in the near future.

Administrative efficiency requires more than organisational reform within the Executive Yuan. The constraint imposed by Taiwan's semi-presidential constitution, which requires the Executive Yuan to be accountable to both the president and the Legislative Yuan, must also be addressed. The relationship between politics and administration is always complex and it is difficult for ministers and senior officers to strike a subtle balance between loyalty to the leader of the country and the leader of the executive, to move the government forwards with due respect and accountability to the legislature, to insist on the professionalism of the civil service and be open to the diversified demands and expectations of the general public, and to establish a productive partnership with local governments so that policy can be faithfully implemented. This can only be achieved in a complex political system with patience, skill and wisdom. The efficiency of a government is never only a matter of organisational restructuring.

In *The Origins of Political Order* (2011) and *Political Order and Political Decay* (2014), Francis Fukuyama contends that a stable modern political order is based on the three pillars of state capacity, rule of law and democratic accountability. State capability (or state building) concerns the capability of a government to manage public affairs with bureaucratic autonomy and administrative efficiency. Political accountability is best achieved when the government is held accountable to a democratically elected legislature that constitutes an effective check to the potential abuse of government power. Yet, as Fukuyama notes, tensions exist among these three elements. Too much democratic accountability may cripple government efficiency, such as the 'vetocracy' of contemporary US politics. Too much administrative discretion, for its part, can hurt the foundation of the rule of law, as is evident in the authoritarian rule of communist China. Rule of law can be a good balance to the arbitrary will of the majority, but 'judicial activism' may be as dangerous as a judiciary system, which is too susceptible to political will (Fukuyama 2014).

From the experience of organisational reform in Taiwan, institutional restructuring and administrative streamlining can help to improve government efficiency. Yet Taiwan's constitutional framework of a 'dual-head' system with distorted relations between the executive and the legislature make the government less able to carry out policies in the interest of the people. If the regime type can be changed from semi-presidentialism to either presidential or parliamentary, the problem of 'confusion of accountability' and 'inconsistency of power and responsibility' could be significantly improved, which in turn should enhance administrative efficiency in Taiwan. In the same vein, if the relations between the executive and the legislative could be modified so that legislative scrutiny became more rational and constructive, it would also promote government efficiency. These remedies, however, require the amendment of the constitution and some fundamental changes in Taiwan's political culture.

References

Cepiku, D & Meneguzzo, M 2011, 'Public administration reform in Italy: a shopping-basket approach to the new public management or the new Weberianism?', *International Journal of Public Administration*, vol 34, no 1, pp 19–25, doi.org/10.1080/01900692.2010.506088.

Christensen, T, Dong, L & Painter, M 2008, 'Administrative reform in China's central government – how much "learning from the West"?', *International Review of Administrative Sciences*, vol 74, no 3, pp 351–71, doi.org/10.1177/0020852308095308.

Chu, J 2012, 'Retrospection and visions for organizational reform of the ROC government, *Archives Quarterly*, vol 11, no 1, pp 4–17 [in Chinese].

Elgie, R, Moestrup, S & Wu, Y 2011, *Semi-presidentialism and Democracy*, Palgrave Macmillan, New York, doi.org/10.1057/9780230306424.

Fukuyama, F 2011, *The Origins of Political Order*, Farrar, Straus and Giroux, New York.

—— 2014, *Political Order and Political Decay: From the Industrial Revolution to the Present Day*, Farrar, Straus and Giroux, New York.

Hauner, D & Kyobe, A 2008, *Determinants of Government Efficiency*, International Monetary Fund, Washington, doi.org/10.5089/9781451870862.001.

Hinrik, J & Sahling, M 2009, 'Varieties of legacies: a critical review of legacy explanations of public administration reform in East Central Europe', *International Review of Administrative Sciences*, vol 75, no 3, pp 509–28, doi.org/10.1177/0020852309337670.

Hsiao, W 2012, 'Historical review and prospect of the organizational reform of the Executive Yuan', *Legal Review of National Zhongcheng University*, no 37, pp 51–116 [in Chinese].

Institute for Management Development 2007–17, *IMD World Competitiveness Yearbook*, Lausanne.

Jiang, Y 2013, 'An interview with the premier: enhancing good governance, facilitating sustainable development', *Public Governance Quarterly*, vol 1, no 1, pp 3–10 [in Chinese].

Meyer-Sahling, J & Yesilkagit, K 2011, 'Differential legacy effects: three propositions on the impact of administrative traditions on public administration reform in Europe east and west', *Journal of European Public Policy*, vol 18, no 2, pp 311–22, doi.org/10.1080/13501763.2011.544515.

Morgeson, F 2014, *Citizen Satisfaction: Improving Government Performance, Efficiency, and Citizen Trust*, Palgrave Macmillan, New York, doi.org/10.1057/9781137047137.

Pollitt, C & Bouckaert, G 2011, *Public Management Reform: A Comparative Analysis: New Public Management, Governance, and the Neo-Weberian State*, 3rd edn, Oxford University Press.

Shen, J, Liu, Y & Zeng, S 2016, 'Promoting cooperation and efficient management between the central and local governments', *Public Governance Quarterly*, vol 4, no 3, pp 118–23 [in Chinese].

Shen, Y & Wu, Y (eds) 2017, *Power Triangle under Semi-presidentialism: President, Parliament, Cabinet*, Wu-nan, Taipei [in Chinese].

Shih, N 2005, 'Moving forward the organizational reform of the Executive Yuan', *Bimonthly of RDEC*, vol 29, no 2, pp 86–104 [in Chinese].

Song, Y & Hsieh, W 2009, 'The design principle and practice of the organizational reform of the Executive Yuan', *Bimonthly of RDEC*, vol 33, no 3, pp 58–71 [in Chinese].

Song, Y, & Hu, Y 2013, 'Public governance and the restructuring of organization and capacity of the Executive Yuan', *Public Governance Quarterly*, vol 1, no 1, pp 61–72 [in Chinese].

World Economic Forum (WEF) 2007–17, *Global Competitiveness Report*, Cologne.

Wu, Y 2016, 'Semi-presidentialism in the ROC: dilemma and choice', in Y Wang (ed), *The Retrospect and Prospect of Democracy in Taiwan*, Taiwan Foundation for Democracy, Taipei [in Chinese].

Yeh, J 2002, 'The goal, principle and facilitating mechanism of the organizational reform of the Executive Yuan', *National Policy Quarterly*, vol 1, no 1, pp 1–22 [in Chinese].

5

PRACTICAL ACTION, THEORETICAL IMPACTS
Aged care and disability services reform in Australia

Mike Woods and David Gilchrist

Introduction

In Western democracies such as Australia, the provision of human services (the care and supports provided to people who fall into specific 'at-risk' cohorts such as the aged or people living with disability) is a central element of the drive to build equity and social cohesion (Frumkin 2002).

In Australia, the consolidation of the concept of the welfare state following World War II was preceded by a half century of initiatives including the development of pensions and the pursuit of welfare through the industrial relations system and parliamentary review. There was similar debate and experimentation in Britain, including publication of the Beveridge Report into social insurance (Beveridge 1942). Constitutional changes in Australia during the mid-1940s empowered the Commonwealth to provide an extended range of income support (including for the unemployed and widows) and benefits (such as for medical and pharmaceutical expenses, child endowment and maternity allowances). This represented a broader acceptance by governments of their responsibility for the provision of human services (Butcher & Gilchrist 2016). The changes formalised many aspects of the almost anti-theoretical approach of policymakers and actors that was recognised as Australian pragmatism and that developed from the time of colonisation (Metin 1977).

Within a decade of the establishment of the welfare state in British-linked Western democracies such as Australia, however, scholarly movements emerged that attacked the fundamental theoretical underpinnings of economic and political science that held sway for the first half of the 20th century at least – namely, institutional theory. Indeed, the primacy of the institution as a vehicle for policy implementation (of which the welfare state was the ultimate exemplar) was undermined by work that took a diametrically opposed view, replacing the institution with the individual as the focus of policy development (Peters 2012).

Much of the subsequent literature dichotomises these two ideas as being polar opposites.[1] For instance, from the mid-1950s, theoretical schools – such as that of public choice (Buchanan 1954) – developed a discourse that elevated the influence of the individual and discounted the influence of the institution. By the 1980s, what had been a primarily scholarly exercise became a political drive reflected in Australia by the advent of neoliberal thinking. In the context of the provision of human services and supports, it emphasised the individual and invoked such ideas as 'mutual obligation' (Mendes 2008).

Based on an analysis of two significant national human services policy reforms in Australia – the restructuring of the provision and funding of aged care services and the introduction of the first national disability services individualised funding scheme – this chapter argues that these two apparently dichotomised theories have been brought together in practice to effect the changes.

We use these two reform processes as a foil to argue that policymakers are seeking to exploit the opportunity inherent in both institutional theory and neoliberal ideas, such as public choice, to influence consumer and service provider behaviour. The objectives include improving individual outcomes and at least stabilising fiscal sustainability by implementing human services delivery and funding arrangements via quasi-market structures.

---

1   Rhetoric of scholarship.

This chapter is divided into four sections. In section two we briefly review the theoretical underpinnings of institutional theory and behavioural – or individualist – neoliberalism. In section three we describe the broad framework for the delivery of aged care and disability services in Australia and the reforms being implemented in terms of the theoretical framework discussed above, using these two sub-sectors of human service delivery to exemplify our argument. We provide concluding remarks in the final section.

Theoretical underpinnings

An ongoing discourse of the first four decades of the 20th century grew out of late 19th-century examinations of the economic state of the working poor, and discussion and experimentation with respect to the best course of action aimed at mitigating the extreme effects of poverty and inequity primarily derived from the consequences of the industrial revolution. This discourse culminated in setting aside the liberal tenets of individualism and self-help that were hallmarks of popular 19th-century economic thinking. It was replaced with 'scientifically' developed ideas pertaining to institutional resolutions to the endemic and wicked problems of inequity and poverty (White 2012; Deane 1980). Predominantly, these ideas were developed and promulgated by people who considered themselves the founders of sociology and who believed that institutions were the appropriate vehicle for the implementation of policy and the management of human behaviour (for example, see Webb & Webb 1965; Tawney 1964).

The popular champions of the move to place the institution at the point of primacy in public policy implementation included Max Weber (1947) from a scholarly perspective and William Beveridge (1942) from a public policy perspective. Beveridge's report *Social Insurance and Allied Services* set out the framework and logic of the United Kingdom's welfare state that was subsequently implemented through the establishment of such institutions as the National Health Service.

This brief analysis of the development trajectory and basis of institutional theory focuses on the central tenets of this school of thought. In particular, the rule of law is a critical precondition providing the necessary foundation for the creation of a civil society – that is, there is a hierarchy of society and a respect for institutions. Institutions are the lever used to develop, guide and manage that society (Peters 2012). Accordingly, structure is considered to drive personal behaviour, shape policy and act as the political frame.

We focus on the two main streams of institutional theory: (1) what might be termed classical institutional theory; and (2) new institutionalism. The former constitutes the original theoretical framework while the latter relates to a revision or revival of institutional theory in response to neoliberal ideas pertaining to individualism such as public choice. Peters (2012) argues that the latter form resulted from a reprise of classical institutional theory that broadened the theory particularly to include informal institutions in order to maintain the centrality of these ideas in the context of the significant advance of neoliberal thinking.

Institutionalism is a normative theoretical framework (Ostrom 2007). Fundamentally, it considers that the institution drives behaviour and that policymakers need to design institutional responses to the wicked problems of human services provision in order to ensure equity of access and outcome. As the 1970s and 1980s wore on, though, the scholarly push to replace institutional theory with neoliberal ideas of individual behaviourism became mainstream. Policymakers argued that individuals, who make preference choices regardless of the nature of the institutions serving them, should be the focus of policy development.

This idea saw a move away from a focus on bureaucratic institutions toward a broader conception of collective action (Denhardt 2011) – which incidentally led thinking away from the idea of government responsibility (the classical welfare state mentality) to collective responsibility in which government is one actor amongst a number. Indeed, in relation to human services provision in Australia, by the mid-1990s public choice theory was the driver of much public policy (Barraket 2008).

This policy framework manifested itself in a number of fundamental and important ways. For instance, the idea of mutual obligation in relation to human service provision and financial support was established at this time.[2] Additionally, as these services are increasingly provided in Australia by not-for-profit and charitable organisations, governments began

---

2   Perhaps re-established is a better phrase as this idea was a significant part of the 19th-century liberal thought that was displaced by institutional theory in the 20th century.

to utilise market-based procurement regimes, including competitive tendering and the use of the term 'client' to describe service users (Alford & O'Flynn 2012).

While, at a policy development level, the acceptance of such neoliberal ideas was almost universal, a number of scholars did not accept the turn that theory and practice had taken. They warned (and continue to warn) of the unintended consequences manifesting as a result particularly of quasi-market funding rationing systems and the primacy of the individual, essentially arguing that 'a rising tide [does not] lift all boats' (Stiglitz 2013: 1; see also, Rainnie et al. 2012; Davidson 2011; Van Slyke 2007; Barraket 2008; McGregor-Lowndes 2008).

Importantly for this chapter, by the second decade of the 21st century, many policymakers in Australia sought to establish quasi-market environments intended to empower consumers and create incentives for providers, while creating institutional structures that sought to correct for market failures. The former aimed to enable the individual service user to make choices about from whom they sourced their services and how they received them, and to own the decision and demand provider performance. Providers were encouraged to respond to 'market signals' thus delivering a better outcome more efficiently. The institutional reforms aimed to improve information and transparency so that service users could make informed choices, to ensure there were sound safety nets for individuals and enforceable quality standards and to instigate alternative interventions in 'thin' markets.

In effect, many policymakers made use of a combination of institutional theory and neoliberalism to elicit the policy outcomes that best served the interests of the community as a whole. In the next section, we examine this phenomenon by way of two policy examples being implemented in Australia.

Reform – aged care and disability services

In Australia, two significant human services reforms are underway relating to the provision of publicly funded aged care services and disability supports and care services – respectively referred to herein as aged care and disability services. In this section, we briefly describe the background to these reforms; examine the framework for reform, including aspects that demonstrate a reliance on both institutional theory and neoliberalism; and discuss the key features of both new structures.

While reform is being carried out in these two sub-sectors contemporaneously, government is, in fact, implementing differing systems for each. Whereas there is a common resort to neoliberalism underpinning both, the way in which institutional theory is drawn on takes a different form in each, with disability services reforms intended to result in greater transparency and accountability through reliance on governance bodies that are independent of the ministerial–departmental nexus that dominates aged care.

Partly this is to do with the historical policy settings that moulded each sub-sector, effectively forcing the Commonwealth government to drive change from different starting positions. Partly it is to do with the fact that aged care, and residential aged care in particular, has historically been the domain of the Commonwealth government, while the provision of disability services has been the domain of the sub-national jurisdictions making up the Australian federation, with each of those jurisdictions adopting different policies and programs. Finally, it is also partly to do with the fact that aged care is fundamentally an elderly and end-of-life care and support system while disability services form a whole-of-life care and support system.

Broadly, these reforms are being carried out by the Commonwealth government, with the involvement of sub-national jurisdictions where necessary – particularly for disability services. In terms of institutions, the reforms impact not-for-profit and for-profit contracted service providers, government departments and regulators at various levels. In terms of policy development, however, a critical element in the reform process is the role of the Australian Productivity Commission (hereafter, the Commission). It has investigated and reported upon aspects of aged care for over a decade, disability services more recently, and the role of the not-for-profit and charitable sectors in Australia as fundamental institutions that support civil society (Productivity Commission 2010).

Background to the aged care and disability care reforms

The current reforms of aged care and disability services have similar origins. Following the election of the federal Labor government in 2007, the Productivity Commission was issued with two terms of reference to undertake broad-ranging public inquiries into the policies, programs, regulations, funding and service quality of both sectors.

The Commission is an independent policy research and advisory body established under an Act of the Commonwealth parliament. It operates at arm's length from government and conducts open and transparent public inquiries and research to inform itself and develop recommendations that are in turn provided to government and, importantly, are published. It accepts its inquiry briefs from the Commonwealth government, however, and those briefs can prioritise, emphasise or curtail investigations in relation to specific areas of interest. As such, there is a tension between the nature of the brief being given and the interests of independent and transparent research and reporting practice. In this respect, the Commission draws on the independence inherent in its legislated powers, when it considers it necessary, to 'also make recommendations in the report on any matters relevant to the matter referred' (Commonwealth of Australia 1998 s.11(4)).

In the case of aged care, the Commonwealth government gave the Commission broad and open-ended terms of reference, asking it to develop options to redesign and reform Australia's aged care system and to recommend a transition path to a new system (Productivity Commission 2011a). More detailed terms of reference were also set out to provide a framework for the inquiry.

In the case of the inquiry into disability services, the terms of reference required the Commission to examine a range of options and approaches for the provision of long-term care and support for people with profound disability (Productivity Commission 2011b). The Commission was required to examine a social insurance model on a no-fault basis, reflecting the shared risk of disability across the population, as well as other options that provided incentives to focus investment in early intervention, as an adjunct to, or substitute for, an insurance model.

The Productivity Commission's report (2011a) *Caring for Older Australians* documented a range of problems in the aged care sector. The issues included high levels of unmet demand; a lack of continuity of care as a person's needs increased; inconsistent pricing of the different types and levels of care; limited incentives for service providers to become more efficient, improve quality or respond to consumer demand; workforce shortages; complex, overlapping and costly regulations; insufficient independence of the complaint-handling process from the Commonwealth Department of Health; and incomplete and overlapping responsibilities within and between jurisdictions.

The disability care story was much the same. The Productivity Commission's report (2011b) *Disability Care and Support* concluded that most families and individuals could not adequately prepare for the risk and financial impact of significant disability. The costs of lifetime care could be so substantial for individual households that the risks and costs needed to be pooled across the community. The Commission found that the disability support system was underfunded, unfair, fragmented and inefficient, and gave people living with disability little choice and no certainty of access to appropriate supports. There was no nationally consistent level of care and support and the stresses on the system were growing, resulting in rising costs for individual households and all governments.

Governance of major policy review and reform

Rationales for government involvement in aged care and disability services exist in the national discourse. These include equity of access to appropriate care, the protection of vulnerable consumers and the correction of market failures such as gaps in the provision of information about available services and, in the case of disability, the probability of an individual having a disability being low but the lifelong costs that could ensue being potentially catastrophic (Gilchrist 2017; Knight & Gilchrist 2015). As such, evidence-based and objective governance over the development, examination and consideration of policy was critical to identifying measures that would provide access to appropriate care and support for service users, incentives for service providers to improve efficiency and effectiveness, and the achievement of greater value for money and fiscal sustainability for taxpayers.

The Commission's institutional processes are well suited to undertaking major policy reviews. The three organisational design pillars of the Commission are that:

1. it is independent (it is ruled by commissioners who are appointed for up to five years and whose independence is protected by law)
2. it conducts its policy inquiries in an open and transparent manner
3. its guiding principle is improvement of the wellbeing of the community as a whole – it acts in the public interest.

Appropriately, the Commission's role does not extend to final decision-making or implementation. This separation of functions is an important element of sound governance design. Accordingly, its recommendations on the reform of aged care and disability services, both published in 2011, were subject to scrutiny by the central departments – as well as by the two departments primarily responsible for aged care (Department of Health) and welfare services (Department of Social Services). In both cases, the government also undertook extensive consultation processes and developed the final reform packages that were agreed to by the cabinet. The *Aged Care (Living Longer Living Better) Act 2013* and the *National Disability Insurance Scheme Act 2013* were subsequently passed.

Following government agreement to these major policy reforms, government service delivery departments and agencies commenced implementation and undertook ongoing monitoring and revision of the detail of the policy and its programs. Different governance arrangements have evolved for aged care and disability services, but each draws on institutional theory and neoliberalism. These elements are explored further in the following subsections.

Governance of service delivery management and accountability

This section examines and contrasts the governance model adopted for aged care, which is administered by the Commonwealth government through the Department of Health, with that of disability services, which is administered jointly between the Commonwealth and participating sub-national governments and a newly created independent institution, the National Disability Insurance Agency (NDIA). The two governance models bring with them differences in arrangements for the oversight of policy and administration, funding and quality control. Notwithstanding, each establishes the institutional framework necessary for the governance of the publicly funded services, and at the same time establishes a quasi-market environment within which services are demanded and supplied.

Aged care: A departmental model within one level of government

The funding and regulation of aged care is largely the responsibility of the Commonwealth government via the Department of Health, which reports directly to the Minister for Aged Care. The *Aged Care Act 1997* and related legislation provides the legal basis for the department's actions and requires the department to report annually on its operations. There are no transparency or accountability requirements for publication of the minister's directions to the department. The department closely manages the performance of all aspects of the aged care programs, from operational policy and regulation of service supply and delivery, to funding and a high level of direct involvement in the regulation of quality.

Although there are several formal non-departmental bodies that contribute advice in relation to policy, management and funding, the Department of Health is involved in their operations, especially by providing the staff for their secretariats. As noted below, only the quality regulator operates as a fully independent statutory authority, but even it works jointly with the department, which is responsible for the enforcement of quality standards through the licensing of providers.

The services provided to service users, either in their own homes or in residential aged care facilities, are delivered by not-for-profit organisations or for-profit businesses (with a small number of facilities still run by sub-national governments) rather than directly by the Department of Health. Aged care subsidies are largely funded from the annual budgets of the Commonwealth government. User co-payments (both capital and operating) are made by services users according to the cost of the services being delivered and their capacity to pay.

Services delivered in users' own homes have been reformed through the introduction of consumer-directed care, with funding being provided to users and providers having to compete for business. Supply-side limits still apply to both home care and to care delivered in residential facilities.

Disability services: An independent agency model across two levels of government

Prior to the recent reforms, each sub-national government provided for the care and supports for people with disability within its jurisdiction. This resulted in there being considerable diversity across jurisdictions in the types of care available for comparable levels of disability, the quantity and quality of services and the amount of funding made available to providers. As such, among other things, people with disability could not move jurisdictions with any assurance that they would receive, or be able to afford, the supports that they required.

All governments have now committed to a National Disability Strategy that aims to support people with disability, to improve their lives as well as the lives of their families and carers, and to provide leadership for a community-wide shift in attitudes towards disability.

Within the National Disability Strategy, the National Disability Insurance Scheme (NDIS) has been established to enact a fundamental change to how supports and services for people with permanent and severe disability are funded and delivered across Australia. The total number of people with disability being supported by the NDIS is limited by the eligibility criteria. Accordingly, considerable responsibility under the broader strategy remains with both sub-national and national health, education and community service agencies. The NDIS is an important part of the system, but it is not the whole system.

As explained further below, the governance structure for the NDIS is different to that for aged care. NDIS is managed by an independent agency that reports to the Council of Ministers from the Commonwealth and state/territory governments. The Commonwealth Department of Social Services coordinates Commonwealth policy advising and budgeting, but has no direct role in funding or regulating disability services.

The NDIS can pay for supports, housing modification, transport assistance, assistance to seek and sustain employment and other services that pass the test of being 'reasonable and necessary'. This means that the services and supports are relevant to a person's disability and are necessary for them to be able to live an ordinary life and achieve their goals. Services are delivered by approved providers who compete for customers in a quasi-market. Local area coordinators for the NDIS can also assist people with disability to access mainstream community services such as medical care and education, and to participate in community activities and services.[3] Sub-national jurisdictions continue to directly support those with disability who are not eligible for NDIS assistance.

Oversight of policy and administration

Aged care

Given the extensive nature of the aged care reforms and the decade-long timeframe in which they are being progressively implemented, the Minister for Aged Care and the Department of Health[4] closely monitor this implementation phase. The cost of the scheme, however, and aged care issues that may impact on broader policy settings such as taxation and the age pension, also attract the attention of the central departments.

The Department of Health has considerable internal capacity to undertake a policy-monitoring role. It has also established an Aged Care Sector Committee[5] comprising members appointed from the major stakeholder groups such as consumers, large for-profit and not-for-profit providers, aged care worker organisations and the department. The department's staff provide the secretariat for the committee.

The committee's Aged Care Roadmap offered advice to the minister on the future directions for aged care. This committee is the only broadly based institution capable of holding the government to account for its overall management of the aged care system; however, its communiqués issued after every meeting (averaging four per year) make only brief mention of matters discussed and do not report on the outcomes of its deliberations on those matters. The terms of reference of the committee require that members respect the confidentiality of the committee proceedings.

Policy monitoring and review was entrenched in the legislation that gave legal force to the reforms. There is a requirement in the *Aged Care (Living Longer Living Better) Act* that the minister initiate an independent

---

3   These arrangements are yet to be effectively implemented and, as can be expected with such a complex and large policy rollout, there have been identified many significant issues in the context of examining the intention and the reality; for example, see Gilchrist (2017).

4   For information relating to the structural components of this department, see 'Aged Care Sector Committee', *Ageing and Aged Care*, Department of Health, Australian Government, agedcare.health. gov.au/aged-care-reform/aged-care-sector-committee.

5   For information pertaining to this committee, see 'Terms of reference: Aged Care Sector Committee', *Ageing and Aged Care*, Department of Health, Australian Government, agedcare.health. gov.au/aged-care-reform/aged-care-sector-committee/terms-of-reference-aged-care-sector-committee.

review of the operation of the reforms provided for under the Act after the first three years of their implementation. The minister appointed the chair of the Aged Care Sector Committee as the independent reviewer and the department provided the research secretariat.

The government released the report of the legislated review in 2017. The review concluded that the reforms it examined (being a subset of the total reform agenda and excluding major issues such as funding and quality regulation) had successfully progressed the achievement of a consumer-driven and sustainable system, but that there was further progress to be made (Department of Health 2017a, 2017b).

The aged care sector's stakeholders, including consumer groups, providers, workforce organisations and health professionals have established the National Aged Care Alliance,[6] which has played a long-term constructive role in improving aged care. It was particularly effective in contributing to the Productivity Commission's 2010–11 inquiry and in subsequently assisting both sides of politics in the parliament to accept the reform framework.

Disability services

Responsibility for disability services policy and administration for those who are eligible for NDIS support is shared between the Commonwealth and sub-national governments in accordance with the various bilateral agreements discussed above. A new governance framework is being developed as part of the establishment of the NDIS.[7]

A ministerial council – the Standing Council on Disability Reform – is the peak level of the strategy as a whole.[8] It comprises the Commonwealth Minister for Social Services and state/territory ministers with disability and treasury portfolios, as well as a representative from the Australian Local Government Association. Building on the framework developed by

---

6   For information pertaining to this organisation, see National Aged Care Alliance, www.naca.asn.au/.

7   As of mid-2017, bilateral agreements with a number of sub-national governments were being negotiated and uncertainty exists with respect to those agreements currently in place. Inevitably, experience of the processes in practice will inform reflection on the original agreements.

8   For information pertaining to this council, see 'Disability Reform Council', *Disability and Carers*, Department of Social Services, Australian Government, www.dss.gov.au/our-responsibilities/disability-and-carers/programmes-services/government-international/disability-reform-council.

the Productivity Commission (2011a), the council ensures the strategy reforms are implemented through an intergovernmental National Disability Agreement.[9]

The National Disability Agreement specifies that all participating governments have joint responsibility for a range of functions: developing national policy and reform directions, as well as funding and pursuing research and providing data that improves the evidence base for policy and reform. The agreement also provides that each jurisdiction can, where appropriate, invest in initiatives to support nationally agreed policy priorities, in consultation with other levels of government. The enabling legislation for the NDIS also required a review to be undertaken after two years of operation of the scheme.

Under the agreement, the Commonwealth is responsible for the provision of employment services for people with disability; income support targeted to the needs of people with disability, their families and carers; funding for the sub-jurisdictional governments to assist them in meeting their obligations under the scheme; and funding disability services for the elderly.

The participating sub-national governments are responsible for providing non-employment disability services; funding and regulating basic community care services, except for the elderly who have a disability; and funding community care packages and residential aged care delivered under Commonwealth aged care programs (again, except for the cohort aged over 65, which is a Commonwealth responsibility. There are, however, mitigating provisions for circumstances when people with disability enter the NDIS prior to turning 65 years of age).

Additional bilateral agreements deal with various matters including, in the case of the Northern Territory, the issue of provider of last resort and, for Western Australia, in relation to the state retaining a more significant decision-making capacity. As described above, however, the rollout of the new arrangements has highlighted significant issues with these agreements.

---

9   Information pertaining to this agreement is available here: 'National agreements', *Council on Federal Financial Relations*, Australia, www.federalfinancialrelations.gov.au/content/national_agreements.aspx.

The NDIS started with a small number of trials in several jurisdictions and is being progressively rolled out across the nation over a three-year period. Oversight is undertaken by the Standing Council on Disability Reform. The Commonwealth minister is responsible for administering the *National Disability Insurance Scheme Act* and exercises statutory powers with the agreement of states and territories, including a power to make the rules for the scheme and direct the newly created NDIA.

The NDIA is an independent statutory authority that was established under the NDIS legislation, rather than as a function of a ministerial department as occurs with aged care. It is governed by a board of directors that is responsible for the efficient and effective performance of the functions of the NDIA and for determining the strategies and policies of the agency. The NDIA reports to the Commonwealth Minister for Social Services as well as the intergovernmental Council of Ministers, and therefore sits within the Commonwealth minister's 'portfolio'. As noted earlier, the Department of Social Services is the 'portfolio' department but has no direct role in NDIS funding or regulation.

The NDIA produces annual reports of its operations together with quarterly reports updating the public on the scheme's rollout. The Commonwealth minister may give directions as well as general strategic advice to the board provided it is in writing and has been agreed to by all participating jurisdictions. To ensure transparency and ministerial accountability, ministerial directions must be published in the NDIA's annual reports.

The Act provides for the appointment of an independent advisory council[10] to advise the board. The council is predominantly made up of people with disability and some carers of people with disability. In effect, the council provides a formal dedicated consumer voice to advise on the operation of the scheme. In contrast to the Aged Care Sector Committee, the disability governance model enforces greater transparency and accountability. The board of the agency is required to consider and respond to all advice from the independent advisory council and to inform the Standing Council on Disability Reform of the actions it is taking.

---

10   Information pertaining to this council can be found at 'IAC', NDIS, Department of Human Services, Australian Government, www.ndis.gov.au/about-us/governance/IAC.

Funding

Aged care

Government subsidies for services delivered to eligible service users are funded directly from the budget of the Australian Government's Department of Health. Service users are subject to a means test and make financial contributions commensurate with their capacity to pay. Consumer contributions are also subject to annual and lifetime self-funding limits, reflecting a social insurance principle, with the government meeting full costs once those limits have been reached.

The government's Aged Care Financing Authority (ACFA)[11] has no funding role but, rather, monitors the financial performance of the aged care system and publishes an annual report on the system's operation. The authority's annual report states: '[its] role is to provide independent, transparent advice to the Australian Government on funding and financial issues in the aged care sector' (ACFA 2017: 20). In effect, the authority is a committee of independent persons and representatives of significant stakeholders that is funded by the department and supported by departmental staff. The minister can request the authority to monitor and report on specific issues relating to the financial performance of the aged care programs such as changes to means-testing arrangements and accommodation payment changes.

Another institution established to regulate certain financial issues in aged care is the Aged Care Pricing Commissioner. This statutory office holder is supported by staff employed by the department. The functions of the commissioner include granting approval, where warranted, to providers who wish to charge capital payments for aged care accommodation that are above a maximum amount set by the minister, and to approve schedules of fees for a range of services that are of a considerably higher standard or scope than is required to be provided under the funded program. These are important risk-mitigating constraints in a quasi-market-based system, given the vulnerability of many consumers of residential aged care and the fact that the service users are ultimately exposed to the supply-side risk of providers failing or otherwise exiting the market. In those instances, the department works closely with other providers with the aim of supporting the elderly who are affected by the closure of a facility.

---

11   See Aged Care Financing Authority (2016).

The level (and cost) of community care delivered in service users' own homes is determined by Aged Care Assessment Teams based on the needs of the person. These teams are funded by the Commonwealth and comprise professional health workers such as doctors, nurses, social workers and occupational therapists. The level of co-contribution by a person deemed eligible for government-subsidised care is assessed according to their income and wealth. Under the quasi-market consumer-directed care reforms, the service user can choose from competing service providers to 'purchase' services from one or more providers, and can change the services and the providers. A user's needs can also be reassessed as their circumstances change. The government protects fiscal sustainability by capping the number of community care packages available at any one time.

For care in residential aged care facilities, the government subsidises the service providers directly and maintains caps on demand (the number of care places) and supply (the number of bed licences issued to providers). This significantly constrains the benefits of market competition in residential care, though the government is committed to removing supply-side constraints and introducing consumer-directed care in the future.

To improve the information available to service users, so that they can exercise their progressively increasing market power, the government has established the *My Aged Care* website and requires service providers to make up-to-date market information available to service users. This represents a bringing together of institutional and neoliberal approaches to reform to benefit empowered consumers and to elicit more competitive behaviour by providers.

Disability services

Funding arrangements for the disability scheme in 2017 reflected the transition from pilot trials to the scheme's progressive nationwide rollout. They are complex due to the nature of disability services themselves and of the agreements in place. The Commonwealth makes National Disability Specific Purpose Payments to the sub-national jurisdictions in order to meet its contribution to the NDIS, while these jurisdictions continue to fund the original system as it is gradually replaced. As the scheme becomes fully operational in each jurisdiction, Commonwealth payments will be redirected to the NDIA.

Disability funding is governed by the intergovernmental National Disability Agreement and the National Partnership Agreement on Transitioning Responsibilities for Aged Care and Disability Services. The NDIA holds all NDIS funds contributed by the Commonwealth and sub-national jurisdictions in a single pool, administers assessments of eligibility and access by participants to the NDIS and approves the payment of individualised support packages. The NDIA's annual report must contain an actuarial statement as to the financial sustainability of the scheme together with any risks to that sustainability and estimates of the future costs of the NDIS.

Assistance from the NDIS is not means tested and has no impact on a person's eligibility for income support such as the disability support pension and carer's allowance. Individuals are required to exhaust private insurance cover prior to accessing NDIS funds.

The NDIA has developed a price list that includes individual service elements grouped together as bundles that can be accessed by eligible service users (Gilchrist 2017). Service users are expected to co-create a care plan with the NDIA with reference to the price list. Once the plan is activated, service users can choose services from competing registered providers. In this way, the NDIS is intended to employ quasi-market principles with incentives to influence service provider behaviour to emphasise the interests of service users. While this neoliberal funding arrangement may well solicit certain outcomes, it is intended that quasi-market behaviour is tempered by the institutions that surround the system, including the NDIA and quality control institutions.

Quality control

Aged care

One of the central elements of performance accountability within the aged care system relates to the quality and safety of the services being delivered to service users. This is especially important given that the client group are some of the most frail and vulnerable in society, with many having limited cognitive functioning. Indeed, approximately half of all residents in aged care residential facilities have a diagnosis of dementia, and many have other impairments and little financial security.

To this end, the Commonwealth government has employed an institutional approach by establishing an independent Australian Aged Care Quality Agency under its own Act, with the power to employ its own staff. The Act and its delegated legislation – the Quality Agency Principles 2013 – sets out the obligations with which approved aged care providers must comply.[12]

This agency is supported by an Aged Care Quality Advisory Council that provides advice to the agency on its functions and operations. The advisory council gives essential advice on safety and compliance so as to help align the quality agenda with community expectations.

But even in this sensitive area, there is a lack of clarity of roles and separation of powers. The government has, instead, created dual administration of quality control by the independent agency and by the department. They both have roles in monitoring the compliance of aged care service providers to the quality standards. Where noncompliance is identified, it is the department that assesses the performance of providers and takes appropriate regulatory action, including revoking a provider's approval to deliver services when their standards of care have been found to be particularly poor.

High-profile failures in the regulation of quality in aged care have prompted the government to commission a public review in 2017. The resulting report of the Review of National Aged Care Quality Regulatory Processes was released late in that year. In the words of the reviewers:

> Our consultations and research highlighted the need for better coordination of regulatory functions, expanded intelligence-gathering capacity and a better system for sharing information on provider performance with the public and aged care service providers, to promote service improvement. We have also recommended changes to accreditation, compliance monitoring and complaints-handling processes to make them more responsive to emerging issues with care quality. (Department of Health 2017b: ii)

---

12 The functions of this agency have been incorporated into the Aged Care Quality and Safety Commission (see www.agedcarequality.gov.au).

The government has also created the role of a minister-appointed statutory office holder, the Aged Care Complaints Commissioner, under the *Aged Care Act*. The role was promoted as creating complaint-handling arrangements independent from the department.[13] The staff of the commissioner are departmental staff.

An advocacy scheme for service users, their families and carers has also been established. This provides them with free, confidential and independent advice on matters relating to aged care and support. It is an important adjunct in helping this vulnerable group to resolve their concerns in circumstances in which they often feel powerless and confused.

Disability care

A core component of NDIS performance management and accountability is the quality of the services being delivered to people with disability. Service users bear supply-side risk in that they are directly impacted by market failure where service providers fail.

The core document is the NDIS Quality and Safeguarding Framework, which is designed to ensure high-quality supports and services delivered in safe environments for all people with disability who are participating in the scheme.[14] The framework was endorsed by the Council of Australian Governments in 2016 and publicly released by the Disability Reform Council in 2017. The framework was developed in consultation with stakeholders, including people with disability, carers, providers and peak bodies. Public consultation helped to inform the final framework.

The framework includes the following new national functions: a code of conduct; provider registration, including quality assurance; a complaint-handling system; investigation and enforcement; and nationally consistent worker screening. The code of conduct will be overseen by the new NDIS Quality and Safeguards Commission, which was announced by the Commonwealth Government in 2017 and funded in the 2017–18 Budget. The commission will have powers to enforce action where providers or workers have engaged in unacceptable behaviours.

---

13   See Aged Care Quality and Safety Commission: www.agedcarequality.gov.au/.
14   'NDIS Quality and Safeguards Commission', *Disability and Carers*, NDIS, Department of Social Services, Australian Government, www.dss.gov.au/ndisqualitysafeguards.

An additional and important private institution, which is a significant contributor to the disability services infrastructure, is National Disability Services. This industry peak body has a crucial role in responding to regulatory, funding and quality issues on behalf of the service provider sector.

Concluding remarks

The advent and implementation of significant reform in the funding and delivery of aged care and disability services in Australia is multifaceted, time consuming and challenging for governments, providers and service users. These are complex, crucial and universal services. Policymakers have considered that neoliberal theories, such as public choice, can be employed to design systems to empower service users with choice and control and create a quasi-market arrangement with embedded incentives for providers to deliver consumer-oriented services with higher quality and lower costs.

A principle aim is to elicit better value for money outcomes for the service users and taxpayers more generally. The benefits derived from quasi-market response behaviours by service providers are also seen as important. Essentially, if the provider is to be successful it is in the provider's interest to respond to the quasi-market signals.

Nonetheless, consistent with institutional theory, institutions have been needed to protect the vulnerability of consumers and correct for market failures, such as by overcoming information asymmetry, improving transparency and intervening in thin markets. A number of institutions and associated government program and regulatory interventions have proven critical in the administration, oversight and evaluation of the policy frameworks. They influence the behaviour of service providers by setting rules relating to funding, quality, service content and service planning.

They also impact behaviour via the requirements for transparency and accountability of governance and the collaboration of institutions and, in the case of disability services, the various bilateral agreements that exist between sub-national and national governments. The latter impact a number of issues that are peripheral to the policy arrangements, but are nevertheless important, such as the impact of oversubscription.

Within the ambit of institutional theory, there has been considerable divergence of approach, with the aged care framework being heavily reliant on a ministerial–departmental nexus while disability services are administered through more independent and clearly delineated institutions, with greater transparency and accountability. While this divergence has arisen in part from the different histories of the two frameworks (the long dominant role of the Commonwealth in aged care and the dominance of the states and territories in disability services until very recently), it is now opportune to reflect upon the merits of the two approaches and to consider what might be 'best practice'.

In both service areas, there exist formal private institutions – called peak bodies – that act as conduits for information, feedback and the exchange of expertise in the implementation of new policy. Provider peak bodies also exert influence on the way their members deliver services.

The research focus of this chapter demonstrates the utility and purpose of applying multiple theoretical frameworks. The two case studies illustrate that the employment of a neoliberal strategy of quasi-market systems and public choice, which aims to empower service users and give service providers incentives to improve efficiency, effectiveness and responsiveness to consumer demand, is being tempered by resort to institutional theory. The latter is based on control by institutions focused on administering the provision of funding and service rules, correcting market failures and enforcing quality standards.

Future research could investigate the extent to which a multiple-theory implementation framework is effective. It may also investigate the degree to which either institutional theory or neoliberal theories impact differentially on scheme performance, and whether either of the two forms of institutional theory deliver the greater public good. That is, does the combination work and, if so, is it critical or does one school of thought dominate the other in terms of driving service provider performance and service user outcomes?

Overall, the complexity inherent in the provision of human services emphasises the importance of such studies in terms of ensuring the policy framework generates the desired outcomes from the point of view of service users who are, after all, at risk and dependent on these service systems as well as the overall public good.

References

Aged Care Financing Authority 2016, *Fourth Report on the Funding and Financing of the Aged Care Sector*, Department of Health, Commonwealth of Australia, Canberra, www.health.gov.au/committees-and-groups/aged-care-financing-authority-acfa.

—— 2017, *Fifth Report on the Funding and Financing of the Aged Care Sector*, Department of Health, Commonwealth of Australia, Canberra, agedcare.health.gov.au/reform/aged-care-financing-authority/2017-report-on-the-funding-and-financing-of-the-aged-care-industry.

Alford, JL & O'Flynn, J 2012, *Rethinking Public Service Delivery: Managing with External Providers*, Palgrave Macmillan, London.

Barraket, J (ed) 2008, *Strategic Issues for the Not-For-Profit Sector*, UNSW Press, Sydney.

Beveridge, W 1942, *Inter-departmental Committee on Social Insurance and Allied Services*, HMSO, Great Britain.

Buchanan, JM 1954, 'Individual choice in voting and the market', *Journal of Political Economy*, vol 62, pp 334–43, doi.org/10.1086/257538.

Butcher, J 2015, 'Australian sub-national compacts with the not-for-profit sector: pathways to cross-sector cooperation', in J Wanna (ed), *New Accountabilities, New Challenges*, ANU Press, Canberra, doi.org/10.22459/NANC.04.2015.10.

Butcher, JR & Gilchrist, DJ 2016, 'Introduction', in JR Butcher & DJ Gilchrist (eds), *The Three Sector Solution: Delivering Public Policy in Collaboration with Not-For-Profits and Business*, ANU Press, Canberra, doi.org/10.22459/TSS.07.2016.01.

Commonwealth of Australia 1998, *Productivity Commission Act, 1998*, doi.org/10.25291/VR/1998-4-VR-459.

Davidson, B 2011, 'Contestability in human services markets', *Journal of Australian Political Economy*, no 68, pp 213–39.

Deane, P 1980, *The Evolution of Economic Ideas*, Modern Cambridge Economics, Cambridge University Press, London.

Denhardt, RB 2011, *Theories of Public Organization*, 6th edn, Wadsworth Cengage Learning, London.

Department of Health 2016, *2015–16 Report of the Operation of the Aged Care Act 1997*, Australian Government, Canberra, gen-agedcaredata.gov. au/Resources/Reports-and-Publications/2016/December/2015%E2%80 %9316-Report-on-the-Operation-of-the-Aged-Care-A.

—— 2017a, *Legislated Review of Aged Care 2017*, Australian Government, Canberra, agedcare.health.gov.au/legislated-review-of-aged-care-2017-report.

—— 2017b, *Review of National Aged Care Quality Regulatory Processes*, agedcare. health.gov.au/quality/review-of-national-aged-care-quality-regulatory-processes-report.

Economic Audit Committee 2009, *Putting the Public First: Partnering with the Community and Business to Deliver Outcomes*, Report to the Government of Western Australian, Perth.

Frumkin, P 2002, *On Being Nonprofit: A Conceptual and Policy Primer*, Harvard University Press, London, doi.org/10.4159/9780674037403.

Galbraith, JK 1952, *American Capitalism: The Concept of Countervailing Power*, Houghton Mifflin Company, Boston.

Gilchrist, DJ 2017, *Person Centred Planning within the NDIS: Current Limitations – Prospective Opportunities*, report for the Independent Centre for Not-For-Profit Research, Perth.

Knight, PA & Gilchrist, DJ 2015, *2014 Evaluation of the Sustainable Funding and Contracting with the Not-For-Profit Sector Initiatives and Associated Procurement Reforms*, Government of Western Australia, Perth.

March, JG & Olsen, JP 1984, 'The new institutionalism: organisational factors in political life', *American Political Science Review*, vol 78, no 3, pp 734–49, doi.org/10.2307/1961840.

McGregor-Lowndes, M 2008, 'Is there something better than partnership?', in J Barraket, *Strategic Issues for the Not-For-Profit Sector*, UNSW Press, Sydney.

Mendes, P 2008, *Australia's Welfare Wars Revisited: The Players, The Politics and the Ideologies*, UNSW Press, Sydney.

Metin, A 1977 (1901), *Socialism without Doctrine*, R Ward (trans), Alternative Publishing Co-operative Ltd, Chippendale.

Office of the Auditor General Western Australia 2000, *A Means to an End: Contracting Not-For-Profit Organisations for The Delivery of Community Services*, audit.wa.gov.au/wp-content/uploads/2013/05/report2000_03.pdf.

Ostrom, E 2007, 'Institutional rational choice: an assessment of the institutional analysis and development framework', in PA Sabatier (ed), *Theories of the Policy Process*, 2nd edn, Westview Press, Cambridge.

Peters, BG 2012, *Institutional Theory in Political Science: The 'New Institutionalism'*, 2nd edn, The Continuum International Publishing Group, New York.

Productivity Commission 2010, *Contribution of the Australian Not-For-Profit Sector*, Research Report, Canberra.

—— 2011a, *Caring for Older Australians*, report no 53, Final Inquiry Report, Canberra, www.pc.gov.au/inquiries/completed/aged-care/report/aged-care-volume1.pdf.

—— 2011b, *Disability Care and Support*, report no 54, Final Inquiry Report, Canberra, www.pc.gov.au/inquiries/completed/disability-support/report/disability-support-volume1.pdf.

Rainnie, SF, Gilchrist DJ & Morris, CL 2012, 'Putting the public first? Restructuring the West Australian Human Services Sector', *International Journal of Employment Studies*, vol 20, no 1, pp 104–25.

Salamon, LM 1995, *Partners in Public Service: Government – Nonprofit Relations in the Modern Welfare State*, The Johns Hopkins University Press, Baltimore.

Stiglitz, J 2013, *The price of inequality: how today's divided society endangers our future*, Penguin, London.

Tawney, RH 1964, *Equality*, Unwin Books, London.

Van Slyke, DM 2007, 'Agents or stewards: using theory to understand the government–nonprofit social service contracting relationship', *Journal of Public Administration Research and Theory*, vol 17, no 2, pp 157–87, doi.org/10.1093/jopart/mul012.

Webb, S & Webb, B 1965 (1894), *Industrial Democracy*, Augustus M Kelly, New York.

Weber, M 1947, *The Theory of Social and Economic Organization*, AM Henderson & T Parsons (trans), The Free Press, London.

White, LH 2012, *The Clash of Economic Ideas: The Great Policy Debates and Experiments of the Last Hundred Years*, Cambridge University Press, London, doi.org/10.1017/CBO9780511998218.

Wilkins, P & Gilchrist, DJ 2016, 'Accountability for the public policy contribution of not-for-profit organisations: who is accountable to whom and for what?', in R Pablo Guerrero & P Wilkins (eds), *Doing Good?: Private Actors, Evaluation and Public Value (Comparative Policy Evaluation)*, Transaction Publishing, doi.org/10.4324/9780203793008-6.

6

ALL THE BEST INTENTIONS

A review of a sub-national attempt at reshaping the not-for-profit/public sector nexus

David Gilchrist

Introduction

There is little doubt that, over the past two decades, governments in developed Western countries have increasingly relied on the not-for-profit (NFP) and charitable sector as an infrastructure framework for the delivery of policy (Frumkin 2002). This is no less the case in Australia, where the NFP sector is articulated effectively into many activity areas that are also the domain of national and sub-national governments.

In the Australian case, in the aftermath of World War II, the implementation of the welfare state broadly followed the example of the United Kingdom and saw governments take an increased responsibility for human services.[1] Governments met this responsibility in one of three ways: (1) they provided services directly (e.g. primary health care); (2) they funded other governments to undertake service provision

---

1   The definition of human services can be fraught as differing contexts may imply different activities that fall into or out of the accepted definition. While the definition is not so important in this chapter, it includes disability services, aged care services, child protection and mental health services, as well as hybrid activities such as the provision of post-incarceration supports.

(e.g. local government service provision funded by state governments, state government health provision funded by the Commonwealth government); and/or (3) they directly funded NFPs to provide services (Butcher & Gilchrist 2016). It is the third case, and the resulting government/NFP nexus, that is my focus here.

At this point, it is appropriate to indicate that there has been considerable discussion in academic and industry circles regarding the government/ NFP nexus (Butcher & Gilchrist 2016; Alford & O'Flynn 2012; McGregor-Lowndes 2008; Mendes 2008). There is a metaphysical and practical aspect to this discourse. It is the outcomes achieved from a practical attempt at strengthening the nexus in an Australian sub-national jurisdiction, however, that is of interest in this chapter (Wilkins & Gilchrist 2016).

In recent years, the nexus between governments and the Australian NFP sector[2] – hereinafter termed the NFP sector or the sector – has undergone changes due to 'traditional' funding arrangements giving way to quasi market systems intended to result in better service delivery and better outcomes for service users (Alford & O'Flynn 2012). While the extent to which the introduction of quasi-market-style arrangements has resulted in the outcomes expected warrants further examination, this chapter is concerned with the broader development of the government/NFP nexus in one Australian sub-national jurisdiction – Western Australia (WA).[3]

In 2008, the newly elected WA Government undertook an economic audit of the state's public sector. The focus of the audit was to identify prospective efficiencies, cost savings and better ways of conducting government business. The audit considered all aspects of government business, including the relationship between the NFPs contracted to

---

2   The Australian NFP sector is composed of an estimated 600,000 organisations that can be incorporated under many differing types of legislation under both state/territory and federal legislative frameworks. Further, charities are a sub-sector of the NFP sector and comprise approximately 55,000 organisations. Charities are the primary regulated NFP sub-sector and they are also most likely to be the type of organisation providing human services in Western Australia. This is because the types of services provided in human services attract charitable status and certain tax advantages. As the tax or other status of the organisations discussed in this chapter is irrelevant to the context and findings, I have retained the use of NFPs throughout the chapter to cover all types of entities that may be impacted by the Delivering Community Services in Partnership (DCSP) policy.

3   Additional changes in recent years have included the establishment of a national charities regulator (the Australian Charities and Not-for-profits Commission) in 2012, the establishment of a new statutory definition of charity (*Charities Act 2013* (Cth)), and the development of federal regulatory requirements for charities including the annual lodgement of financial and operational data.

provide government-funded services and the government agencies procuring those services – the WA Government/NFP nexus. This aspect became a major subsection of the final economic audit report.

Specific recommendations relating to the government/NFP nexus (Economic Audit Committee 2009) were adopted, including that a partnership forum should be established of senior representatives from the NFP and government sectors that would: (1) act as a policy and practice driver; (2) seek to recognise the value of the NFP sector; and (3) establish a number of subcommittees – including a contracting subcommittee – focused on practical improvements. The various recommendations that were developed as part of the economic audit were wrapped into what became the Delivering Community Services in Partnership Policy (or DCSP) (Government of Western Australian 2011).

The initiative was also to be evaluated on an annual basis; subsequently, assessment of the outcomes achieved, having been identified as a result of this annual evaluation, was to be reported to parliament. Since its inception, the author has carried out three evaluations on behalf of the WA Government and reported the largely quantitative aspects of these evaluations in previous publications (Gilchrist 2016; Knight & Gilchrist 2015; Gilchrist 2013; Gilchrist & Knight 2013a). Now, over a decade after the establishment of the Partnership Forum, and after the election of a new government, the forum has been discontinued and a new, replacement, structure is being introduced.[4]

It is appropriate, then, for this chapter to look at the Partnership Forum structure and to analyse the impact it has had at a policy level, and whether or not it has achieved its intended outcomes. I do this by reviewing the most recent evaluation (together with previous evaluations where useful) within the context of the government/NFP nexus.

---

4   While not strictly relevant to this chapter, the new WA Government's policy framework is entitled the Supporting Communities Program and it will focus on procurement processes but include the establishment of a Supporting Communities Forum to be made up of senior government and sector personnel but also including service user representatives (see www.wacoss.org.au/wp-content/uploads/2017/06/Draft-Terms-of-Reference.pdf). Amongst other things, this new arrangement is intended as a response to the Partnership Forum's failings by including service users, appointing and prioritising participation in forum deliberations of senior public sector personnel, and appointing a local chair.

This chapter is divided into four sections. In section two, I consider the government/NFP nexus with respect to human services, and place the DCSP in that context. In this section I also briefly describe the structures that made up the Partnership Forum. In section three, I analyse the forum's achievements by considering the 2016 report to the WA parliament and, in section four, I provide concluding remarks.

The government/NFP nexus: The WA Partnership Forum

While this chapter is concerned specifically with the WA experience and while this sub-national government has sovereignty with regard to its response to human services challenges, due to the nature of the Australian national polity, this response is also tempered by the impact of federal government policy and funding as well as by practice in other Australian jurisdictions. It is necessary, therefore, to consider a broader, national framework before narrowing the view to the WA experience.

The development of funding and practice relating to human services has not been uniform across Australia[5] or within each sub-sector of the sector – nor, indeed, has it been uniform worldwide (Young 2006; Salamon 1995). Broadly, however, the NFP sector has been involved in direct service delivery for over three decades, during which time there has been a general reduction in the level of direct government involvement. It has also been the case in Australia that governments have traditionally provided different services to varying degrees, but the trend is now toward a reduction in direct government services and an increase in the role of NFPs as service providers (Butcher & Gilchrist 2016).

Indeed, over the past five or so years, Australian governments have increasingly sought to transfer their services delivery activity (including in relation to assets and staff) to the NFP sector (Alford & O'Flynn 2012).

---

5   For clarity, Australia is a federation of six states and two territories, while the federal government also controls a number of territories that are external to the continent of Australia. Each state and territory has a set of responsibilities relating to human services delivery and these responsibilities can be both concomitant with those of the federal government or they can be separate and specifically a state/territory responsibility. Because of Australia's vertical fiscal imbalance – where the states/ territories have many responsibilities but the federal government has the chief income sources – it can be difficult to disaggregate the roles of the federal government and that of the states and territories. For our purposes, I have restrained my discussion to the WA nexus and the DCSP.

This objective has been pursued because: (1) savings can be made – NFPs are cheaper and more efficient than government in the delivery of services; (2) clinical and other service delivery risk can be transferred to the NFP sector (although, importantly, it is questionable as to whether political risk can be effectively transferred); (3) NFPs are more connected to the communities in which they operate and, therefore, better understand service needs and effective delivery techniques; and (4) NFPs are able to be defunded and policy is able to be changed without the need for changes to machinery of government and the industrial relations issues that arise from such changes (Productivity Commission 2010; Mendes 2008).

Due to the considerable costs associated with the provision of human services in Australia, watchdog agencies, particularly auditors-general (for instance, see Victorian Auditor-General 2013; Office of the Auditor General Western Australia 1998, 2000, 2003, 2012 and 2013; National Audit Office 2005), have also subject the government/NFP nexus to review. Concomitantly, there has been a move to change the government/NFP nexus in recent years, particularly in terms of procurement arrangements. Indeed, this development has seen the replacement of 'traditional' service funding arrangements – including government control, acquittal processes, funding in advance and often in quarterly tranches, and limited input from service users – toward the development of quasi-markets in human services. In such funding rationing structures, the various governments providing funding in support of service delivery do so in a way that is reminiscent of the operation of markets so that, in the ideal scenario: (1) service users are able to exercise choice and control; (2) procuring government agencies pay a price per iteration of service provision, often via the service user, and after the service has been provided; (3) and service providers are intended to be user responsive and more commercial in their outlook but recompensed to an extent that is reflective of the true cost of service delivery (Knight & Gilchrist 2015; Alford & O'Flynn 2012; Productivity Commission 2010; Mendes 2008).

The costs of service delivery in Western Australia are no less significant than elsewhere (Gilchrist & Knight 2017a) and the resources provided by the state's Treasury support a considerable level of service delivery provided largely by NFPs on behalf of the state government (Government of Western Australia 2016). Given the significance of the sector's work and its cost to the state government, it is logical for the government to look at alternative ways of driving efficiency and effectiveness in relation to the nexus. The introduction of quasi-market-funding rationing systems is one such alternative. There are other aspects driving government policy, however, including in relation to managing the nexus itself.

Indeed, in the WA context, the economic audit resulted in a set of recommendations intended to modernise and rationalise the relationship between the state government and the NFP sector. This included the Partnership Forum's establishment as a standing committee with the authority to receive reports and make recommendations regarding the government/NFP nexus, including in relation to the procurement of services, red tape reduction and broader human services policies.

The DCSP was the WA Government's policy response to the recommendations it accepted and this policy impacted the contextual framework within which the government and NFPs operated, both at a metaphysical level and at a practical level.

The DCSP provided for a number of changes in the way that the government procurement process impacted the delivery of human services in Western Australia with the intention of changing the relationship between government and the sector as well as impacting the service-user focus of human service providers. In short, the DCSP set the scene for the government to hand more of its services over to the NFP sector on the basis that: (1) the NFP sector was best placed to provide services due to its closeness to the community; (2) the provision of funding should be made such that resources are to be provided to individuals using the services so that they can make provider decisions based on their needs and their perception of provider responsiveness to them (individualised funding); (3) recipients then have control over decision-making regarding the services they access (person-centred care); and (4) the evaluation of funded programs should be focused on the assessment of outcomes rather than the provision of outputs (Government of Western Australian 2011).

Further, the DCSP also provided for a policy framework that encouraged state government agencies to exit service delivery, it confirmed that the price offered for service procurement should be sustainable from the perspective of the NFP providers, and that the administrative burden experienced by the government procuring agencies and the NFP sector should be reduced. It also established a policy framework within which to provide additional funding – in the form of $600 million paid to the sector in a number of tranches according to need – intended as a response to the apparent real reduction in funding experienced by the sector over previous years.

The DCSP also provided for the creation of the Partnership Forum, which was established with considerable political commitment being made by the then premier of Western Australia who saw this infrastructure as the pinnacle roundtable for shaping the government/NFP nexus. Figure 6.1 provides an overview of the elements making up the forum and the context in which it operated. As can be seen, the premier saw himself as having a central role, while members of the forum were recruited from the NFP sector via cabinet appointments – they naturally included representatives from sector peak bodies, but there was no design from the sector's perspective in terms of who should be around the table – and from the public sector by reference to the roles, rather than specific people, required to be in attendance.

The Department of Premier and Cabinet, at the centre of government, acted as secretariat and directors-general and senior policy personnel were required to attend on behalf of government. By and large, NFP representatives were either peak body policy personnel or sector leaders with a high profile. However, on the sector side representation changed over time, while the sector peaks remained as part of the structure at all times.

The Partnership Forum created a number of subcommittees charged with widening the opportunity for specialist input into policy relating to key elements such as procurement and funding. These were especially important in the context of the implementation of the DCSP and its impact on government purchasing, funding acquittals and so on. As can be seen in Figure 6.1, the procurement subcommittee was supported by the Department of Finance as the central department with primary responsibility for facilitating the reform of the procurement process. Procurement personnel from key agencies and relevant sector personnel were appointed to this subcommittee.

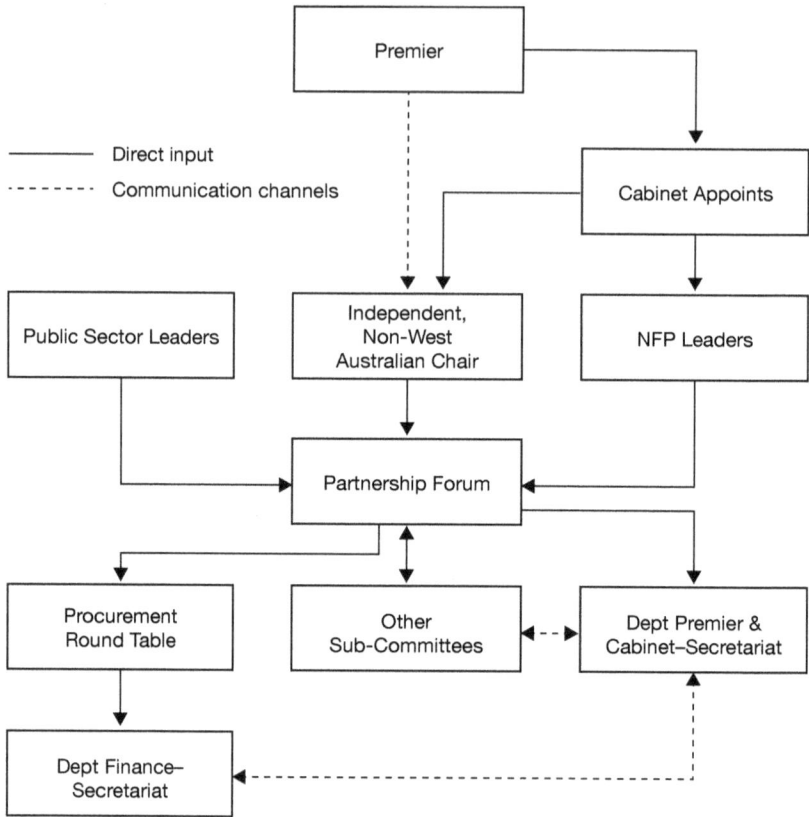

Figure 6.1. Partnership Forum structure
Source. David Gilchrist

Importantly, while the Partnership Forum was seen to be an important roundtable and facilitator of communication between the government and the NFP sector, it had no financial or human resources available to it to deploy in order to examine alternative policy frameworks, assess or evaluate existing practice or with which to drive its own agenda. As such, the Partnership Forum had limited real autonomy.

It is the impact of the Partnership Forum that is of interest in this chapter. In order to accept the policy framework and the concomitant funding increase that accompanied it, the parliament of Western Australia insisted that the government must annually evaluate the DCSP, its implementation and impact, and provide a report communicating the evaluation outcomes to the parliament. I have taken the results reported in the latest evaluation (Government of Western Australia 2016) related to the nexus and the objectives of the DCSP as a proxy for the success or otherwise of the Partnership Forum. In short, the evaluation process examines the extent to which the DCSP was achieved in the context of the Partnership Forum infrastructure. The evaluation methodology, findings and commentary are provided in the following section.

Annual policy evaluation and commentary

As indicated above, the WA parliament required an annual evaluation of the DCSP in relation to the relative improvements achieved through the policy's implementation. The evaluation took place each year for four years – the first three evaluations were undertaken by the author and the fourth evaluation – the focus of this chapter – was undertaken by the WA Treasury (Government of Western Australia 2016). The evaluation was carried out in 2016 but considered 2015–16 data due to the need to use lag data in this process. In this section, all references relate to this evaluation unless otherwise stated.

In 2015, approximately 1,500 individual contracts were established between approximately 400 NFPs delivering human services on behalf of 14 government agencies. These contracts had a value of approximately $1.65 billion while the median contract value was $250,000.

In summary, if the DCSP was impactful we would expect to see outcomes such as the increased transfer of services from government to the NFP sector, increased sustainability of the NFP sector as a result of the increased prices that should have been applied, and a reduction in administrative burden. These outcomes should be found to have increased sustainability, improved outcomes and reduced cost for both government and the NFP sector.

To undertake the evaluation, the WA Treasury implemented four key data-gathering processes: (1) a review of the 2015–16 whole-of-government NFP contract database; (2) a survey of NFP organisations delivering human services on behalf of the WA Government via contracts established under the DCSP; (3) a roundtable discussion with procurement staff representing applicable government agencies; and (4) a review of a sample of 20 human services contracts developed under the DCSP.

The inclusion in the evaluation process of government agencies procuring services was a critical aspect because the intent was to see an improvement on both sides of the nexus. This evaluation constituted an important confirmation of the government's genuine intent with respect to the delivery of the expected advantages of the DCSP. This section is divided into four subsections, the first examines the impact of the DCSP on government agencies, the second examines the impact on NFPs, while the third section examines the deficiencies identified by Treasury and that relate to government agencies and the NFP human services sector. The final section considers the evaluation findings and draws conclusions regarding the Partnership Forum.

Importantly, all of these findings were also reported to the Partnership Forum and their lack of resolution is also likely to be an indication of the relative success of that body.

The impact of the DCSP on government agencies

In many respects, the impact of the DCSP is highlighted via an examination of what has not been achieved by government. This is partly because the key value of the DCSP from the perspective of procuring agencies is a decrease in administrative burden and partly because the complexity of the DCSP means that new skills need to be acquired and new processes need to be implemented in order to achieve the outcomes sought.

In terms of the deficiencies identified, the evaluation made it clear that, notwithstanding the DCSP was under its fourth evaluation, insufficient investment was made in training and systems to develop the intellectual capital and infrastructure required to ensure the DCSP achieved the desired results. The lack of government resulted in the DCSP's limited impact in relation to a number of key result areas thus also limiting the capacity of procuring agencies to evaluate the purchases they made from the NFP sector – a critical element in any public sector accountability regime (Wilkins & Gilchrist 2016).

Specifically, Treasury identified a need to improve how service level outcomes – an important aspect of the DCSP given its focus on the need to achieve service delivery outcomes from the user's perspective – are defined and measured in human services contracts. This finding is not necessarily an indictment of the commitment of the WA Government in relation to the DCSP, however, as outcomes are notoriously difficult to identify, measure and report upon (Gilchrist & Knight 2017b). Notwithstanding, the need for investment in training and systems is an important consideration for government if it expects to achieve the DCSP's desired outcomes; the evaluation results are strongly suggestive of a lack of investment in this regard.

Additionally, the evaluation identified insufficient machinery necessary for managing the increased number of contracts – under the person-centred care and individualised funding paradigm, service users signed separate contracts resulting in an exponential increase in the numbers of contracts managed by procuring agencies – and for evaluating the extent to which the contracts achieved the intended outcomes. The contract management processes evinced by agencies needed improvement in order to undertake value-for-money evaluation. Once again, however, this deficiency is a result of a lack of investment. Without such investment, the additional cost of administering greater numbers of individualised contracts and assessing outcomes achieved adds cost to the process rather than reducing it. Thus, technology and know-how are critical to ensuring the containment of costs.

An extension of the identified infrastructure deficiency was that of a need to provide for data linkages between government agencies. NFPs providing human services can contract with more than one government agency depending on the breadth of services they offer. Therefore, Treasury identified a need for data sharing to assist with the analysis of a program's efficiency, effectiveness and appropriateness.

A need was also found for government agencies procuring services from the NFP sector to support that sector in developing skills and awareness with respect to undertaking collaborations. It is widely held that such collaborations are likely to increase the integration of services and develop better approaches to service delivery while also enhancing efficiencies, thereby ensuring the right resources are allocated to the right areas at the right time (Butcher & Gilchrist 2016). As such, this issue identified that the procuring agencies have a responsibility for supporting the NFP sector, which obviates against the rhetoric of commercialisation and quasi-markets that underpins much of the discussion relating to the DCSP.

The impact of the DCSP on human services NFPs

The deficiencies identified in the previous section were found to manifest on the NFP side of the nexus – they invariably had limited capacity with respect to identifying and measuring outcomes; they did not have the capacity to invest in training, change management or systems; and they were impacted negatively by the growing administrative costs associated with the management of a substantially increased number of contracts and involved in identifying and reporting on outcomes.

There were also, however, some NFP-specific deficiencies identified by Treasury in its evaluation in 2016. These included that the sustainability of NFP organisations' was brought into question because 57 per cent of their income in 2014–15 was raised via WA contracts; Treasury described this as an excessive proportion. Clearly, this is also a finding specific to the cohort reviewed given that other research has identified that approximately 71 per cent of the income of Western Australia's charities is raised from government sources, including federal government sources (Gilchrist & Knight 2017a). It is accepted, however, that diversity in income sources is an important indicator of financial sustainability (Zhai et al. 2017).

The Treasury evaluation also found, however, that NFPs were confident in their capacity to meet both current and future demand for their services. This confidence included the issue of individualised funding. The positive perspective was also extended to the NFPs' belief regarding their desire and ability to work with other NFPs and government in the development and provision of services. This positivity suggests that, where government was found to have a need to invest in and support the development of NFPs' capacity for collaborative work, any response to this need by government would meet fertile ground.

Joint deficiencies identified – the challenges of outcomes measurement

The deficiencies identified above were particular either to the WA Government agencies or NFPs. As already described, however, a deficiency on one side of the nexus usually impacts the other. In this case, both sectors felt the lack of real investment needed to support change.

Specifically, outcomes measurement always represents challenges because outcomes can be difficult to identify, measure and report, especially when they are related to human services (Gilchrist 2018a, 2018b; Gilchrist & Knight 2017b). For instance, while government and NFPs may agree on specific outcomes, when it comes to human services, valid outcomes do not always neatly allow for annual reporting against contractual requirements, can be difficult to aggregate to allow for corporate governance regarding service delivery due to differences between individual service users, and the collection and measurement of individual outcomes can be difficult as well as expensive in time and infrastructure.

As such, investment is needed in upskilling agency procurement staff and NFP personnel, to establish outcomes measurement frameworks that are satisfactory to government and NFP providers, to establish the infrastructure required (such as IT platforms) for data gathering, and to develop the skills necessary for appropriate analysis of the data and a suitable response.

The co-design of services between government and the NFP sector was also identified as an important goal. Indeed, the Treasury report posited that the co-design of services would likely result in better targeted services that represent better value for money. The communications channels and collaboration between government procurers and the NFP sector, however, were identified as unsatisfactory and further work was needed in order to ensure the realisation of the advantages of collaborative work. Such an improvement would likely require investment on the part of government, as would the mitigation of additional concerns raised by Treasury.

For instance, a need was identified to recognise the expenses associated with the process of outcomes reporting. Data collection can take up time from a service delivery perspective, and there is administrative cost and time associated with identifying and implementing outcomes for individual service users (Gilchrist 2018a, 2018b; Gilchrist & Knight 2014). While the outcomes framework is accepted as an improvement with respect to the prospects for individualised funding and person-centred care, it is also true that the framework increases the administrative burden because all of these activities need to be conducted at an individual service-user level rather than a corporate level.

An increase in the administrative burden also requires a change in perspective relative to administrative and governance costs associated with human services delivery – it is almost universally agreed that the aspiration of person-centred care and individualised funding are worthy goals, yet the cost of administering the service design and reporting responses to this aspiration are not accepted. These costs are important elements in the success of outcomes and need to be accepted as such rather than simply as unnecessary red tape.

The evaluation further identified the need for additional skills development to support government agencies and NFPs to collaborate in identifying and operationalising outcomes measures. Guides and exemplars would add capacity on both sides of the nexus and there was a need for additional expertise to be applied at a sector level. Treasury expects that such upskilling and exemplars will improve the prospects for collaborative outcomes identification and measurement, thus improving the effectiveness of government service purchases.

The final element raised by Treasury, which appeared likely to be an ongoing issue for the DCSP, was the need for administrative streamlining and reform. While it has already been observed that elements of the DCSP, such as individualised funding and person-centred care, will naturally result in an increase in administrative effort, a fundamental recommendation of the audit review that resulted in the DCSP was that administrative burden ought to be reduced with respect to the government/NFP nexus. Co-design between government purchaser and NFP supplier, shared data and genuine joined-up government are required if administrative costs are to be meaningfully reduced.

The impact of the Partnership Forum

Clearly, the deficiencies identified endured through the first three evaluations and continued into the period covered by the fourth, with no expectation that change was imminent. Fundamentally, the Partnership Forum was supported by the government and the NFP sector. It is clear, however, that there were a number of aspects of the forum that impacted negatively on its capacity to effect change, notwithstanding the almost universal support it enjoyed.

While the Partnership Forum was intended to be the peak venue for guiding the government/NFP nexus in Western Australia, it was effectively restrained by the central agencies of government as it did not have a budget of its own or an independent secretariat. This restraint was not 'negative' in that the central agencies did not necessarily move to constrain the forum or reduce the opportunity for realising the DCSP. Rather, as his government aged, the premier's attention was focused elsewhere, and the subsequent lack of political focus on the DCSP meant that the necessary resources for change were withheld.

Without a budget, the forum was neither able to develop an implementation plan to guide the functional introduction of the DCSP, nor examine alternative policy settings or undertake research or other work in its own right. Additionally, the lack of executive capacity meant that, while four annual evaluation reports consecutively described the same problems and prescribed the same solutions, there was no appetite or capacity to respond positively.

The lack of an implementation plan combined with the absence of executive capacity and effectively sidelined the Partnership Forum, with anecdotal evidence suggesting that senior government personnel routinely sent subordinates to represent them at forum meetings – an indication of the failing relevance of the body.

Additionally, the Partnership Forum was chaired by a non-WA resident – who arguably lacked context as a result – and provision was not made for a contribution by service users or their advocates. Consequently, the gradual dissipation of influence meant that, when the government changed in April 2017, the forum was suspended.

Following initial consideration by the new government, the Partnership Forum was disbanded and the Supporting Communities Forum has been established. Among other things, this new body will include service users' advocates, be chaired by a Western Australian with an understanding of the human services sector and include senior government and sector personnel. Importantly, it appears that the body will not have any financial or human resources at its disposal, suggesting that the same problems that arose with the previous body may be replicated in this new one.

Concluding remarks

The establishment of the DCSP in 2011 was identified as a paradigm shift in Western Australia's government/NFP nexus. Expectations were raised that the Partnership Forum would husband the change sought, and implementation of annual evaluation of both sides of the nexus was an important signal that the government was serious about driving effective change to the state's provision of human services – change that would benefit those relying on supports funded by government and provided by NFPs.

The four subsequent annual evaluations, however, including the evaluation undertaken by the WA Treasury in 2016 that forms the basis for this chapter, confirm that the government did not supply sufficient funding for investment and change management. The need for capital to support change was highlighted by the fact that the necessary infrastructure and skills sets remained deficient, even though the policy itself was in place for six years and preceding evaluations raised similar concerns.

Additionally, the prospects for improving the effectiveness of the government/NFP nexus seemed strong at the commencement of the DCSP. Annual evaluations, however, highlighted the need for improved collaboration between government procurers and the NFP sector to co-design services and identify and report on outcomes.

Of course, the prospects for improvement might have increased if there was also a fundamental reconstruction plan in place that could have been used to prioritise the allocation of resources, guide the development of service frameworks and guide reporting and other requirements for ongoing improvement. Such a plan was, and remains, likely to identify investment needs, establish a logical timeframe and allow for government and sector change processes.

The implementation of a policy framework of the significance of the DCSP required broader consideration at a whole-of-government and a whole-of-sector level. The change impacted two intertwined sectors that have worked together within the context of a policy framework that has been in existence for decades, making it difficult to change cultures as well as practices. Continued government enthusiasm at the highest levels is critical to ensuring the prospects for the expected outcomes associated with the DCSP can be realised, even under the new Supporting Communities Forum. Unfortunately, it is clear that the prospects for positive change expected out of the DCSP have, to date, not been fully realised.

References

Alford, JL & O'Flynn, J 2012, *Rethinking Public Service Delivery: Managing with External Providers*, Palgrave Macmillan, London.

Butcher, JR & Gilchrist, DJ (eds) 2016, *The Three Sector Solution: Delivering Public Policy in Collaboration with Not-For-Profits and Business*, ANU Press, Canberra, doi.org/10.22459/TSS.07.2016.

Economic Audit Committee 2009, *Putting the Public First: Partnering with the Community and Business to Deliver Outcomes*, Report to the Government of Western Australian, Perth.

Frumkin, P 2002, *On Being Nonprofit: A Conceptual and Policy Primer*, Harvard University Press, London, doi.org/10.4159/9780674037403.

Gilchrist, DJ 2013, *2012 Evaluation of the Sustainable Funding and Contracting with the Not-for-profit Sector Initiatives and Associated Procurement Reforms*, Government of Western Australia, Perth.

—— 2016, 'Partnerships between government and the third sector at a sub-national level: experience of an Australian sub- national government', in JR Butcher & DJ Gilchrist (eds), *The Three Sector Solution: Delivering Public Policy in Collaboration with Not-For-Profits and Business*, ANU Press, Canberra, 2016.

—— 2018a, *Outcomes: Research into Practice: Working Paper No. 3*, report to Grant Thornton Australia, Melbourne.

—— 2018b, *Outcomes: Research into Practice: Working Paper No. 4*, report to Grant Thornton Australia, Melbourne.

Gilchrist, DJ & Knight, PA 2013a, *2013 Evaluation of the Sustainable Funding and Contracting with the Not-For-Profit Sector Initiatives and Associated Procurement Reforms*, Government of Western Australia, Perth.

—— 2013b, *Annual Funded Sector Report*, report for the Disability Services Commission, Government of Western Australia, Perth.

—— 2014, *Community Employers, Person Centred Care and Individualised Funding – Final Report*, joint report undertaken with Community Employers WA, Perth.

—— 2017a, *WA's Not-For-Profit Sector 2017: The First Report on Charities and Other Not-For-Profits in WA*, report for the Western Australian Council for Social Service, Perth.

—— 2017b, *Outcomes Research into Practice: Working Paper No. 2*, report to Grant Thornton Australia.

Government of Western Australia 2011, *Delivering Community Services in Partnership: A Policy to Achieve Better Outcomes for Western Australians Through the Funding and Contracting of Community Services*, Perth.

—— 2016, *Sustainable Funding and Contracting with the Not-for-profit Sector Initiative 2015 Evaluation Report*, Perth.

Knight, PA & Gilchrist, DJ 2015, *2014 Evaluation of the Sustainable Funding and Contracting with the Not-For-Profit Sector Initiatives and Associated Procurement Reforms*, Government of Western Australia, Perth.

McGregor-Lowndes, M 2008, 'Is there something better than partnership?', in J Barraket (ed), *Strategic Issues for the Not-For-Profit Sector*, UNSW Press, Sydney.

Mendes, P 2008, *Australia's Welfare Wars Revisited: The Players, The Politics and the Ideologies*, UNSW Press, Sydney.

National Audit Office 2005, *Working with the Third Sector*, www.nao.org.uk/wp-content/uploads/2005/06/050675.pdf.

Office of the Auditor General Western Australia 1998, *Accommodation and Support Services to Young People Unable to Live at Home*, report no 11, audit.wa.gov.au/wp-content/uploads/2013/05/report98_11.pdf.

—— 2000, *A Means to an End: Contracting Not-For-Profit Organisations for The Delivery of Community Services*, audit.wa.gov.au/wp-content/uploads/2013/05/report2000_03.pdf.

—— 2003, *Contracting Not-For-Profit Organisations for Delivery of Health Services*, audit.wa.gov.au/wp-content/uploads/2013/05/report2003_02.pdf.

—— 2012, *Working Together: Management of Partnerships with Volunteers*, audit.wa.gov.au/wp-content/uploads/2013/05/report2012_01.pdf.

—— 2013, *Sustainable Funding and Contracting – Component I Funding to the Not-For-Profit Sector*, audit.wa.gov.au/wp-content/uploads/2013/09/report2013_13-Component-1-Funding.pdf.

Productivity Commission 2010, *Contribution of the Australian Not-For-Profit Sector*, Research Report, Canberra.

Salamon, LM 1995, *Partners in Public Service: Government – Nonprofit Relations in the Modern Welfare State*, The Johns Hopkins University Press, Baltimore.

Victorian Auditor-General 2013, *Implementation of the Strengthening Community Organisations Action Plan*, www.audit.vic.gov.au/sites/default/files/20131016-Community-Action-Plan.pdf.

Wilkins, P & Gilchrist, DJ 2016, 'Accountability for the public policy contribution of not-for-profit organisations: who is accountable to whom and for what?', R Pablo Guerrero & P Wilkins (eds), *Doing Good?: Private Actors, Evaluation and Public Value (Comparative Policy Evaluation)*, Routledge, New York. doi.org/10.4324/9780203793008-6.

Young, DR 2006, 'Complimentary, supplementary or adversarial: nonprofit – government relations', in ET Boris & CE Streuerle (eds), *Nonprofits & Government: Collaboration and Conflict*, 2nd edn, The Urban Institute Press, Washington.

Zhai, L, Watson, J, Gilchrist, DJ & Newby, R 2017, 'Nonprofit vulnerability: an exploratory study', *Financial Accountability and Management*, vol 33, no 4, pp 1–18, doi.org/10.1111/faam.12129.

.

7

GOVERNANCE FOR INTEGRITY AGENCIES IN AUSTRALIA

An examination of three models of influence

Annwyn Godwin

Institutional structures influence the way in which organisations and individuals interact. While the leaders of organisations may respond differently, the structures themselves can encourage or stifle collaboration, openness and innovation, and can constrain or promote independence. Leaders of integrity organisations may also have some discretion about the approach they take to their statutory responsibilities, including whether to emphasise the promotion of good behaviour or the policing of bad behaviour; there is room, at times, for integrity agencies to collaborate to get the balance right.

During my 10 years as a statutory office holder in the Merit Protection Commissioner role, I witnessed an evolution in the understanding of governance – public accountability and performance – for non-core agencies. This chapter outlines some of the major influential factors that I observed in Australia generally, and for statutory integrity agencies in particular.

In examining governance changes, this chapter draws on my experience in the Office of the Merit Protection Commissioner (MPC) to illustrate the influence of three models promulgated since the early 2000s. The first model was presented in the Uhrig Report – after its leader, John Uhrig – which was commissioned by the Australian Government to review the corporate governance of Commonwealth authorities. The second model was outlined by Jocelyne Bourgon, a former head of the Canadian civil service, in her keynote address to the Institute of Public Administration Australia (IPAA) national conference in Sydney in June 2008. The third model was presented in a paper by Maryantonett Flumian, another former senior Canadian public servant and president of the Public Governance Exchange (PGEx), at the Public Sector Governance Conference hosted by the Australian Institute of Company Directors in October 2009.

My own experience, drawing on these models, is that public sector governance arrangements, including for integrity organisations, continue to evolve. While such agencies require a considerable degree of independence and autonomy, it is not easy to categorise them or apply a common or fixed approach to their accountability or management arrangements for optimising performance.

The Uhrig Report

Uhrig completed his *Review of Corporate Governance of Statutory Authorities and Office Holders* in 2003. It was influential at the time in attempting to develop a broad template of governance principles for statutory agencies that drew upon best-practice models in the public and private sectors.

The report's context was the financial management reforms enacted in the 1990s. At the time there was limited consideration of the implications of the significant machinery of government (MoG) changes that occurred in 1987 and the expansion of statutory authorities under new public management (NPM) reforms. The 1987 changes included the establishment of mega-departments and 'portfolios' that grouped agencies (including statutory authorities) under 'portfolio ministers' and gave the 'portfolio department' implicit responsibility for coordinating portfolio budgets and policy advice. The administrative, reporting and accountability arrangements to parliament changed as a result of the creation of the roles of assistant ministers and parliamentary secretaries to support portfolio ministers. As John Nethercote noted in 1999:

there has continued to be considerable organisational change within portfolios, especially through hiving off, corporatisation and privatisation, for instance, by creation of Centrelink, based on the regional networks of the departments of Social Security and Employment, Education and Training, or establishment of bodies such as the Civil Aviation Safety Authority and the Australian Maritime Safety Authority within the Transport Department. (Nethercote 1999)

The establishment of a wide range of statutory organisations over this period was not just a political response to the issues of the day, but also a response to broader developments in public sector management. These developments included NPM's focus on results including through wider principal–agent arrangements, the new role of regulation that emerged with commercialisation, privatisation and competition policy, and increasing interest in 'integrity' and the oversight of public sector governance values, especially following NPM's devolution of authority.

The statutory bodies, encompassing regulatory, service delivery and government oversight functions, used a range of governance structures. Most were subject to the *Commonwealth Authorities and Companies Act 1997* for the purposes of formal financial management and accountability and some were subject to the *Public Service Act 1999*.

The key recommendations of the Uhrig Report may be summarised as:

1. a firmer and more consistent approach to accountability with two main governance templates, one being via an executive board the other via a single accountable CEO, where any board would be advisory only

2. notwithstanding statutory independence, some recalibration of the line of accountability through the minister to the parliament by having a ministerial statement of expectation of how the authority is to exercise its responsibilities and a corresponding statement of intent by the authority

3. a firmer role for the 'portfolio' secretary of the relevant department in advising on appointments and coordinating the agencies within the portfolio.

I regarded the Uhrig review as having led, at least for a short while, to an alignment at the highest level between management rhetoric and management practice, in terms of a stronger focus on governance arrangements and management accountability. I held a senior departmental management position in 2003 and the mantra of 'let the managers manage' felt real, including the expectation of being held to account. This meant senior managers needed sound evidence to support decision-making and could be expected to demonstrate this if called to explain. It may of course be coincidental that this period was also when a wide range of accountability reforms came to fruition including, for example, the charter of budget honesty (1998), the integrated accrual accounting framework (1999–2000) and the consolidated *Commonwealth Procurement Guidelines* (2004).

One impact of these developments was increasing standards of public accountability for officials rather than ministers only. Dr Derek Drinkwater drew upon his experiences at the Australian Public Service Commission (APSC) and in the department of the Senate when researching his paper on parliamentary scrutiny of the Australian Public Service (APS). He reported that since 1996 'more and more, senior public servants at the table, rather than ministers, were being required to answer questions and explain decisions, and to do so at an unprecedented degree' (Drinkwater 2015: 61). This trend was arguably underway for much longer, particularly since the strengthening role of parliamentary committees and their focus on questioning officials. The shift was to some extent inevitable, of course, for statutory officers with statutory independence from ministerial direction who must be held accountable directly for the exercise of those responsibilities.

In many respects, Uhrig brought to a head a growing disconnect between public sector managers' accountability and the traditional Westminster ministerial accountability to parliament. Uhrig, however, applied private sector practice to the issue in his terminology and focus on CEOs and boards and, arguably, he did not appreciate sufficiently the public sector environment. But he exposed a potential accountability vacuum and suggested a particular way of addressing it. This involved the exchange of statements of expectations and intent between ministers and the statutory authorities 'that identified agreed outcomes and priorities without compromising the authorities' statutory independence'.

Another grey area concerned responsibility for appointments to individual statutory officer roles. Section 19 of the *Public Service Act* specifically prohibits a minister from directing an agency head with regard to APS staffing decisions. From its beginnings, selection into the APS was consciously designed for people to compete and be assessed on their ability on the basis of the merit principle. The *Public Service Act* includes explicitly a provision that employment decisions be based on merit, but this does not apply to the employment of agency heads. The prime minister appoints departmental secretaries (following a report by the secretary of the Prime Minister's Department) and ministers appoint the heads of other agencies (in practice, the decisions are subject to cabinet endorsement); there is no formal statutory requirement to consider or apply merit.

Uhrig recommended that portfolio secretaries advise ministers on the appointment of statutory office holders in the portfolio. While this would not enforce a merit-based approach, it would inform ministers of the relative merit of those considered by the portfolio secretary, while leaving the final decision to ministers. While this recommendation was generally implemented, it is not clear that it was widely influential in the final decision. In early 2008, however, the APSC published *Merit and Transparency: Merit-Based Selection of APS Agency Heads and APS Statutory Office Holders* (APSC 2012), a policy document agreed by the then government.

This document affirmed merit as a basis for selection of most APS agency heads and other statutory office holders working in, or in conjunction with, APS agencies, giving formal authority to portfolio secretaries in their advising role in consultation with the Public Service Commissioner. There were exceptions to the application of the policy, notably with regard to the APS Commissioner, the Commissioner of Taxation, the Auditor-General, the CEO of the (then) Australian Customs Service and the Australian Statistician. These positions, of a similar status to portfolio secretaries, had an expectation of appointment on merit (in the case of the auditor-general, consultation with the relevant parliamentary committee is required).

In the context of governance and Uhrig, this policy document was another recognition of the changing nature of the relationships and accountabilities between ministers and portfolio secretaries. For the first time the roles of a secretary, the APS Commissioner and the minister in a statutory appointment process were explicitly identified. Importantly, portfolio secretaries have responsibility for the processes of appointments within their portfolios and for advising the minister of the recommendations from those processes. While there is an expectation that the minister will accept those recommendations, there are important exception clauses where the minister (and the government) can override the recommendations.

These developments, influenced by Uhrig, did not settle other grey areas that have emerged over the years in the relationship between ministers and senior officials. The other key trend has been the growth in numbers and influence of ministerial staff outside the public service. After attempts by the APSC to clarify the respective roles of public servants and ministerial staff (APSC 2003, 2005), in 2008 the then government introduced a formal (but not statutory) code of conduct for ministerial staff that includes the provision the APSC had previously articulated that such staff do not have the power to direct APS staff or make decisions: such power lies exclusively with ministers and public servants. That code (slightly amended) still applies, though its title has changed to *Statement of Standards for Ministerial Staff*.[1]

Uhrig and the Office of the Merit Protection Commissioner

Uhrig's terms of reference 'required an examination of structures for good governance, including relationships between statutory authorities and the responsible Minister, the Parliament and the public, including business' (Uhrig 2003: 1). Importantly, Uhrig's report attempted to place some boundaries and insert a consistent nomenclature around the plethora of authorities and structures that had flourished. Once departments of state and executive agencies were accounted for, the term 'statutory authority' was a convenient way to cover the remaining structures created by law. While not a way of classifying different statutory authorities, the report defined the following selection of terms (more than one term may apply to the same organisation):

- **Department of state**

  A department created by the Administrative Arrangements Order made by the Governor-General.

- **Executive agency**

  An agency established under section 65 of the *Public Service Act 1999*.

---

1   Statement of Ministerial Standards available at www.smos.gov.au/statement-standards-ministerial-staff.

- **Statutory authority**

  A public sector entity created by a specific law of the Commonwealth. For the purposes of this report the term includes a statutory agency having statutory office holders.

- **Statutory agency**

  A body or group of positions declared by an Act to be a statutory agency for the purposes of the *Public Service Act 1999*.

- **Regulatory authorities**

  Those entities that administer legislation on behalf of government to regulate the behaviour of individuals and/or organisations.

- **Commission**

  A statutory authority with a full-time executive management structure that is directly accountable to a Minister. (Uhrig 2003: 121–24)

Likewise, Uhrig defined office holders as:

> those persons appointed to statutory positions in the governance structure of a statutory authority. Depending on an authority's particular structure, these positions would include the CEO or managing director, commissioners and members of a board of directors.

The role of a statutory office holder is principally to implement legislation. Given how difficult it usually is to remove an officer from office once appointed, it is a position of considerable trust and stewardship.

For example, the office of the Merit Protection Commissioner is one of only two individual offices specifically named in the *Public Service Act* (the Public Service Commissioner being the other). My appointment was made via a national and open merit-selection process. As required under sections 61 and 62 of the Australian Constitution, my name was put forward to the executive council for appointment by the governor-general.

The independence of the role is enshrined in the legislation and the normal five-year term safeguards against political or other interference as it is longer than the usual term (around three years) of an Australian federal government.

Section 54 of the *Public Service Act* states:

Removal from Office

1. The Governor-General may remove the Merit Protection Commissioner from the office if each House of the Parliament, in the same session of the Parliament, presents an address to the Governor-General praying for the removal of the Merit Protection Commissioner on the grounds of misbehaviour or physical or mental incapacity.

2. The Governor-General must remove the Merit Protection Commissioner from the office if the Merit Protection Commissioner does any of the following:

   a. becomes bankrupt;

   b. applies to take the benefit of any law for the relief of bankrupt or insolvent debtors;

   c. compounds with his or her creditors;

   d. assigns his or her remuneration for the benefit of his or her creditors.

The terms of the appointment are designed to reinforce the Merit Protection Commissioner as free of influence and able to uphold public sector governance values whilst fulfilling the statutory requirements. Consistent with the APSC's Merit and Transparency policy, the final decision-maker regarding the appointment is at arm's length from the independent recommendations put forward as a result of the selection process.

Post-Uhrig work on governance

Australian governance structures have evolved considerably since the Uhrig Report. Among the criticisms of the report and its private sector focus was its failure to clarify whether and when statutory authorities should be under the *Public Service Act* and which financial management and accountability legislation should apply (the *Financial Management and Accountability Act 1997* or *the Commonwealth Authorities and Companies Act 1997*). The Department of Finance issued some guidance on these matters in 2005, and a more substantial internal review in 2012 (the Commonwealth Financial Accountability Review (CFAR)) recommended action that led to the replacement of both financial management laws with the *Public Governance, Performance and Accountability Act 2013* (PGPA). The PGPA Act and its definition of Commonwealth entities for financial purposes had flow-on effects for the governance structures of entities and, in particular, Finance's issuing of guidance about the establishment of new entities.

While Finance's definitional terminology in its policy guidance on governance structures has some similarities to Uhrig's, it has been simplified and sharpened; for example, 'A statutory authority is a generic term for an Australian Government body established through legislation for a public purpose. This can include a body headed by, or comprising, an office holder, a commission or a governing board'.[2]

Finance guidance now includes measures relating to the circumstances in which alternative organisational structures may be required. Through an assessment tool, it has identified seven considerations when establishing an alternative governance structure. These are summarised as, does the activity:

1. require enabling legislation which cannot be altered without parliamentary authorisation
2. involve exercising coercive (enforcement) or regulatory powers usually for a specific field or industry and may include regulatory fees, imposing penalties, conducting investigations and/or compelling production of evidence
3. have core policy (and/or non-commercial) government functions, as this may be better served within an existing non-corporate Commonwealth entity
4. have a commercial focus
5. need to hold money outside the Commonwealth
6. necessitate a governing board or multi-member accountable authority
7. require a level of independence, based on an assessment of risk.

Finance goes on to acknowledge that 'It is enabling legislation that provides the level of independence of Commonwealth entities, not the type of entity ... Ultimately it is the level of risk in undertaking the activity that will dictate the level of independence for the body'.[3]

---

2   Available at www.finance.gov.au/about-us/glossary/governance/term-statutory-authority.
3   Finance advice on governance structures is available at www.finance.gov.au/government/managing-commonwealth-resources/structure-australian-government-public-sector/commonwealth-governance-structures-policy-governance-policy.

Some public servants and commentators considered the Uhrig Report too private sector–oriented and too narrow in its understanding of the range of government functions and possible structures. The two main templates for accountability – via a board or a single CEO point – held little flexibility to assimilate non-core functions and political circumstances. While it exposed gaps in the existing system, the recommended solutions didn't always work as expected. The seeds of Uhrig can be seen, nonetheless, in the more flexible but coherent PGPA Act following CFAR, and its principles-based approach provided a new paradigm for governance.

Jocelyne Bourgon and Maryantonett Flumian

The second and third models that had a major influence on me in my role as Merit Protection Commissioner were both from Canada. Bourgon's model was enunciated in her 2008 paper 'Future of the public service: a search for new balance' and further developed in her collaborative book *A New Synthesis for Public Administration* (2011), which is based on seven case studies.

Bourgon provides an evolutionary framework to make sense of developments in public administration, including through NPM and subsequent reforms. She first acknowledges the origins and contribution of public administration in democratic governments:

> Many of our public institutions were born in the latter part of the 19th century and early 20th century; a period characterised by the industrial revolution, the emergence of bureaucracies in democratic societies and the influence of scientific management.

> Public sector organisations were expected to perform *predictable* tasks under prescribed rules. The power structure was top down and hierarchical. Rigorous controls ensured performance and accountability for delegated authorities. (Bourgon 2008: 5)

The structures of public accountability and performance in Australia (and Bourgon's Canada) are inherited from the United Kingdom. The Westminster parent gave its colonial children institutions based on the rule of law, respect for democracy, due process, transparency and accountability.

Bourgon's model draws upon the broad base of conceptual thinking that challenged this 'classic model' of public accountability, including NPM's focus on accountability for results and subsequent emphasis on whole-of-government and networking beyond government. Christopher Hood's 1990 article 'De-Sir Humphreyfying the Westminster model of bureaucracy: a new style of governance?' was followed by another thought piece on the intellectual provenance of NPM (Hood 1991). Rod Rhodes wrote about policy networks, reflexivity and accountability in the late 1990s (Rhodes 1997) and Stephen Osborne argued in 2006 that NPM was a transitory phase in public administration (PA) before it emerged as new public governance (NPG). Bourgon constructively links these emerging ideas of the late 1990s and early 2000s in her framework; she doesn't categorise traditional PA, NPM and NPG but rather 'synthesises' (her term) them in a modern and more integrated approach. She offers jurisdictions at different stages of development or facing different challenges the flexibility to move between different paradigms and to balance approaches to suit their circumstances. Figure 7.1 illustrates Bourgon's 'synthesis' concept.

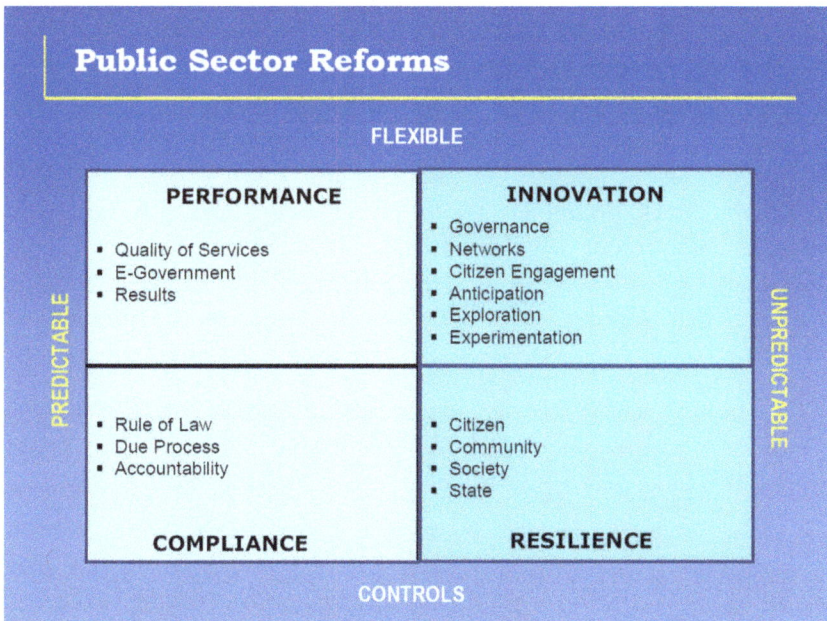

Figure 7.1. Categorising public sector reforms
Source. Bourgon 2008

She notes that 'A combination of vertical accountability for the exercise of delegated authority and of network management improves the capacity of the public sector to achieve system-wides results' (Bourgon 2008). Bourgon's model offers a whole-of-government approach to governance – acknowledging all the competing parts – rather than identifying any single approach that may be optimal to a specific function of government; at the same time, she recognises the continuing value of the traditional emphasis on compliance and NPM's emphasis on performance.

Like the UK and Canadian models, Australia's public sector institutions were established before the availability of the internet and before artificial intelligence. Our structures, expectations and accountability mechanisms were based on old paradigms of bureaucracy. In the early 2000s, at the time when Bourgon presented her synthesis, the emerging governance questions were:

1. Are the current hierarchical and lineal structures flexible enough to address evolving community and parliamentary expectations?
2. If not, how can we structurally encourage tailored and immediate responses to complex and interconnected issues?

This was a time when the APS trialled a variety of new practices in an attempt to dismantle siloed responses to 'wicked problems'[4] including, for example, how to encourage meaningful cross-agency collaboration when one agency supplied the resources and another was accountable for the outcomes. Bourgon's view of the evolving nature of management provided new ways of thinking about the needs of the public sector and the range of potential responses. Her ideas exposed the inherent tension within modern management of traditional accountability structures for non-hierarchical, non-traditional relationships.

While these ideas did not have a particular impact on me as the Merit Protection Commissioner, they did influence me and many other senior Australian public servants about the way we worked across and beyond government.

In 2009, Maryantonett Flumian's outlined 'The new reality of "distributed governance"', which she described as having three main dynamics (Flumian 2009):

---

4   www.apsc.gov.au/publications-and-media/archive/publications-archive/tackling-wicked-problems

1. governments have been transforming to accommodate the realities of a faster paced, networked and globalised world
2. redistribution of the functions of government from traditional command-and-control core bureaucracies to public models of governance distributed across a variety of factors based on performance
3. a significant shift in the organisational design of public institutions and a significant increase in the number, size and significance of organisations along a much longer governance continuum.

She summarised the impact, both positive and negative, of these on governance, as shown in Table 7.1.

Table 7.1. The impact of 'distributed governance'

Governance impacts	
Intended	**Unintended**
Devolution	Less direct relationship with citizens
Increase in distributed governance	Role confusion / mandate diffusion
Deregulation	Decreased accountability capacity
Re-centralisation	Who's got the ball
Redefined relationships	Indirect accountability
Clarified mandates / performance targets	Increased importance of departmental silos
Effectiveness?	Effectiveness?

Source. Flumian 2009

Flumian's work was a natural and logical extension of Bourgon's, but with more specific relevance to the Merit Protection Commissioner's role and accountability. The evolving nature of the operating environment led to shifts in formal roles and accountability methods. Agencies realised that the traditional arrangements established for highly centralised and hierarchical models didn't reflect the use of alternative organisational models and degrees of independence. This led to a rethinking of how different agencies interact along a governance continuum; in particular, the need for a conceptual model to capture and map organisational independence and institutional control across the public spectrum, from the centre to the most autonomous models. Even within and along the continuum, however, roles and relationships may vary and overlap. Flumian's model is summarised in Figures 7.2, 7.3 and 7.4.

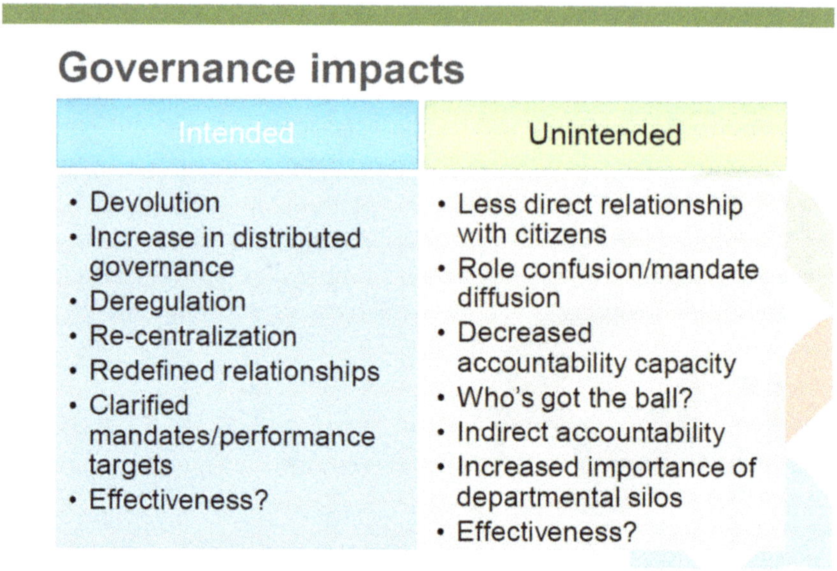

Governance impacts

Intended	Unintended
• Devolution • Increase in distributed governance • Deregulation • Re-centralization • Redefined relationships • Clarified mandates/performance targets • Effectiveness?	• Less direct relationship with citizens • Role confusion/mandate diffusion • Decreased accountability capacity • Who's got the ball? • Indirect accountability • Increased importance of departmental silos • Effectiveness?

Figure 7.2. Traditional hierarchical and contemporary accountability relationships

Source. Flumian 2009

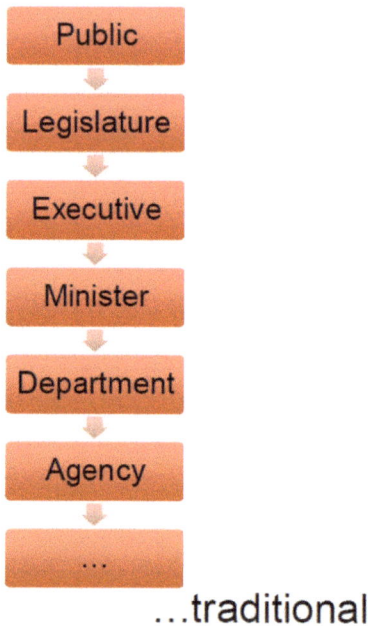

Public
↓
Legislature
↓
Executive
↓
Minister
↓
Department
↓
Agency
↓
...

...traditional

Figure 7.3. Institutional control – operational autonomy continuum

Source. Flumian 2009

Functions place organizations along the Continuum

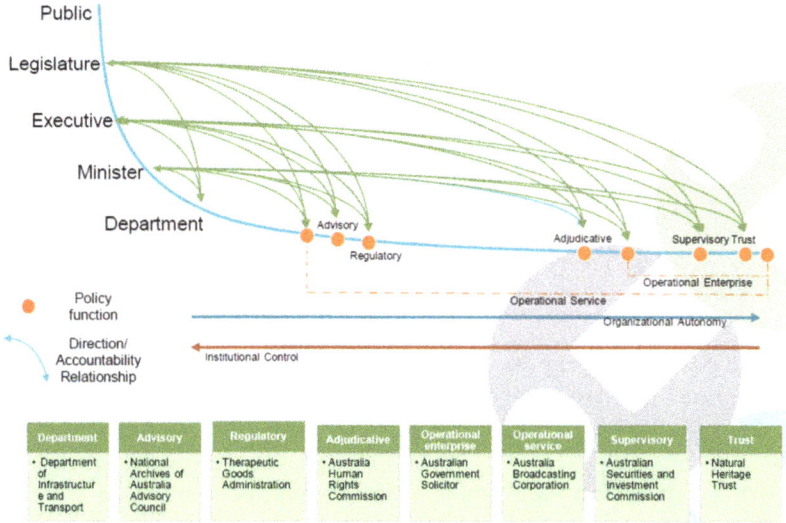

...as well as relationships

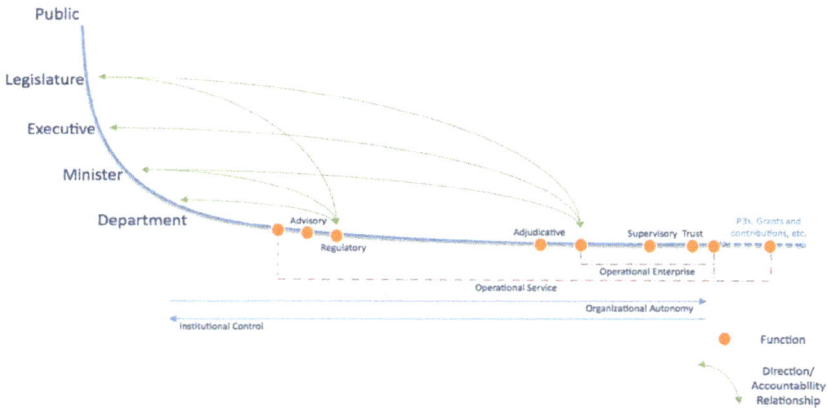

Figure 7.4. Mapping organisations' functions and relationships to the continuum

Source. Flumian 2009

This model brought together the thinking behind the Uhrig Report and subsequent Finance guidance about the establishment of different structures, and Bourgon's ideas about structures evolving to meet new requirements. Flumian's framework combined these elements, offering a way to map and integrate different structures in interconnected systems.

While Flumian's model made intuitive sense, it didn't neatly map to the wide range of Australian public sector organisational forms (see Table 7.2). While Flumian's operational service and enterprise categories may be a matter of interpretation (corresponding broadly to service delivery agencies and government business enterprises), there was greater difficulty with mapping Australian structures to her regulatory, adjudicative and supervisory categories. In particular, Australia's 'integrity bodies' cover a wide range of organisational forms and functions that potentially overlap several of Flumian's categories (Table 7.3 identifies the multiple roles of a selection of integrity bodies).

Table 7.2. Mapping the Flumian model to Australian practice

Flumian model	Australian translation
Ministry: traditional generalist department	Departments (central and line)
Advisory: publicly provides advice to government	Special research and policy-advising authorities (statutory bodies)
Regulatory: establishes and/or enforces rules of conduct in a particular sector of activity against obligations set out in existing statutes and/or regulations	Regulatory bodies, integrity bodies, independent commissions and tribunals
Adjudicative: renders impartial quasi-judicial decisions to resolve disputes	
Operational service: delivers programs and services to the public in a primarily non-commercial manner within a well-defined policy framework determined outside the organisation itself	Executive agencies and service delivery authorities (also, often departments)
Operational enterprise: sells programs and services to the public in a primarily commercial manner	Government business enterprises and other commercial units
Supervisory: impartially oversees activities on behalf of another entity with authority over those activities and reports on its findings	Integrity bodies, independent commissions
Relationship trust: invests or otherwise administers funds on behalf of the public, other groups and entities.	Non-government organisation (NGO) bodies linked with government

Source. Flumian 2009 and author's assessment

Under Flumian's model, integrity agencies, including the Merit Protection Commissioner, lie towards the independence end of the spectrum, though there remain uncertainties about the degree of independence and operational autonomy of different integrity agencies.

Australian integrity agencies and the Integrity Agencies Group

The collective idea of 'integrity organisations' is not institutionalised at the federal level, though the term has been used by some state governments (e.g. Western Australia). Senator John Faulkner as Special Minister for State, used the term in a ministerial speech in 2008 when he said:

> One of our first steps was to bring under a single minister integrity agencies across the Commonwealth such as the ANAO [Australian National Audit Office], the Inspector-General of Intelligence and Security, the ombudsmen [sic], the Public Service Commissioner, the Archives and the like. (Faulkner 2008)

With this as the context, the then Public Service Commissioner, Lynelle Briggs established the Integrity Agencies Group (IAG). The original membership included the relevant statutory office holders that focus on integrity-related matters from within the portfolio of Prime Minister and Cabinet. The goal was to support a 'joined-up' approach to whole-of-APS integrity-related issues within the portfolio. As agencies moved in and out of the portfolio, so too did the membership. For example, the Australian Electoral Commissioner, while upholding the integrity of the electoral process and thereby the legitimacy of government, is no longer an IAG member; however, when the Office of the Australian Information Commissioner was created, the three commissioners – Privacy, Freedom of Information and Australian Information – became members.

With subsequent machinery of government, policy and legislative changes and a new APS Commissioner, the IAG evolved to reflect a clearer understanding of the integrity framework, though there is no longer a minister with explicit responsibility for integrity organisations. IAG membership and its role have varied over time and are no longer based on the portfolio of Prime Minister and Cabinet. The nature of the group changed significantly around 2012 with the extension of jurisdictional coverage of the Australian Commission for Law Enforcement Integrity (ACLEI) to include specific agencies that employ staff under the *Public Service Act*. ACLEI joined the IAG around this time.

Under APS Commissioner Stephen Sedgwick, the IAG responded to two cases of integrity organisation inquiries: the Home Insulation Program inquiry by the Australian National Audit Office and specific activity that ACLEI identified involving Australian Customs Service employees at Sydney international airport. The IAG recognised the intrinsic links between culture, leadership and behaviour and how a tolerance of low-level indiscretions and general misconduct can, and does, influence an organisation's (and the APS's) overall integrity risk profile.

The overlapping roles of IAG members were recognised as part of an education-to-enforcement continuum for integrity in the APS. As Sedgwick stated before the ACLEI Committee in 2014:

> One of the things we have learned out of the experience that ACLEI has had … has been the availability of forensic skills to investigate quite complex issues and that has been valuable to resolving those matters. An environment in which you have a modulated series of responses, for example, makes sense in terms of the relationship between the risk that is being borne and the costs that are involved. We have a number of agencies that operate in this space … We [the APSC] promote the values and the employment principles, the ethical framework and the code of conduct … We work at one end of the spectrum, if you like; ACLEI works at the other – ACLEI or the AFP [Australian Federal Police], depending on the nature of the issues. (Parliamentary Joint Committee on the Australian Commission for Law Enforcement Integrity 2014)

The education–enforcement continuum is just that, a risk-based sliding scale. It guides organisations to identify the appropriate response to a situation at both inter- and intra-agency levels. For example, at an internal level, when the Merit Protection Commissioner reviews agency decisions on code of conduct breaches and makes a recommendation, there is the potential for:

- an education intervention – to help a public servant learn from the outcome and hopefully ensure he or she is unlikely to repeat the mistake

  or

- an enforcement intervention – to punish wrongdoing as an example to others, with the downside risk of creating a vexatious employee with attitude!

In my experience as Merit Protection Commissioner, the two extremes – complete education or complete enforcement – are not where most effort is spent. Rather, an approach resting between the two is used. Depending on the intervention, this approach tries to engage the person concerned as a positive partner, not as a negative influencer. The intent is to have as many individuals and teams working with, not against, the system. This reduces workload, creates a peer cohort of support and allows the Merit Protection Commissioner to focus on areas of high and serious risk that require enforcement. Again, the approach is to target the intervention and the sanction.

In the APS environment, the overlapping and complementary roles of specialist integrity agencies have been promoted as a basis for a strong and appropriate response to upholding integrity in our specific environment. The interagency continuum framework enabled targeted and escalating interventions as appropriate. The IAG played a significant role in providing a level of assurance that a multi-pronged approach to the APS integrity framework is indeed integrated. Under this umbrella, information and insight has been shared and the experience, knowledge and contribution of all members to the integrity framework has been recognised and valued. The IAG has no formal role or status and its contribution is based on the assumed goodwill and understanding of the principal members.

Considering the roles of Australian integrity agencies along the education–enforcement continuum (educative, regulatory, adjudicative, enforcement) provides insight into why it is difficult to map their multipurpose roles strictly against the Flumian model (see Table 7.3).

For example, the APSC's role in encouraging the embedding of the APS Values as a means of supporting a positive workplace culture is at the education end of the spectrum, and ACLEI, with its forensic fraud investigations, is an example of the enforcement end. The Merit Protection Commissioner and most other integrity agencies are bridges somewhere in between. All are focused on learning and preventing the recurrence of inappropriate behaviour.

Table 7.3. Authority, powers and accountability arrangements of a selection of integrity agencies

Agency/office holder	Officer independence	Legislation	Communicate in own right	Performance accountability	Financial resources	Main focus
Australian Commission for Law Enforcement Integrity	• Statutory officer • Maximum sum of 7 years, can be multiple appointments	Law Enforcement Integrity Commissioner Act 2006	• Annual report • Matters of expertise • Special reports to the minister to lay before parliament	• To parliament via Minister for Justice • Attorney-General's portfolio	• Appropriation • Offset payments from agencies covered by legislation	• Regulatory • Enforcement
Australian National Audit Office	• Statutory officer • Independent officer of the parliament • Appointed for a term of 10 years	Auditor-General Act 1997	• Annual report • Matters of expertise • Special reports to parliament	• To parliament via the prime minister • Prime Minister and Cabinet (PMC) portfolio	• Appropriation • Offset payments from agencies covered by legislation	• Regulatory • Supervisory • Enforcement • Educative
Commonwealth Ombudsman	• Statutory officer • Maximum sum of 7 years, can be multiple appointments	Ombudsman Act 1976	• Annual report • Matters of expertise • Special reports to parliament	• To parliament via Minister for Justice • PMC portfolio	• Appropriation • Fee for service such as ACT government	• Regulatory • Enforcement
Australian Public Service Commissioner (APSC)	• Statutory officer • Up to 5 years, no limit on reappointment	Public Service Act 1999	• Annual report • Matters of expertise • State of the service report to be tabled in parliament	• To parliament via Minister Assisting the Prime Minister for the Public Service (MAPM) • PMC portfolio	• Appropriation • Fee for service	• Regulatory • Supervisory • Educative
Merit Protection Commissioner (MPC)	• Statutory officer • Up to 5 years, no limit on reappointment	Public Service Act 1999	• Annual report • Matters of expertise	• To parliament via MAPM • PMC portfolio • Not an agency for Public Governance and Performance Accountability purposes	• Memorandum of understanding with the APSCer • Fee for service	• Regulatory • Adjudicative • Educative

Source. www.aclei.gov.au; www.anao.gov.au; www.ombudsman.gov.au; www.apsc.gov.au; www.meritprotectioncommission.gov.au

Mapped against the Flumian model, the Australian integrity agencies are statutory agencies under the *Public Service Act* and tend to clump around the 'regulatory' and 'adjudicative' sections of the curve, though some may be categorised under Flumian's model as 'supervisory'. Even ACLEI seems to fall into the regulatory and adjudicative sections of the spectrum as it must employ staff under the *Public Service Act* and cannot prosecute under its own legislation. As it must work in tandem with a relevant law enforcement agency to lay charges of criminal activity, it is unclear to me how operationally autonomous it is when mapped to Flumian's model.

The Flumian regulation and adjudicative categories tend to have a particular governance style; for example, focusing on policy autonomy, the leader's term of appointment, their specific statute and legal personality, as well as having a governing board. This may reflect Flumian's Canadian heritage and public service experience. The dimensions of her categorisation are also linear in nature and assume a level of structural discipline that may work well in theory but not necessarily in practice.

Independence is a relative term – independence from whom or to do what? There may be value in developing a public administration continuum that maps degrees of autonomy and control. For example, dimensions could identify how much control or autonomy an organisation has in practice to make budget and financial decisions, appoint staff and manage personnel, conduct research and release communications.

From my experience as the Merit Protection Commissioner, an independent complaint/investigation-type agency also faces certain underlying strategic issues, including:

- providing credible assurance on the integrity and fairness of decision-making while simultaneously exposing endemic issues to be addressed
- building relationships and networks to influence policy change while retaining impartiality and independence.

To these I would add the administrative issue of improving cost-effectiveness and reducing red tape while ensuring the legality of due process.

There is no right or wrong approach to balancing these issues; achieving the balance is a result of leadership, vision and judgement depending on the evidence available at the time. My experience as a commissioner revealed to me that balancing the above is difficult in a media savvy, fast-paced environment where the prized quality of a timely response can come at the expense of proper investigation. It can also be difficult to maintain a media or other profile without being perceived as 'crying wolf' over every incident; picking the cases not to promulgate is more difficult than it may seem.

Conclusion

Having had the luxury and privilege of two terms in the statutory role as Merit Protection Commissioner, it is easy to observe through Uhrig, Bourgon and Flumian that requirements and expectations are continuing to evolve. In Australia, the role of integrity agencies is not easy to categorise and new dimensions may assist in reflecting the complexity and sophistication of our environment.

Acknowledgements

I would like to acknowledge the assistance of the staff made available to the Office of the Merit Protection Commissioner and Ms Lorna Kunz, in particular, in the preparation of the original presentation. I would also like to acknowledge and thank Professor Andrew Podger for his assistance in translating the presentation into a chapter for publication.

References

Australian Public Service Commission (APSC) 2003, *APS Values and Code of Conduct in Practice: A Guide to Official Conduct for APS Employees and Agency Heads*, www.apsc.gov.au/aps-values-and-code-of-conduct-practice.

—— 2005, *Supporting Ministers – Upholding the Values*, www.apsc.gov.au/supporting-ministers-upholding-values.

—— 2012, *Merit and Transparency: Merit-Based Selection of APS Agency Heads and APS Statutory Office Holders*, 4th edn, Australian Government, www.apsc.gov.au/sites/default/files/Merit-and-transparency.pdf.

Bourgon, J 2008, 'Future of the public service: a search for new balance', key note address, Institute of Public Administration Australia (IPAA) National Conference, Sydney, June, doi.org/10.1111/j.1467-8500.2008.00597.x.

—— 2011, *A New Synthesis of Public Administration: Serving in the 21st Century*, Kingston School of Policy Studies and McGill-Queens University Press.

Commonwealth of Australia 1998, *Charter of Public Honesty Act 1998*, www.legislation.gov.au/Details/C2020C00126.

Department of Finance 2004, *Commonwealth Procurement Guidelines*, www.legislation.gov.au/Details/C2010L00022.

Drinkwater, D 2015, 'Parliamentary scrutiny of the Australian Public Service', in J Wanna, EA Lindquist & P Marshall (eds), *New Accountabilities, New Challenges*, ANU Press, Canberra, p 61, doi.org/10.22459/NANC.04.2015.03.

Faulkner, J. 2008, 'Ministerial Statements: Restoring integrity to government', Speech in *Journals of the Senate*, No. 52, 4 Dec, parlinfo.aph.gov.au/parlInfo/genpdf/chamber/hansards/2008-12-04/0206/hansard_frag.pdf;fileType=application%2Fpdf.

Flumian, M 2009, 'Global perspective on public sector governance: the governance continuum as a dynamic tool', conference paper, Public Sector Governance Conference, Australian Institute of Company Directors, Canberra, October, slide 5.

Hood, C 1990, 'De-Sir Humphreyfying the Westminster model of bureaucracy: a new style of governance?' *Governance: An International Journal of Policy and Administration*, vol 3, no 2, April, pp 205–14, doi.org/10.1111/j.1468-0491.1990.tb00116.x.

—— 1991, 'A public management for all seasons?', *Public Administration*, vol 69, no 1, March, pp 3–19, doi.org/10.1111/j.1467-9299.1991.tb00779.x.

Joint Committee of Public Accounts and Audit Committee 2002, *Review of the Accrual Budget Documentation*, www.aphref.aph.gov.au_house_committee_jcpaa_accrualbudget_chapter1.pdf.

Nethercote, J 1999, *Departmental Machinery of Government since 1987*, Research Paper 24 1998–99, Politics and Public Administration Group, Parliamentary Library Research, Australian Parliament House, Jun, www.aph.gov.au/About_Parliament/Parliamentary_Departments/Parliamentary_Library/pubs/rp/rp9899/99RP24.

Osborne, SP 2006, 'The new public governance?', *Public Management Review*, vol 18, no 3, doi.org/10.1080/14719030600853022.

Parliamentary Joint Committee on the Australian Commission for Law Enforcement Integrity 2014, Official Committee Hansard, Commonwealth of Australia, 26 Sep, parlinfo.aph.gov.au/parlInfo/search/display/display. w3p;db=COMMITTEES;id=committees/commjnt/5006a599-6dd7-4ac0-a69f-49b317ca84af/0003;query=Id:%22committees/commjnt/5006a599-6dd7-4ac0-a69f-49b317ca84af/0011%22.

Public Service Act 1999, Federal Register of Legislation, www.legislation.gov.au/Details/C2017C00270.

Rhodes, RA 1997, *Understanding Governance: Policy Networks, Governance, Reflexivity and Accountability*, Open University Press, Philadelphia.

Uhrig, J 2003, 'Executive summary', *Review of the Corporate Governance of Statutory Authorities and Office Holders*, Commonwealth of Australia, Jun, p 1, nla.gov. au/nla.obj-922761191/view?partId=nla.obj-924528151#page/n8/mode/1up.

8

THE ROLES OF COMMUNITY-BASED NON-PROFITS IN THE CONTEXT OF COLLABORATIVE GOVERNANCE IN HONG KONG AND TAIWAN

José Chiu-C Chen and Helen K Liu

Introduction

Essential social programs, such as elderly care and assistance for low-income earners, have been introduced through community-based initiatives in Taiwan and Hong Kong. For example, over the past two decades, reforms to Taiwan's long-term care policy (Nadash & Shih 2013) and the Community Care Stations project (Wang 2013; Wang 2016), and to Hong Kong's Lump Sum Grant Initiative (Lee 2005), have increased the role of community-based organisations (CBOs) in the provision of social services at the local community level (Lee & Liu 2012; Liu 2019). These policies aim to provide personalised services and ease of access for the elderly or disabled (Hunter & Ritchie 2007) by working with organisations that have strong connections with the community. This chapter stems from a need to explore how well these policies work and to investigate further the role of CBOs in local communities and their impact on accountability and performance when used to deliver publicly funded services, especially in the context of moves towards collaborative governance.

Marwell (2009: 32) described CBOs as 'a particular kind of neighbourhood organisation: uniquely oriented to the external economic and political world, yet closely tied to specific geographic places and the local residents who are their constituents'. Chaskin and Greenberg (2015) have since provided a framework to examine the roles of CBOs in the context of governance, identifying three key roles: resource provision and allocation, representation, and deliberation. First, through contracting with local government agencies or foundations, CBOs may implement public policies by delivering essential services to local residents (Smith & Lipsky 1993; Grønbjerg & Salamon 2002). Second, by sitting on the boards of local committees or conducting advocacy activities, CBOs play the role of representing local residents (Marwell 2007; Mosley 2011); they may also negotiate decisions that are relevant to their communities' interests (Ostrander 2013). Third, by engaging local residents, CBOs provide a space for deliberation among them and influence the agenda for community affairs (Chaskin 2001; Chaskin & Greenberg 2015).

As we move from the new public management (NPM) reforms towards more collaborative governance, existing studies on CBOs can help us understand community governance by reviewing how CBOs fulfil these three roles (Marwell 2007; Mosley 2011; Chaskin & Greenberg 2015). This conceptual framework not only helps us to understand how CBOs operate and contribute to public policy, but also draws attention to the importance of the external relationships CBOs must build to contribute more broadly to governance issues in local communities. We ask research questions similar to those raised by Chaskin and Greenberg (2015), but in the context of Hong Kong and Taiwan. To what extent do the CBOs perform and balance the roles of service delivery, advocacy, public engagement and political exchange? How do their external relationships affect their roles in the governance of the local community?

Following the methods used in Galaskiewicz's (1979) and Liu and Chen's (2015) studies, we selected 96 CBOs for in-depth, face-to-face interviews with directors or top managers in four urban poor communities in Taiwan and Hong Kong. The interview questions covered basic information about the organisation and its functions, its advocacy and public policy participation activities, and the CBO's external relationships with governments, funders and other non-profits. More specifically, our study examines the varied roles of these CBOs and explores factors that might influence their roles in Taiwan and Hong Kong, particularly in terms of their resources and external relationships.

The development of collaborative governance in Hong Kong and Taiwan

New public management reforms

Western and Asian countries have adopted NPM reforms with different focuses, depending on the political institutional arrangements, culture and socioeconomic conditions of the given country (Pollitt & Bouckaert 2000). Previous studies have emphasised some common characteristics of the NPM reforms, including public–private partnerships, the introduction of competition and performance evaluations (Osborne & Gaebler 1993; Hood 1995). Given the differences in political institutional arrangements and socioeconomic conditions between Hong Kong and Taiwan, the focus of NPM reforms has taken slightly different turns in both countries, including in terms of the emphasis on local community actors.

In Hong Kong and Taiwan from the 1990s, governments began to contract out to external service agencies, especially to community-based non-profits delivering various social services to local communities. The literature shows that non-profits can provide free or low-cost services to their beneficiaries, and they can act as service providers, advocates, value guardians and social capital creators for the community (Kramer 1981; Salamon 1997). The act of contracting out social services from the government to non-profits shifts the mode of service provision from uniform and standard systems to systems with greater flexibility and variety (Ferlie, Ashburner, Fitzgerald & Pettigrew 1996). In these more flexible systems, differently sized agencies can be selected to address the varying demands for the types of public services required (Gruening 2001: 7). From the government's perspective, contracting out has the additional advantage of attracting professionals who are not otherwise available to participate in service delivery (Christensen & Lægreid 2001: 83).

The selection of not-for-profit partners is a challenge in managing partnerships. To ensure the quality, efficiency and accountability of services, the government introduced competitive bidding to select potential community partners. In Hong Kong during the 1990s, the Social Welfare Department introduced the Lump Sum Grant Initiative, a short-term competitive grant, to replace the long-term Standard Unit Cost Model grant (Lee 2005; Lee & Liu 2012). Non-profit organisations that receive funding to provide various social services (such as social security; family and child welfare; clinical psychology; rehabilitation; and aged, youth and community services) must prove that they meet established program goals before they can receive additional grants. In Taiwan, a competitive bidding process was created to select community partners to carry out social, youth, elderly, health and other community services on behalf of local governments (Wu 2011).

Contracting non-profits are required to demonstrate their performance in meeting set targets and goals (Ferlie et al. 1996). The performance approach results in a list of measurable outcomes to evaluate social services and a high degree of professionalism in the workforce (Meyer & Zucker 1989). For instance, in Hong Kong, a series of public management reforms in the 1990s – including a service performance monitoring system, service quality standards, and funding and service agreements – were created as guidelines to measure and monitor non-profits that received government funding (Painter 2005; Lee & Liu 2012; Wang 2013). In Taiwan, non-profit organisations were also required to be accountable and provide evidence-based outcomes to demonstrate their performance before being able to secure government contracts (Wu 2011).

Moving toward collaborative governance

Collaborative governance is an approach in which the government openly and inclusively involves various stakeholders in dynamic processes of communication and adjustment to work toward a common goal (Ansell 2003; Emerson, Nabatchi & Balogh 2012). Jing and Hu (2017) argue that contractual relationships between the government and non-profits under NPM evolve naturally into collaborative governance among stakeholders in the provision of social services. While the NPM reforms in both Hong Kong and Taiwan involved competition and performance evaluation, different policies and systems emerged over time to collaboratively build the capacities of the community-based non-profits to carry out social services on behalf of governments.

In Hong Kong, under the influence of NPM, the Social Welfare Department prompted local community centres to deliver integrated services through so-called one-stop service centres. These centres provide specialised integrated services, including to children, youth and the elderly; in-home care; mental wellness; and family services. These centres are designed to integrate multiple local government agencies and non-profits into one unit and allow clients to access specialised services at a single location. This change has also created a top-down system and entails a greater dependence of the community-based non-profits on local government welfare agencies.

In Taiwan, as a continuous initiative since 1997, the government has introduced a series of reforms to establish long-term care management centres in certain districts leading to the *Promotion of Community Care Development Act* (Wu 2011). The previous long-term care reforms established a foundation for the development of a 10-year Phase 1 and Phase 2 long-term care program with the aim of building community capacity through contracting directly with community-based non-profits to deliver essential social services (Wu 2011). Community care in Taiwan has its roots in the development of long-term care reforms with resources flowing to community actors who play essential roles in providing direct social services to residents. The focus of community care and home care is a bottom-up system requiring city governments to build and strengthen the capacity of CBOs. This system is similar to community care systems in other countries, such as that operating under the United Kingdom's *National Health Service and Community Care Act 1990* (Ackroyd, Kirkpatrick & Walker 2007).

While the structures of community networks might be different, the governments in Hong Kong and Taiwan both face governance challenges, because managing collaborative systems requires the administration to go beyond traditional boundaries (Kettl 2006). Resolving citizens' needs requires the collaboration or cooperation of multiple agencies, sometimes from different sectors. This means that the government, the private sector and the CBOs must be adaptive and able to manage complex relationships in the institutional environments where they operate (Agranoff & McGuire 1998). Previous studies have focused on how governments address emerging collaborative initiatives and integrated services (Agranoff & McGuire 1998; Liu & Chen 2015). Here, we focus on the roles of CBOs in implementing collaborative initiatives and integrated services in Hong Kong and Taiwan.

The roles of CBOs in implementing collaborative governance

Studies on CBOs illustrate how they fulfil various roles in carrying out social services and engaging the public in a complex institutional environment (Osborne 2006; Marwell 2007; Mosley 2011; Chaskin & Greenberg 2015). Chaskin and Greenberg (2015) provide a framework for illustrating the roles of CBOs in the context of governance. First, after contracting with the local government agencies or foundations, CBOs carry out policies and deliver essential services for local residents (Smith & Lipsky 1993; Grønbjerg & Salamon 2002).

Second, by sitting on the boards of local policy committees or conducting advocacy activities, CBOs represent local residents (Marwell 2007; Mosley 2011) and negotiate decisions that are relevant to their communities' interests (Ostrander 2013). For instance, CBOs often have an agenda with regard to local affairs and wish to resolve their issues of concern through a particular political channel (Crenson 1983). Sometimes, the government intentionally builds relationships with reputable CBOs, seeking to engage a particular target group of residents and build a participatory system through those CBOs (Berry, Portney & Thomson 1993). Kuan, Lee and Hsieh (2006) also found that CBOs in Taiwan act in accordance with residents' interests to address local issues, such as development, unemployment and social inclusion. Following some CBOs' successful influence over local policies, the government reached out to the CBOs for regular consultation.

Third, by engaging local residents, CBOs provide a space for deliberation among them and for setting agendas for community affairs (Chaskin 2001; Chaskin & Greenberg 2015). While the nature and scope of the deliberation varies across communities and types of CBOs, often a wide range of community actors are engaged to participate (Chaskin & Greenberg 2015). The physical presence of the CBOs' offices in the local community can allow residents to get together through local activities and discuss various issues (Marwell 2004). Kuan et al. (2006) also found that the governing boards of CBOs are composed of local volunteers, enabling deliberation on community issues to take place within the CBO setting.

Chaskin and Greenberg's conceptual framework enhances not only the understanding of the different roles of CBOs, but also addresses how their construction of different external relationships might influence governance issues in local communities. Marwell's (2004, 2007) community studies further elaborate the roles of CBOs in the context of governance. Building on other studies (Chaskin 2001; Chaskin & Greenberg, 2015), Marwell's (2004) work argues that CBOs generate greater contract revenue by adding electoral politics to their traditional roles of providing services and building communities.

This model produces a new kind of CBO: the political machine (Marwell 2004, 2009; Liu 2019). By reciprocally distributing services to residents and binding residents to the organisation, political machine CBOs create reliable voting constituencies for local elected officials. These officials trade these constituencies at higher levels of the governmental system and steer government human service contracts to favoured CBOs. This suggests that some CBOs might intentionally form relationships with local elected officials to obtain funding and resources, especially those CBOs that have closer and more direct relationships with community residents.

Network roles under collaborative governance

In addition to understanding the functional roles of CBOs, Ansell (2003) argues that it is necessary to measure how organisations are embedded within a broader collaborative governance structure. Granovetter (1985) explains how embeddedness in social relations allows exchange among actors within the system, with less dependence on organisational hierarchy. Network embeddedness also enhances the capacity of organisations to make exchanges through relational and informal mechanisms, such as trust, reciprocity and norms (Powell 1990; Gulati & Gargiulo 1999; Uzzi 1996; Ansell 2003). The social embeddedness of organisations is associated with the construction of social capital through a horizontal network among organisations that engage the public actively in public affairs (Putnam 1993).

The social embeddedness of an organisation refers to its embedding within a set of social relationships or networks (Ansell 2003). The more central an organisation is within a set of social relationships in a network, the more it is embedded in the network (Gulati & Gargiulo 1999). Network theory uses centrality as a measure of organisations' embeddedness. Centrality can be measured in several ways (Freeman 1979). Degree centrality refers to the number of ties an organisation sends to others (outdegree) or receives from others (indegree). This captures the importance of the organisation. More specifically, a high outdegree indicates that an organisation is networking actively with other organisations while a high indegree indicates that an organisation is prestigious or powerful, with others seeking partnership with it. Previous research suggests the following distinct roles, divided according to the degree of centrality: 'prestigious organisation', 'boundary spanner' and 'peripheral organisation'.

While previous studies have laid a strong theoretical foundation for understanding the roles of CBOs in the context of collaborative governance, as yet we know little about the roles of CBOs in Hong Kong and Taiwan, which face similar transitions from NPM's competitive model to new governance's emphasis on collaboration. This study applies case study and social network analysis to examine how CBOs in Hong Kong and Taiwan perform and balance the roles of service delivery, advocacy, public engagement and political exchange, as well as the influence of external relationships on their roles.

Methods and data

According to Yin (2004), a unique and relevant case might not be representative in a given research site, but it could serve a purpose by advancing theory through the understanding of a specific phenomenon. Consistent with this view, this study focuses on four communities in the poorest districts of the cities, namely Kwun Tong and Shek Kip Mei (Hong Kong), Taipei and Old Train Station (Taiwan). For data collection, following methods in Galaskiewicz's (1979) and Liu and Chen's (2015) studies, we selected 96 directors or top managers of CBOs in the four urban poor communities for in-depth, face-to-face interviews. The subjects of the interview questions included organisational functions and basic organisational information, advocacy and public policy participation activities, and the external relationships of the CBOs with governments, funders and other non-profits.

Our primary focus was to examine partnership selection among CBOs, following Provan and Milward's (1991, 1995) procedures. To assist our examination of relationships, we created a table listing all the CBOs within each of the relevant communities and asked the respondents to select the organisations with which they had working relationships, and to identify the direction of the relationship. To illustrate the relationships, four sociomatrices with multiple relationships were developed. We did not assume symmetrical relationships for the sociomatrix representing partnership selection because the directional ties allowed us to examine the power dynamics (White, Boorman & Breiger 1976; Ansell 2003). To illustrate the structure of this network, we adopted a network analysis technique to visualise the four networks and their associated characteristics (Wasserman & Faust 1994).

Results

The characteristics of social service provisions in Hong Kong and Taiwan

Professionalism and competition

There is increasing demand on CBOs to deliver social services in Hong Kong and Taiwan, both to respond directly to the actual needs of society and to meet the demands for services that are being passed on by government. Our findings on the roles of the CBOs in service provision are consistent with existing findings on non-profits in general (Lee & Liu 2012; Xian, Kuan & Lu 2009). For instance, in a study of large non-profit databases and their missions, Xian et al. (2009) found social service organisations that received government funding serve mainly in the social welfare and education sectors and with increased professionalism in service delivery. Our survey found a trend also for those CBOs that focus on social provision to be more professional. For instance, in Hong Kong, most CBOs receiving government funding have joined the Hong Kong Council of Social Service, which sets the standard for the provision of social services in Hong Kong (Lee 2005).

Furthermore, our study found that most of the CBOs in Hong Kong and Taiwan have small- and medium-size funding amounts, as they are frontline centres and receive only limited support from their local headquarters. More than half of these organisations self-reported from our open-ended questions about financial difficulties and lack of managerial experience, small-scale, limited mobilisation ability, inadequate ability to sustain operations, confined quarters, lack of communication skills for coordinating with other organisations, insufficient scale of participation or intervention, and deficient understanding of their social and economic environment. The larger CBOs have greater capacity to secure funding, despite the competitive environment.

Political influence and social embeddedness

A previous study shows that most of the CBOs studied in Hong Kong do not carry out advocacy activities or have political involvement (Centre for Civil Society and Governance 2010), whereas the CBOs in the two cities in Taiwan have greater political activity and engage residents in signing petitions and joining organised protests (Lin, Chuang, Liu & Hwang 2012). Consistent with our findings, but with some variations (see 'Discussion' below for details), many small local or regional organisations have appeared in recent years, forming an indispensable grassroots force in different regions. Given their size, CBOs in Taiwan must mobilise networks to gain support from the community for petitioning or advocacy activities. Thus, this type of CBO tends to form external relationships with actors of diverse backgrounds.

Network roles of non-profits

Next, by analysing social networks in four communities (two in Hong Kong and two in Taiwan), we examined degree centrality as a measure of organisations' embeddedness (Ansell 2003). As explained above, degree centrality refers to the number of ties an organisation sends to others (outdegree) or receives from others (indegree). We classify the roles that CBOs play based on their number of outdegree and indegree ties with other CBOs as partners in local communities. These roles can be described as prestigious, boundary spanning and peripheral CBOs (Table 8.1). We then examine the network roles and the average organisational characteristics of these network types across the four communities (summarised in Table 8.2).

Table 8.1. Four social service networks in Hong Kong and Taiwan and their network roles as measured by degree centrality

Roles	Sau Mau Ping, Hong Kong	Sham Shui Po, Hong Kong	Beitou, Taipei	Central Taicheung
Prestigious	27.6%	19%	32%	20%
Boundary	41.4%	33.3%	28%	40%
Peripheral	31%	47.6%	40%	40%

Source. Surveys conducted by authors

Table 8.2. Network roles and associated organisational characteristics in Hong Kong and Taiwan

	Prestigious		Boundary		Peripheral		P
	N		N		N		
Overall	**24**	**25%**	**35**	**36.5%**	**37**	**38.5%**	**0.832**
Hong Kong	12	23.5%	20	39.2%	19	37.3%	
Taiwan	12	26.7%	15	33.3%	18	40%	
Size[1]	**24**	**136.17**	**35**	**28.26**	**36**	**23.64**	**0.201**
Hong Kong	12	29.75	20	14.5	19	22.74	0.116
Taiwan	12	242.58	15	46.6	17	24.65	0.365
Annual budget	**17**	**$4,318,319**	**27**	**$938,651**	**29**	**$645,365**	**0.398**
Hong Kong	9	$1,550,466	14	$362,978	14	$1,036,065	0.460
Taiwan	8	$7,478,300	13	$1,568,696	15	$297,205	0.301
Service delivery	**24**	**100%**	**34**	**97.1%**	**34**	**91.9%**	**0.268**
Hong Kong	12	100%	19	95%	18	94.7%	0.725
Taiwan	12	100%	15	100%	16	88.9%	0.208
Advocacy	**6**	**25%**	**12**	**34.3%**	**7**	**18.9%**	**0.329**
Hong Kong	2	16.7%	7	35%	3	15.8%	0.300
Taiwan	4	33.3%	5	33.3%	4	22.2%	0.723
Engagement	**7**	**29.2%**	**17**	**48.6%**	**12**	**32.4%**	**0.229**
Hong Kong	1	8.3%	8	40%	5	26.3%	0.150
Taiwan	6	50%	9	60%	7	38.9%	0.480

[1] Average number of employees of the studied organisation.

Source. Surveys conducted by authors

Prestigious CBOs

Prestigious CBOs have stronger ties with government and sufficient resources but are less flexible

In social network analysis, prestige can be measured by the indegree number. In other words, the higher its indegree number, the more prestigious the given CBO is. Our data shows that about 25 per cent of CBOs are prestigious within their community networks (Table 8.1). In Hong Kong and Taiwan, we find that service delivery is the primary function of prestigious CBOs and they tend to collaborate with other CBOs that are also primarily service providers, and they are not particularly involved in political activities, such as petitions, advocacy or citizen engagement (Table 8.2).

One explanation for this could be that CBOs receiving significant government funding must follow service quality guidelines and remain non-partisan. Thus, they organise events and exchange resources within their existing networks but are reluctant to share their resources with actors outside this system. They enjoy not only reliable funding from the government, but also a high level of prestige, as evidenced by the many ties that they enjoy. There are, however, few reciprocal ties from this type of CBO to others. As a result, the integrative system designed originally by the government to build networks in the community has become a more inclusively networked social service system.

Boundary spanners

Boundary spanners connect with everyone but have less resources and political motivations

The term 'boundary spanner' refers to those who have connections with different types of actors within communities. For instance, a boundary spanner would not only have a higher degree of outdegree relationships but also connect with different types of organisations according to the nature of their service. In our data, we found about 36.5 per cent of CBOs are boundary spanners. The data also shows that boundary spanners are, moreover, mostly politically affiliated (either with a local district councillor/representative or they are founded by politicians) and tend to have more ties with CBOs of diverse backgrounds. For instance, in Hong Kong, district councillors and politically affiliated CBOs serve a bridging role in poor urban communities because they actively build relationships with different community members.

As in Marwell's (2004) study, the current study identified an exchange relationship among local politicians, politically affiliated CBOs and other informal neighbourhood associations. Politically affiliated groups build working relationships but are also keen to gain resources and access to local residents to expand their political interests. This was especially observed in Hong Kong (Liu 2019) and is similar to the case in Taiwan, where local elected representatives work with specific CBOs to deliver meal services and perform elderly visits in exchange for gaining potential political support from community residents, as reported by the local representative office in Beitou, Taipei. Political interference, however, was reflected more clearly in our open-ended survey in Hong Kong, where the interviewees noted that politics represented a major obstacle to building mutual trust and understanding in their community (see 'Discussion' below).

Peripheral CBOs

Peripheral CBOs have fewer connections with actors in their communities

Our analysis showed that 38.5 per cent of the CBOs are peripheral, based on their network connections. These CBOs are either smaller or informal, have fewer connections with other CBOs and do not occupy an important position within their own community networks; they also are less involved in advocacy (Table 8.2). Such informal CBOs are, however, often gathering points for local residents and provide access to a specific group with a particular ethnicity or special need, such as the deaf, single mothers or private community foundations. Such CBOs tend to have fewer resources (see Table 8.2) and are reached by the politically affiliated CBOs rather than the social welfare CBOs.

In sum, the preliminary results show that CBOs serve the roles of social service provision and allocation, representation and deliberation, yet differences between Taiwan and Hong Kong exist. For instance, the CBOs in Hong Kong reported that they play a minimal role in advocacy and policy participation, while those in Taiwan reported a relatively higher degree of advocacy and policy participation. This study explores the extent to which CBOs are involved in the policymaking process or in advocacy activities and how this varies depending on their resources, community influence and external relationships with government. In doing so, the study shines some light on the implications for community governance in Hong Kong and Taiwan.

A few limitations should be noted before the findings are discussed. First, the empirical cases selected for this study are based on theoretical relevance. The target communities do not represent typical communities. Instead, our research team chose low-income communities at each site. This narrows the application of our findings, but it allows us to examine the roles of CBOs in serving the poor.

Discussion

Differences between Hong Kong and Taiwan

Top-down versus bottom-up approach

Due to social and political differences, the governance structures of the community networks in Hong Kong and Taiwan were created differently. One major difference is Hong Kong's more top-down rather than bottom-up structure. As noted, in the early 2000s, the Hong Kong Government established service integration centres to provide one-stop services for children, youth and the elderly; in-home care; mental wellness; and family services. These centres integrate local government agencies and non-profits into one unit and allow clients and service users to access different specialised services at one location. For instance, multiple agencies that we interviewed in Hong Kong were co-located in the same office building and provided services to the same low-income families. The government in Hong Kong allows rent deduction for non-profits that choose to be located on public housing estates so their clients can readily access services. Because of policy incentives and geographic convenience, both of the communities studied in Hong Kong presented a top-down structure of social service provision.

In Taiwan, NPM reforms in welfare policy took a different turn and put more emphasis on community care and community-building. For instance, before the 2000s, a 10-year Phase 1 and Phase 2 long-term care program was intended to build community capacity by contracting directly with community-based non-profits to deliver essential social services (Wu 2011). Instead of establishing hub centres, Taiwanese policies, like those on long-term care and community care, focused on capacity-building and service-training programs for the local CBOs. Furthermore, through a series of decentralised funding processes and resource decisions for local city and district governments, the amendment of some service contracts to make them more manageable in terms of scope and boundaries allowed CBOs to bid for government contracts.

Engagement versus advocacy

To increase its role in government coordination, the Hong Kong Government actively engages local CBOs. Table 8.3 shows the differences in engagement channels utilised by CBOs in Hong Kong and Taiwan. Surprisingly, CBOs in Hong Kong reported a higher percentage of government engagement through sitting on central or local government boards/committees and participation in public consultation or government panels. For instance, we found a higher percentage (37 per cent) of CBOs in Hong Kong have a representative on local coordinating committees than in Taiwan (13 per cent).

Table 8.3. Differences in the engagement channels utilised by CBOs in Hong Kong and Taiwan

	Hong Kong		Taiwan		Total		
Engagement channels	N	%	N	%	N	%	P
Government board/committee	11	21.57	9	20.45	20	20.83	0.000
Government panel/consultation	17	33.33	12	27.27	29	30.21	0.000
Regional committee	19	37.25	6	13.64	25	26.04	0.000
Public consultation	15	29.41	10	22.73	25	26.04	0.000

Source. Surveys conducted by authors

There are two possible reasons for this disparity. First, the development of social service provision differs historically between Hong Kong and Taiwan. In Hong Kong, beginning in the British colonial period, the government adopted a cooperative strategy and invited large and influential non-profit organisations to sit on government committees (Lee 2005). Hong Kong district councils were designed to cooperate with influential non-profits and they continue to play an essential coordinating role in local communities (Leung 2010). These committees are an important communication channel between the government and the non-profit sector. Taiwan's political transformation from an authoritarian state to a democratic system resulted in non-profits emerged more gradually.

Second, and perhaps related to the different histories, CBOs in the two jurisdictions have different approaches to, and use different means of, engagement and advocacy (see Table 8.4). In Taiwan, CBOs are more involved in advocacy (only 23 per cent report that they did not conduct advocacy activities, compared to 59 per cent in Hong Kong), and they use a wider range of channels. The CBOs in Hong Kong advocate mainly through their member networks (29 per cent), with limited use of other means such as the internet (16 per cent) and street petitions (14 per cent). CBOs in Taiwan relied less on their member networks (16 per cent) and much more on the internet (52 per cent), TV ads (20 per cent), public media (18 per cent) and mailed advertisements (18 per cent). Both made some use of street petitions.

Table 8.4. Differences between CBOs in Hong Kong and Taiwan in their adoption of advocacy methods

Advocacy methods	Hong Kong		Taiwan		Total		
	N	%	N	%	N	%	P
Member network	15	29.41	7	15.91	22	22.92	0.000
Email/phone text	3	5.88	7	15.91	10	10.42	0.000
Social media	8	15.69	23	52.27	31	32.29	0.000
Direct mail	1	1.96	8	18.18	9	9.38	0.000
Street ads	7	13.73	5	11.36	12	12.50	0.000
TV ads	2	3.92	9	20.45	11	11.46	0.000
Public media	1	1.96	8	18.18	9	9.38	0.000
Others	10	19.61	11	25.00	21	21.88	0.000

Source. Surveys conducted by authors

The implementation challenges of collaborative governance

The development of effective collaborative governance systems in local communities poses a challenge to policymakers as well as to the CBOs that implement them. Previous studies have focused more on finding the right combination for collaboration to be effective. As discussed previously, governments have transformed and redesigned social service provisions to be more collaborative and effective, creating one-stop services in the United States, community care in Taiwan, the No Wrong Door policy in the United Kingdom, and integrative service in Hong Kong. This study finds that frontline CBOs struggle to balance their roles of service provision, engagement, advocacy and creating relationships with others to gain additional resources and information to survive in the competitive environment. By understanding the role played by CBOs in implementing collaborative governance in the local community, our findings reveal a number of challenges.

Resource-distribution asymmetry

Under the NPM reforms, governments adopted a competitive bidding process to allocate resources and funding. Our interviews show, however, that resources and funding are allocated mainly to larger and more established non-profits. These CBOs have extended networks and affiliated non-profits that provide similar services or share the same religious or political backgrounds. These clusters of medical and elderly service organisations make the competition for contracts more difficult for newly established non-profits, because it is difficult for them to access clients and build the capacity to bid for contract work. For instance, interviewees from organisations that were established in Hong Kong after 2000 reported difficulty in obtaining service contracts from the government because their client base was smaller than that of larger organisations. To be competitive, these new service organisations had to emphasise their innovativeness and personalised services for the elderly.

Lack of coordination with diverse non-profits

When policy requires them to extend their working boundaries to be more accessible to clients, CBOs are likely to seek less costly relationships or form networks with similar organisations rather than the most effective or efficient ones. Such less costly relationships with similar organisations are usually confined within the existing boundaries of missions, capacities, resources, responsibilities, accountability and networks, as Kettl (2006) found. Not surprisingly, even well-intended policies cannot be accomplished without taking into account the costs of building relationships with organisations with different networks.

Political involvement creates distrust among CBOs

A surprising finding from our open-ended questions was the negative aspect of political engagement. The negative effects of the political involvement of CBOs are particularly significant in Hong Kong. Some interviewees reported that politics is a major obstacle to building mutual trust and understanding in their community. The following observation was reported from an interview in Hong Kong with a librarian at a local public library: 'An organisation's political partners reduce opportunities for cooperation.'

This perception hinders the development of networking relationships between governments and politically affiliated non-profits. The organiser of a neighbourhood community association voiced the following complaint: 'Political polarisation divides society and, consequently, affects mutual trust between organisations and the trust between citizens and organisations as well.' This view was confirmed by a local service centre serving the deaf, which stated that: 'Political affiliation divides the community.' Political interference was mentioned less by the interviewees from the two cities in Taiwan.

Implications for the greater China region

It can be inferred from the cases of Hong Kong and Taiwan that CBOs in the greater China region differ from those of the West due to the historical and political development of the region. The transition from NPM to collaborative governance in China is changing the role of contracting non-profits in social service provision: how can non-profits be both competitive contractors and collaborators that create consensus (Jing & Hu 2017)? While the literature shows that both roles can be taken on at the same time, performance measurement of non-profits as contractors that provide social services in China does not account for collaboration and, thus, creates barriers to it, as found in Shanghai (Jing & Hu 2017), Hong Kong (Lee & Liu 2012; Liu & Chen 2015) and Taiwan (Liu, Kuo & Lin 2018). More importantly, non-profits' disproportionate dependence on government in greater China also deprives them of autonomy and constrains network building, thus reducing their governing capacity (Jing & Hu 2017).

Our empirical findings on Hong Kong and Taiwan have implications for the transition from NPM to collaborative governance in China. Unlike the findings of the literature on the hollow state (Milward & Provan 2003), in our study, CBOs in Hong Kong and Taiwan reported that they seek leadership from local government. From our open-ended questions, a discussion of leadership surfaced, and the local CBOs expressed the view that it is essential to have leadership that can coordinate different non-profits in the community to avoid unnecessary competition and promote information sharing.

The interviews indicated that the relationship between governments and non-profits should be improved so as to increase coordination. Only about one-quarter of CBOs studied here have participated in government-led forums and consultation meetings, and only one-third have been consulted by government. In particular, a higher percentage (37 per cent) of CBOs in Hong Kong reported having representatives on local coordinating committees, than in Taiwan (13 per cent). Due to historical development, the Hong Kong Government cooperates more actively with local CBOs while, over the last few decades, the Taiwan Government has gradually allowed the CBOs to express their perspectives on issues through a variety of channels to accurately represent the views and demands of local residents.

Internationally, governments play leadership roles by adopting strategies to improve coordination and collaboration among service providers in order to assure the level of service especially in competitive policy environments, such as community development block grants (Agranoff & McGuire 1998), information and communication technology platforms (Urban Institute 2012), and insurance schemes, such as the Australian National Disability Insurance Scheme (Green, Malbon, Carey, Dickinson & Reeders 2018).

On the other hand, CBOs in Hong Kong were much less involved in public advocacy and more often relied on formal links with government. Perhaps both models have merits for the greater China region when constructing social service provision arrangements for local communities and establishing effective communication channels between governments, CBOs and local residents.

Our findings for CBOs in Hong Kong and Taiwan have implications for understanding governance capacity and service quality in local communities. The People's Republic of China's recent Five-Year Development Plan listed 'Winning the battle against poverty' as an essential policy target for the near future. In particular, the government will focus on working with cross-sector actors to improve the self-sufficiency of low-income families and assure their upward mobility. The collaborative governance models adopted and the experiences accumulated in both Hong Kong and Taiwan have important implications for this commitment.

To improve governance capacity and to facilitate collaboration and exchange among different CBOs, the government needs to provide legitimacy to bureaucrats and CBOs to build their connections with actors in the communities and remove barriers to forming connections with groups from different backgrounds. For instance, block grants in the United States (Reingold & Liu 2009) and Hong Kong's Community Investment & Inclusion Fund have demonstrated that governments can create cross-sector collaboration by providing separate funds (in addition to funding to services) for facilitating collaboration-related activities (Leung 2010); this might help promote community participation through community network building.

Similarly, increasing the participation of local CBOs and neighbourhood associations in the policymaking process and ensuring fair participation through self-regulation are essential. Huther and Shah (2005: 40) argue, 'the quality of governance is thus determined by the impact of this exercise of power on the quality of life enjoyed by its citizens'. Our social network analyses reveal that the way in which institutions of governance exercise their power in local communities can influence the quality of service provisions. For instance in Hong Kong, unlike in the United States, the existing laws that govern the non-profit sector do not specify the type of political activities in which a non-profit can engage.[1]

Our open-ended survey also suggests that CBOs with a strong individual political motive diminish social capital, because they work for a political agenda rather than the needs of the community. Thus, more specific and fairer regulation of those CBOs can reduce the negative impacts of political machines and clientelism and ensure that the provision of social services by community actors is based on public need rather than individual politicians' political interests. More importantly, diversifying different channels for local CBOs to express their concerns and needs may also reduce the influence of the larger and more influential CBOs and, thus, reduce resource-distribution asymmetry.

References

Ackroyd, S, Kirkpatrick, I & Walker, RM 2007, 'Public management reform in the UK and its consequences for professional organization: a comparative analysis', *Public Administration*, vol 85, no 1, pp 9–26, doi.org/10.1111/ j.1467-9299.2007.00631.x.

---

1   US regulations for 501(c)(3) charity non-profits require them not to participate in any campaign activity for or against political candidates. Political non-profits, however, can file claims under 501(c)(4) and 501(c)(6).

Agranoff, R & McGuire, M 1998, 'Multinetwork management: collaboration and the hollow state in local economic policy', *Journal of Public Administration Research and Theory*, vol 8, no 1, pp 67–91, doi.org/10.1093/oxfordjournals. jpart.a024374.

Ansell, C 2003, 'Community embeddedness and collaborative governance in the San Francisco Bay Area', in M Diani & D McAdam (eds), *Social Movements and Networks: Relational Approaches to Collective Action*, Oxford University Press, Oxford, New York, doi.org/10.1093/0199251789.003.0006.

Berry, JM, Portney, KE & Thomson, K 1993, *The Rebirth of Urban Democracy*, Urban Institute Press, Washington, DC.

Centre for Civil Society and Governance 2010, 'Serving alone: the social service sector in Hong Kong', *Annual Report on the Civil Society in Hong Kong 2009*, The University of Hong Kong.

Chaskin, RJ 2001, 'Building community capacity: a definitional framework and case studies from a comprehensive community initiative', *Urban Affairs Review*, vol 36, no 3, pp 291–323, doi.org/10.1177/10780870122184876.

Chaskin, RJ & Greenberg, DM 2015, 'Between public and private action: neighborhood organizations and local governance', *Nonprofit and Voluntary Sector Quarterly*, vol 44, no 2, pp 248–67, doi.org/10.1177/0899764 013510407.

Christensen, T & Lægreid, P 2001, 'New public management: the effects of contractualism and devolution on political control', *Public Management Review*, vol 3, no 1, pp 73–94, doi.org/10.1080/14616670010009469.

Crenson, M 1983, *Neighborhood Politics*, Harvard University Press, Cambridge, Massachusetts, doi.org/10.4159/harvard.9780674188112.

Emerson, K, Nabatchi, T & Balogh, S 2012, 'An integrative framework for collaborative governance', *Journal of Public Administration Research and Theory*, vol 22, no 1, pp 1–29, doi.org/10.1093/jopart/mur011.

Ferlie, E, Ashburner, L, Fitzgerald, L & Pettigrew, A 1996, *The New Public Management in Action*, Oxford University Press, New York, doi.org/10.1093/ acprof:oso/9780198289029.001.0001.

Freeman, L 1979, 'Centrality in social networks: conceptual clarification', *Social Networks*, vol 1, pp 215–39, doi.org/10.1016/0378-8733(78)90021-7.

Galaskiewicz, J 1979, *Exchange Networks and Community Politics*, Sage Publishing House, Beverly Hills, California.

Granovetter, M 1985, 'Economic action and social structure: the problem of embeddedness', *American Journal of Sociology*, vol 91, no 3, pp 481–510, doi.org/10.1086/228311.

Green, C, Malbon, E, Carey, G, Dickinson, H & Reeders, D 2018, *Competition and Collaboration between Service Providers in the NDIS*, Centre for Social Impact, UNSW Sydney.

Grønbjerg, KA & Salamon, LM 2002, 'Devolution, marketization, and the changing shape of government–nonprofit relations', in LM Salamon (ed), *The State of Nonprofit America*, Brookings Institution Press, Washington, DC.

Gruening, G 2001, 'Origin and theoretical basis of new public management', *International Public Management Journal*, vol 4, no 1, pp 1–25, doi.org/10.1016/S1096-7494(01)00041-1.

Gulati, R & Gargiulo, M 1999, 'Where do interorganizational networks come from?', *American Journal of Sociology*, vol 104, no 5, pp 1439–93, doi.org/10.1086/210179.

Hood, C 1995, 'The "new public management" in the 1980s: variations on a theme', *Accounting, Organizations and Society*, vol 20, no 2–3, pp 93–109, doi.org/10.1016/0361-3682(93)E0001-W.

Hunter S & Ritchie, P 2007, *Co-production and Personalisation in Social Care: Changing Relationships in the Provision of Social Care*, Jessica Kingsley Publishers, London.

Huther, J & Shah, A 2005, 'A simple measure of good governance', in A Shah (ed), *Public Services Delivery*, The World Bank, Washington, DC.

Jing, Y & Hu, Y 2017, 'From service contracting to collaborative governance: evolution of government non-profit relations', *Public Administration and Development*, vol 37, pp 191–202, doi.org/10.1002/pad.1797.

Kettl, DF 2006, 'Managing boundaries in American administration: the collaboration imperative', *Public Administration Review*, vol 66, no 1, pp 10–19, doi.org/10.1111/j.1540-6210.2006.00662.x.

Kramer, RM 1981, *Voluntary Agencies in the Welfare State*, University of California Press, Berkeley.

Kuan, YY, Lee, YH & Hsieh, LY 2006, 'The governance of community-based foundations in Taiwan: the comparative study between Hsin-Kong Foundation and Yang-Sun Foundations', *Journal of Public Administration*, vol 18, pp 21–25 [in Chinese], doi.org/10.1177/095207670602100303.

Lee, EWY 2005, 'Nonprofit development in Hong Kong: the case of a statist–corporatist regime', *VOLUNTAS: International Journal of Voluntary and Nonprofit Organizations*, vol 16, no 1, pp 51–68, doi.org/10.1007/s11266-005-3232-z.

Lee, EWY & Liu, HK 2012, 'Factors influencing network formation among social service nonprofit organizations in Hong Kong and implications for comparative and China studies', *International Public Management Journal*, vol 15, no 4, pp 454–78.

Leung, J 2010, 'Social capital and community: a review of international and Hong Kong development', in SH Ng, SY Cheung, & B Praksah (eds), *Social Capital in Hong Kong: Connectivities and Social Enterprises*, City University of Hong Kong.

Lin, XT, Chuang, LH, Liu, SJ & Hwang, YS 2012, 'Making the community work: the correlation between social capital and community participation', *Taiwanese Journal Social Welfare*, vol 10, no 2, pp 161–210 [in Chinese].

Liu, HK 2019, 'The impact of transition from British to Chinese rule on social service delivery systems in Hong Kong', *Policy & Politics*, vol 47, no 2, pp 331–52, doi.org/10.1332/030557318X15407316999851.

Liu, HK & Chen, B 2015, 'The challenges of implementing collaborative governance in Hong Kong: case study of a low-income family community', in Y Jing (ed), *The Road to Collaborative Governance in China*, Palgrave Macmillan, New York, doi.org/10.1057/9781137542182_3.

Liu, LC, Kuo, HW & Lin, CC 2018, 'Current status and policy planning for promoting age-friendly cities in Taitung County: dialogue between older adults and service providers', *International Journal of Environmental Research and Public Health*, vol 15, no 10, pp 2314–40.

Marwell, NP 2004, 'Privatizing the welfare state: nonprofit community-based organizations as political actors', *American Sociological Review*, vol 69, no 2, pp 265–91, doi.org/10.1177/000312240406900206.

—— 2009, *Bargaining for Brooklyn*, University of Chicago Press.

Meyer, M & Zucker, L 1989, *Permanently Failing Organizations*, Sage Press, Newbury Park.

Milward, HB & Provan, K 2003, 'Managing the hollow state collaboration and contracting', *Public Management Review*, vol 5, no 1, pp 1–18, doi.org/10.1080/1461667022000028834.

Mosley, JE 2011, 'Institutionalization, privatization, and political opportunity: what tactical choices reveal about the policy advocacy of human service nonprofits', *Nonprofit and Voluntary Sector Quarterly*, vol 40, no 3, pp 435–57, doi.org/10.1177/0899764009346335.

Nadash, P & Shih, YC 2013, 'Introducing social insurance for long-term care in Taiwan: key issues', *International Journal of Social Welfare*, vol 22, no 1, pp 69–79, doi.org/10.1111/j.1468-2397.2011.00862.x.

Osborne, D & Gaebler, T 1993, *Reinventing Government: How the Entrepreneurial Spirit is Transforming the Public Sector*, Penguin, New York.

Osborne, S 2006, 'The new public governance?', *Public Management Review*, vol 8, no 3, pp 377–87, doi.org/10.1080/14719030600853022.

Ostrander, SA 2013, 'Agency and initiative by community associations in relations of shared governance: between civil society and local state', *Community Development Journal*, vol 48, no 4, pp 511–24, doi.org/10.1093/cdj/bss051.

Painter, M 2005, 'Transforming the administrative state: reform in Hong Kong and the future of the developmental state', *Public Administration Review*, vol 65, no 3, pp 335–46, doi.org/10.1111/j.1540-6210.2005.00458.x.

Pollitt, C & Bouckaert, G 2000, *Public Management Reform: A Comparative Analysis*, Oxford University Press.

Powell, W 1990, 'Neither market nor hierarchy: network forms of organization', *Research in Organizational Behavior*, vol 12, pp 295–336.

Provan, KG & Milward, HB 1991, 'Institutional-level norms and organizational involvement in a service-implementation network', *Journal of Public Administration Research and Theory*, vol 1, no 4, pp 391–418.

—— 1995, 'A preliminary theory of interorganizational network effectiveness: a comparative study of four community mental health systems', *Administrative Science Quarterly*, vol 40, no 1, pp 1–33, doi.org/10.2307/2393698.

Putnam, RD 1993, *Making Democracy Work: Civic Traditions in Modern Italy*, Princeton University Press, doi.org/10.2307/j.ctt7s8r7.

Reingold, DA & Liu, HK 2009, 'Do poverty attitudes of social service agency directors influence organizational behavior?', *Nonprofit and Voluntary Sector Quarterly*, vol 38, no 2, pp 307–32, doi.org/10.1177/0899764008316967.

Salamon, LM 1997, *Holding the Center: America's Nonprofit Sector at a Crossroads*, New York, Nathan Cummings Foundation.

Smith, SR & Lipsky, M 1993, *Nonprofits for Hire: The Welfare State in the Age of Contracting*, Harvard University Press, Cambridge, Mass.

Urban Institute 2012, *The Community Platform: Engagement, Analysis, and Leadership Tools*, Washington, DC.

Uzzi, B 1996, 'The sources and consequences of embeddedness for the economic performance of organizations: the network effect', *American Sociological Review*, vol 61, pp 674–98, doi.org/10.2307/2096399.

Wu, YQ 2011, 'Review and prospect of long term care policy for the elderly in Taiwan: federation for the welfare of the elderly's perspective', *Community Development Journal*, vol 136, pp 251–63.

Wang, GX 2016, 'Exploration of the relationship between the service delivery quality of Community Care Stations and successful aging: the moderation of cognition on government role', *Journal of Public Administration*, vol 50, pp 77–115 [in Chinese].

Wang, ST 2013, 'The coordination of nonprofit organizations in community care service: a research for the Community Care Stations', *NTU Social Work Review*, vol 27, pp 185–228.

Wasserman, S & Faust, K 1994, *Social Network Analysis: Methods and Applications*, Cambridge University Press, New York, doi.org/10.1017/CBO9780511815478.

White, HC, Boorman, SA & Breiger, RL 1976, 'Social structure from multiple networks. I. Blockmodels of roles and positions', *American Journal of Sociology*, vol 81, no 4, pp 730–80, doi.org/10.1086/226141.

Xian, XP, Kuan, YY & Lu, WP 2009, *Nonprofit Sector: Organization and Operation*, Chuliu Press, Taipei [in Chinese].

Yin, RK 2004, *Case Study Research: Design and Methods*, Sage, Los Angeles.

9

ASSESSING THE VERTICAL MANAGEMENT REFORM OF CHINA'S ENVIRONMENTAL SYSTEM

Progress, conditions and prospects

Fanrong Meng, Zitao Chen and
Pichamon Yeophantong

Introduction

Despite China's rapid economic development over the past 30 years, the country's current patterns of economic growth are not environmentally sustainable. From the severe smog that blanketed Beijing in early 2017 to the serious industrial pollution of major waterways such as the Yangzi and Yellow rivers, China is experiencing an environmental crisis in the making. In response, the Chinese Government has recognised the need for exigent environmental reforms. In a bid to mitigate and reduce environmental degradation, the central government has put in place a range of policy initiatives, having also enacted a series of national plans, policies and laws since the late 1990s (Sims 1999). These policies largely focus on enhancing administrative capabilities to improve environmental protection and legislation, with a clear emphasis on coordinating a 'win–win' balance between economic development and environmental protection (Zhang, Wen & Peng 2007). To this end, the structure and institutional authority of the country's chief environmental agency was considerably strengthened through the transformation of the State Environmental Protection Agency (SEPA) into a fully-fledged Ministry of Environmental Protection (MEP), which was renamed as the Ministry of Ecology and Environment (MEE) in 2018.

China's system of environmental management and the implementation of environment-related policies, however, still suffer from sizable challenges and inefficiencies, as problems of noncompliance and the inconsistent enforcement of laws and regulations persist. This, in part, stems from issues relating to the nature of national legislation, local protectionism, as well as local bureaucratic and enforcement procedures. Some scholars have concluded that environment laws in China are of a low legislative quality, have too many general instructions and that they are basic and difficult to enforce (Wang 2009). Additionally, the lack of attention to environmental indicators in the 'cadre evaluation' system has led to limited capacity in local Environmental Protection Bureaus (EPBs) because of insufficient funding and personnel for monitoring and enforcement (Wang 2013; Jin, Andersson & Zhang 2016). The lack of coherence among environmental regulations, conflicting interests at different levels of administration, and insufficient technical capacity and resources further complicate the ability of state environmental protection authorities to carry out their duties (Van 2006).

It is within this context that demands have arisen for stronger steps to be taken to tackle endemic problems of weak enforcement. During the Fifth Plenary Session of the 18th Communist Party of China's (CPC) Central Committee in October 2015, the CPC pledged to update the current system of governance among the different levels of environmental protection authorities, and to adopt a new vertical management system that has since come into effect under the auspices of the country's 13th Five-Year Plan (2016–20). 'Vertical management' refers to a system in which an agency implements policies within a hierarchical, internal process, and negotiates its roles and duties in relation to other environmental protection authorities. Here, agencies and departments situated on the lower rungs of the chain of command are required to report directly to those on the upper rungs, as opposed to local governments at the same level (Li 2016).

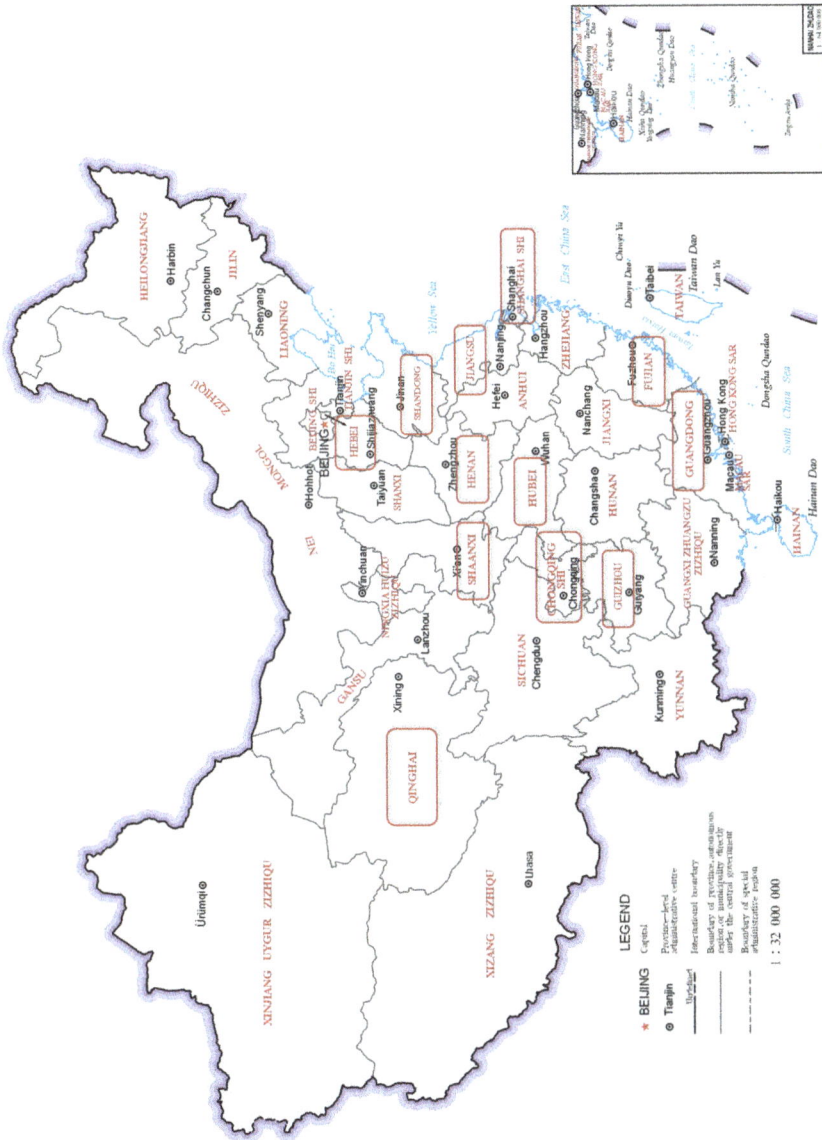

Figure 9.1. Vertical management pilot provinces in environmental protection system

Source. Fanrong Meng and Zitao Chen

Following the development of this system, 12 provinces across the country have since applied to be vertical management pilot regions. These provinces are Hebei, Shanghai, Jiangsu, Fujian, Shandong, Henan, Hubei, Guangdong, Chongqing, Guizhou, Shaanxi, and Qinghai (Figure 9.1). This chapter interrogates the key drivers behind these provinces' application to become vertical management pilot provinces and explores the key elements of China's vertical management reform alongside a review of the evolution of the country's system of environmental management. We then consider whether this reform can potentially fix problems related to administrative inefficiency within the bureaucratic system and improve policy efficiency. As explained later, by applying a qualitative comparative analysis (QCA) method, the chapter compares official field data and documents from 31 provinces across China to reveal the significance of internal and external determinants in informing provincial decisions to apply for the vertical management pilot.

The evolution of China's environmental management system

Prior to transforming into the MEE, MEP had been the sole national body responsible for environmental management. First established in 1974 as a unit under the State Council, with a staff of 20 people, a reorganisation in 1998 led to the creation of SEPA, which came directly under the State Council. In March 2008, as a significant step towards improving environmental management, SEPA was elevated to the ministerial level. The MEP's functions included preparing and implementing national policies, legislation and regulations related to water and air quality, solid waste management, nature protection and nuclear/radiation safety.

The MEP was also in charge of formulating environmental quality criteria and pollutant discharge/emission standards at the national level, organising environmental quality monitoring, and collaborating with local environmental authorities to initiate enforcement activities. It coordinates plans for addressing trans-boundary environmental problems and organising scientific research and development.[1] Apart from the MEP, a range of environment-related issues was further managed separately by other ministries and agencies of the State Council. For example, the

---

1   See www.mee.gov.cn/zjhb/zyzz/

National Development and Reform Commission (NDRC) has played a key role as the agency responsible for developing and implementing Five-Year Plans. In this capacity, the NDRC integrates environmental issues into China's overall planning system, and into sector-specific policies such as those on energy.

Even so, the primary responsibility for implementing environmental policy remains at the sub-national – that is, provincial and local – level. There are around 2,000 EPBs with approximately 60,000 employees at the provincial, prefecture/municipal, district/counties and township administrative levels. Other administrative units of local governments that are engaged in environmental policy implementation include the Environmental Protection Committees of the local People's Congress, the Environmental Protection Commissions of local governments, mayor offices, planning commissions, finance bureaus and a range of industrial bureaus. These all play important roles in endorsing local environmental regulations, coordinating EPBs' work with other government organs, taking key decisions on large investment projects involving industrial development and environmental protection, integrating these projects into local economic and social development plans, as well as managing pollution-discharge fee systems, among other functions.

Historically, the Chinese system of governance was characterised by the division between the vertical line, which means that the agencies of bureaucracy are directly controlled by their functional administrative superiors (*Tiao*), and the horizontal line (*kuai*), in which the agencies are also administered by the local government rather than the higher levels with certain functionalities. In this system, a municipal-level EPB reports to its 'vertical' superiors (i.e. the provincial EPB and MEP) while also being subject to the leadership of its 'horizontal' boss (i.e. the mayor of the municipality). Currently, different departments within local governments shoulder the responsibility of carrying out environmental protection, and sub-units within the environmental agencies are responsible for reporting individually to the government. It is the local government offices that appoint the heads of these agencies and provide financial support. China's environmental reform program has been carried out under this 'parallel management system' for the past 35 years and it is clear that the system is responsible for some of the main structural obstacles to effective environmental policy implementation at the local level.

The first is the interference of local protectionism and weak environmental compliance assurance. The central government has increasingly delegated responsibilities to local governments for addressing local problems, and they are expected to draw upon and allocate local funds for this purpose. This encourages governments to defend local industries in order to secure revenues, even at the cost of environmental enforcement – basically, engaging in a form of local protectionism. This becomes particularly problematic when the goals of environmental protection conflict with the targets of economic development (Ma & Ortolano 2000). While EPBs had received guidance from the MEP, they remained institutionally and financially subordinate to provincial and local governments. Thus, the actions of EPBs were directed more by sub-national governments than by the MEP, as local governments tended to favour economic development over environmental considerations, with EPBs also ranking low in the government hierarchy. Pressures to demonstrate economic growth are powerful and compelling (Wang & Lin 2010). Even with the introduction of a wider range of environmental targets in socioeconomic planning, and despite innovations in the evaluation system for government officials, there was an ever-present risk that 'fake data' might be produced to preserve the political status quo.

The second structural obstacle to effective environmental policy implementation concerns budget allocation. China's decentralised administrative system means that most EPB financial resources come directly from the local government (Jahiel 1998; Ma & Ortolano 2000). As a result, EPBs are often weak with minimal funding and limited authority (Lo & Leung 2000: 677; Ma & Ortolano 2000: 81). Since the late 1990s, EPB authority has improved somewhat nationally – this is especially the case in richer coastal areas – but funding continues to represent a major constraint. Until 2003, EPBs were dependent on the revenue from the pollution levy to finance their operations.

Without adequate funds, EPBs have been unable to carry out sufficient inspections, or to execute sanction decisions. The remainder of the EPBs' resources are taken from pollution discharge fees and are thus dependent on continued pollution. It is in this way that a lack of funding effectively hampers enforcement: staff resources and materials, such as cars needed for inspections, are in chronic shortage. With inefficient staff who are also increasingly overburdened, EPBs are often unable to carry out regular and proactive inspections of polluting enterprises, and are forced to rely heavily on receiving complaints before investigating.

Third, fragmented authority and blurred accountability further hinder cooperation among local government agencies. The fragmented nature of China's bureaucratic system has been debated since the 1980s, and continues to hamper effective environmental management even now (Brombal et al. 2015). China's environmental protection and conservation efforts are managed by different government departments. For example, soil and water conservation activities are guided by the Bureau of Water Resources, dust management on construction sites is regulated by the Bureau of Housing and Construction, and vehicle exhaust is monitored by the Bureau of Transportation. The EPB's authority on such matters is limited by the need for it to seek consensus among its constituent members, consisting of representatives from more than 20 bureaus.

The EPB cannot compel cooperation because it lacks a formal mechanism that would otherwise allow it to do so. On the other hand, local government leaders continue to give limited attention to environmental performance and there remains an underlying bias towards GDP growth within the evaluation and rewards system for government officials. The lack of clear responsibilities and indicators for assessing local government leaders' environmental performance results in the systematic neglect of environmental protection that is seen in China today.

The fourth problem is the challenge of low implementation capabilities at the local level. The lack of knowledge and skills can result in certain national policies being misinterpreted by local governments. Partly, this lack of local capacity is due to the nature of the decentralisation process in China, where sub-national agencies are given decision-making authority but no accompanying financial resources. Even though a large number of civil servants are trained every year, training opportunities for environmental staff are unevenly allocated. In poorer counties and townships where the local government cannot even pay the salaries of their officials, training becomes a non-essential 'luxury', as opposed to a critical necessity.

Reviewing China's approach to vertical management reform

In order to reduce the interference of local governments in the work of local environment departments, overcome the institutional and procedural barriers that hinder environmental protection, and strengthen integrated management by treating both the symptoms and root causes of environmental problems, in September 2016 the General Offices of the CPC Central Committee and the State Council published and distributed *Guidelines for the Pilot Reforms for a Vertical Management System for the Environmental Monitoring, Supervision, Inspection, and Enforcement by the Environmental Protection Branches below Provincial Level* (hereafter, the Guidelines). As one official of the MEP observed:

> The vertical administration system will adjust not only the administrative jurisdiction, but also the division of powers among the local governments at different levels, the functional departments of a local government and the departments in charge of environmental protection. The system will also improve the basic mechanism of environmental governance. (Xinhua News 2016)

Following from the development of the central government's management procedures, 12 provincial divisions applied for and were selected as the vertical management pilot regions amongst 31 provinces. They were urged to carry out the reforms based on their practical circumstances, and to accomplish the reform objectives by the end of June 2017.

The main distinction between the two types of political relationships in horizontal and vertical management refers to those governed by binding orders, and those based on non-binding instructions (Figure 9.2). In horizontal management, the local party committees and governments at each level itemise the responsibilities of EPBs at their level, give full support for their initiatives, and provide supervision and inspections to enhance accountability in environmental protection tasks. On a vertical scale, the Guidelines highlight the unified supervision and management of the environmental protection departments, which is intended to improve overall efficacy. The Guidelines emphasise the regulation and establishment of environmental protection departments and teams, while optimising environmental functions at the provincial, municipal and county levels. The EPBs are primarily responsible for unified supervision and management, as well as for localised management, whereas other relevant departments are expected to take up responsibilities based on their respective jurisdictions.

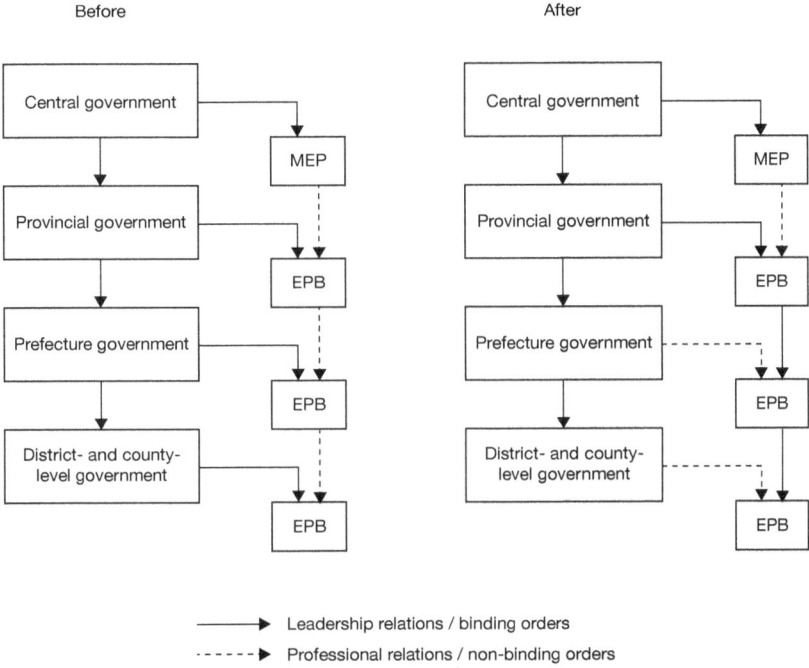

Figure 9.2. Before and after vertical management

Source. Fanrong Meng, Zitao Chen and Pichamon Yeophantong

The purpose of the reforms to a vertical management system is twofold: to address the pressing problems found in existing vertical and horizontal management systems as used in local environmental management, as well as to change the current situation where some local governments either give too much weight to economic development and make light of environmental protection; or intervene in environmental monitoring, inspection and supervision, and enforcement. This, in turn, leads to hurdles in performing environmental protection tasks, failure to observe laws, sloppiness in environmental enforcement and insufficient accountability for law-breaching activities. The key tasks and the corresponding problems are listed in Table 9.1.

Table 9.1. Key tasks in vertical management

Key tasks	Problems
Strengthen the environmental protection responsibilities of the local party committees, governments and relevant departments and urge them to fulfil such responsibilities, conduct authoritative and effective environmental supervision and inspection, and step up accountability and other measures.	Difficulty in overseeing local governments and relevant departments.
Centralise the eco-environmental quality monitoring and environmental supervision and inspection functions in order to wield such powers only at a provincial level, and manage the environmental enforcement teams at municipal level.	Difficulty in stopping the influence of local protectionism over environmental monitoring, supervision, inspection and enforcement.
Build capacity at provincial and municipal levels in making overall plans for and regulating environmental issues, and explore such measures as establishing cross-watershed and cross-region environmental protection bodies.	Difficulty in meeting the new requirements for addressing cross-watershed and cross-region environmental issues in a comprehensive manner.
Enrich the structure and staff of environmental protection institutions, and enable the environmental protection teams to be more specialised.	Difficulty in regulating and enhancing team-building among local environmental protection departments.

Source. Fanrong Meng, Zitao Chen and Pichamon Yeophantong

The integration of a vertical management system into environmental agencies is not entirely new. In 2002, Shaanxi province piloted the 'vertical management' of environmental bureaus at the municipal level and below, which led to 'better law enforcement at the county level' (Yue 2016). But the trial also met with resistance from the counties, which resented the fact that, with the concentration of authority, the original budget attached to this authority was 'sucked upwards'. In 2006, the central government took a bigger step by creating 11 dispatch inspection centres all over China – an idea modelled on the regional offices of the US Environmental Protection Agency. These inspection centres, though based locally, report directly to, and are funded by, the political centre. But as 'dispatch' centres, they do not feed into the existing power structure at the local level, and are sometimes seen as interfering with local governments' ability to exercise their legitimate authority. Since then, the MEP has made little progress vis-à-vis vertical management.

The 2008 upgrade of SEPA into a full ministry required the MEP to assuage fears of an even greater concentration of decision-making power. Accordingly, a key obstacle to pushing through the vertical management reform was the concern that it may further fragment and undermine governance at the local level. With an increasing number of departments reporting to the top, there is a risk of excessive regulatory interference at the expense of catering to local needs.

Within the political science discipline, prior attempts at vertical management amount to experiments from which examples of best practice might be identified (Zhu 2014). The effects of a new policy cannot always be predicted, however, and it may be better, therefore, not to rely on a single approach (Ostrom 2005). Nonetheless, the experiments can potentially provide proof of principle, help shape any new policy and, thereby, provide the basis for policy diffusion.

But how is one to account for the variation in the levels of policy interest among different provinces? Some provinces are more hesitant, yet others appear to be more enthusiastic adopters when it comes to applying to be a vertical management pilot region. Provincial governments face many environmental problems but, at present, there is limited knowledge of how policymakers have responded to this problem. As more environmental problems fall under the purview of provincial governments, it is increasingly important to explore their capacity to develop comprehensive responses to those problems. This chapter explores the determinants of variations in the policy capability of these pilot provinces relative to other provinces and examines the ability of provinces to develop a multifaceted vertical management system.

Theoretical framework
Policy innovation and diffusion
Political scientists have long been fascinated by the puzzle of why local governments adopt certain policies or reforms (Dye 1966; Gray 1973; Savage 1978; Walker 1969). Policy diffusion refers to an understanding of policy innovation that emphasises the spread of novel policy approaches. New approaches are only innovative if and when they enter into widespread use and are adopted by or diffused into many jurisdictions. Diffusion theory is an established field of academic enquiry, which suggests that policymaking activity at the national level can occur either through internal processes, or by building on what has occurred in other states (Berry & Berry 1999; Gray 1994; Walker 1969).

The reasons for innovation and the mechanisms of inter-regional diffusion are complicated. Previous studies generally can be grouped under three models: internal determinants, horizontal influence and vertical interventions (Nice 1994; Elkins et al. 2006; Berry & Berry 2007; Walker et al. 2011). The internal determinants include social, economic, political and historical traditions; traits of leaders; and internal policy networks (Berry & Lowery 1987; Mintrom 1997). The major horizontal influential factors come from competition and pressure among governments (Rogers 1995; Cao 2012; Rose 2005). In contrast with these two models, the vertical intervention model emphasises the role of higher levels of government in powerful hierarchical systems, which may spread and accelerate policy diffusion to local governments through mandated measures (Newman et al. 2000; Nutley et al. 2012).

In China, vertical intervention from the superior government is more complicated than in democratic decentralised countries. The central government has strong powers and considerable influence on the behaviours of local governments and on the careers of local officials. Xufeng Zhu (2014) revealed how different diffusion patterns of innovation are adopted by subordinate local governments under various vertical intervention mechanisms that are established by the central or superior governments within an authoritarian structure. The central or superior governments may adopt two major intervention methods to impose the necessary effect: intervention via administrative command and competition using performance evaluation.

Internal and external determinants of policy adoption

Considering the above theoretical perspective, we establish two broad explanations for policy adoption in this study: internal and external determinants. Internal determinant models suggest that the adoption of policy innovation depends on a state's internal characteristics (Berry & Berry 1999). These characteristics, such as socioeconomic resources, political ideology, the severity of the problem and interest-group pressure, may influence state policymaking (Wright et al. 1987; Ringquist 1994; Williams & Matheny 1984). They are often related directly to the 'motivation to innovate, the strength of obstacles, and resource availability' (Berry & Berry 1999). In view of this literature, we test two specific aspects of the internal determinants explanation of provincial pilot reform:

- **Problem severity:** The emergence of a problem or crisis requires a change to existing circumstances and increases the likelihood of policy adoption. Moreover, the likelihood of adoption and the rate of diffusion increase if the innovation is perceived to be compatible with current circumstances and the generally accepted values and norms of the social system (Rogers 1995). We speculate that the more serious a province's environmental problems, the more likely it will adopt environment management reforms.

- **Resources:** Policy innovation and implementation often carry high costs. Researchers consistently report that larger and wealthier states adopt new programs faster than smaller and poorer states (Gray 1994; Walker 1969). Necessary legitimacy and resources (legal, financial) can facilitate the development of long-term project visions, stimulate and oversee local approaches, and support the implementation of ambitious programs (Bell & Hindmoor 2009). Thus, the availability of resources may increase the motivation of decision-makers to initiate a search for new ideas, study their effectiveness and apply them in practice (Berry & Berry 1999; Jensen 2004). The social and legal viability of the state is not the only established resource required for policy adoption. A sound ecological foundation – which in this chapter refers to the ecological restoration and conservation of land and water resources – also constitutes an essential factor in environmental policy adoption and innovation.

Aside from the internal determinants, diffusion theory also considers how external factors can likewise have a positive influence on policy adoption. In other words, states are more likely to adopt policies or programs when other governmental units have already adopted them (Berry & Berry 1999). The possible reasons are: (a) states learn about different policies from other states, (b) states compete with each other, and (c) public pressure may force a state to adopt a policy that neighbouring states have adopted (Berry & Berry 1999). Given this, we hypothesise three external determinants:

- **Horizontal competition:** Some diffusion theorists suggest that there is a greater likelihood of states adopting policy innovation if a neighbouring state has already done so (Berry & Berry 1999; Gray 1994; Mooney & Lee 1995; Walker 1969). Innovation adoption is not always predictable, as some states have a greater desire to be on the 'cutting edge' and are willing to take risks, while other states prefer to wait until an innovation is 'standard practice' before considering adoption (Dusenbury & Hansen 2004). Competition occurs when units react to, or anticipate, the other's policy actions in an attempt to attract or retain resources. As a pilot region, a province could obtain more political and financial resources, but also face unpredictable risks. Such competition would then affect the choices of other governments.

- **Vertical learning:** Along with the pressure from other state governments, national policymaking can also be affected by upper level government units. Vertical or top-down pressure is often suggested in diffusion research, but seldom examined in an explicit manner (Berry & Berry 1999). The vertical influence model does not view learning and competition as key elements to policy diffusion, but rather situates the influence of national governments as a central factor. Therefore, it is more likely that states will adopt the policies heralded by the national government, rather than emulate the policies of other states (Berry & Berry 1999). More specifically, the vertical influence model posits that states are most likely to adopt policy innovation in response to federal mandates. In fact, adoption is even more likely when it is attached to federal funding and incentives (Berry & Berry 1999). Innovation adoption is also influenced by the national government's expectation that states conform to standards (Brown 1981). Accordingly, supporting the central government is particularly important for local officials seeking to obtain favourable consideration of their future promotion.

- **Public participation:** Popular environmental movements are usually the result of serious public concerns over social and ecological impacts, and can help to compel governments to expedite the search for solutions to environmental problems. National environmental policymaking might also be subject to pressure from interest groups, albeit this is likely to be marginal in China in contrast with Western democracies (Davis & Feiock 1992; Gray & Lowery 1996; Potoski 2001). On this view, new environment policies are likely to emerge under conditions marked by active public participation within the policymaking process.

In sum, we identify seven internal and external determinants – namely, problem severity, social development, legal development, ecological foundation, horizontal competition, vertical learning and public participation – as explanatory variables that may influence provincial decisions to apply to become vertical management pilot regions (i.e. the dependent variable).

Methods, data and measurement

We use QCA in order to empirically assess the relative weight of the determinants of policy adoption. This method is particularly well-suited for a 'small-N' research design, which allows for the examination of multi-causal analysis and the interaction of causal variables (Ragin 1987). A basic premise of QCA is that there may be multiple paths or causal combinations leading to the same outcome. It is a combination of independent variables ('conditions', in QCA terms) that eventually produces the phenomenon to be explained. Several different combinations of conditions can produce the same outcome and, depending on the context (i.e. 'conjuncture'), a given condition may have a different impact on the outcome.

This suggests how different causal paths – each path being relevant in a distinctive way – may lead to the same outcome. Hence, by using QCA, one is urged not to 'specify a single causal model that fits the data best', but rather to 'determine the number and character of the different causal models that exist among comparable cases' (Ragin 1987: 167). Although QCA is often considered a non-standard method, it is steadily gaining ground in comparative research in sociology and political science (Rihoux & Ragin 2009).

China's highest level of administrative division is at the provincial level. There are 31 such divisions spread across the country: 22 provinces, four municipalities and five autonomous regions. This study examines how these 31 divisions decided whether or not to be candidates for vertical management pilot regions within China's broader environmental protection system. We regard attempts to apply to become a pilot region as a manifestation of policy adoption. By using a mix of statistical and qualitative approaches, we identify associations between provincial conditions and policy adoption behaviour. The study utilises data from official field statistics that present the environmental and social–legal conditions of China's 31 provincial level regions.

Table 9.2 lists the indicators that were adopted from the statistical analysis, and which are used to operationalise the seven conditions of internal and external determinants. Problem severity refers to the number of serious environmental events or crises within a province. A province is classified as having a serious environmental problem that requires urgent attention and mitigation if it has experienced more than 10 serious environmental events or crises that were criticised by the MEP or which exhibit levels of air pollution above pm $2.5 \geqq 50 \mu g/m^3$ (the national standard).

The human development index (HDI) is used as an indicator of social development and provides a composite statistic of life expectancy, education and per capita income indicators. Legal development refers to the degree to which public concerns are considered by policymakers, and is measured here by the number of local People's Congress proposals on environmental protection issues. Ecological foundation is measured with respect to whether there is an 'ecological' city, county or district within the province. Horizontal competition is measured on the basis of applications for pilot regions from neighbouring provinces. The indicator for vertical learning is measured by the number of local regulations vis-à-vis central government requirements on soil, water and air protection. Finally, public participation reflects popular participation in and influence on environmental policymaking, and is measured by the number of public petitions on environmental protection.

Table 9.2. Variable calibration and sources

Variables	Calibration	Values	Source
PS (problem severity)	Serious environmental events $\geq$10, PM2.5 $\geq$ 50µg/m³	1, or 0	China Environmental Annual Statistics 2016, PM2.5 Rank of 359 cities in China in 2016
SD (social development)	Human development index (HDI) $\geq$ 0.70	1, or 0	China National Human Development Report 2016
LD (legal development)	Local environment laws or regulations $\geq$ 20 (median)	1, or 0	China Environmental Annual Statistics 2015
EF (ecological foundation)	Number of ecological cities, counties or districts in the province $\geq$1	1, or 0	List of national ecological sites by city, county and district
HC (horizontal competition)	Number of neighbouring provinces applying for vertical management $\geq$ 1	1, or 0	MEP website
VL (vertical learning)	Number of regulations in soil, water and air protection in the light of central government requirement $\geq$ average	1, or 0	MEP website
PP (public participation)	Number of petitions on environment protection $\geq$ average	1, or 0	China Environmental Annual Statistics 2012–15, Environment Report 2016

Source. Fanrong Meng and Zitai Chen

With regard to coding, there are multiple forms of QCA; however, for this study, we used crisp-set QCA (csQCA) in which variables or conditions can take only two values. Each case is evaluated according to the presence (1) or absence (0) of a condition and outcome, and this information is arranged in a truth table (Ragin 1987). QCA is a theory-driven method and the selection of conditions depends on the theoretical questions at hand. We coded the indicators for seven conditions that have been identified in the literature. The coding in csQCA necessarily simplifies the complexity of the cases because it uses a binominal scale. Even though the coding is binominal, the coding process takes into account the complexities of the different conditions.

Analysis and results

The QCA begins with the construction of a 'truth table' (Table 9.3) that registers the possible determinants expected to affect provinces' responses. For each province in our sample, these factors are recorded in accordance with the coding procedures explained above. The truth table is then *minimised* to generate Boolean equations.

Minimisation consists of a set of logical rules that reduce the complexity of the combinations of conditions and outcomes. The objective is to eliminate irrelevant factors. In other words, the QCA produces the shortest possible description of different constellations of conditions and outcomes. We used (fuzzy-set) fsQCA 2.0 software to analyse the truth tables (with our crisp-set data) to specify the different combinations of conditions linked to the selected outcome, as based on the features of the positive cases that consistently distinguish them from the negative cases. We further assess the consistency for crisp sets, which is the percentage of cases in each row displaying the outcome. Consistency scores of either 1 or 0 indicate perfect consistency for a given row. A score of 0.5 indicates perfect inconsistency. Cases with greater than 0.9 consistency are considered likely to be necessary conditions.

Table 9.3 shows that horizontal competition (HC) has 0.9167 consistency and should be considered a necessary condition for a province to apply to be a pilot for vertical management of environmental regulation.

Table 9.3. Truth table

Province	VM	HC	VL	PS	SD	LD	PP	EF
Beijing	0	1	1	1	1	0	1	1
Tianjin	0	1	1	1	1	0	1	1
Hebei	1	1	1	1	1	1	0	0
Shanxi	0	1	1	1	1	1	0	0
Inner Mongolia	0	1	0	0	1	1	0	0
Liaoning	0	1	0	1	1	1	1	1
Jilin	0	0	1	0	1	0	0	0
Heilongjiang	0	0	0	0	1	1	0	0
Shanghai	1	1	1	1	1	0	1	1
Jiangsu	1	1	1	1	1	1	1	1
Zhejiang	0	1	1	1	1	1	1	1
Anhui	0	1	1	1	1	1	0	1
Fujian	1	1	1	1	1	0	1	1
Jiangxi	0	1	0	0	1	0	0	1
Shandong	1	1	1	1	1	1	1	1
Henan	1	1	1	1	1	1	1	1
Hubei	1	1	1	1	1	1	0	1
Hunan	0	1	1	1	1	0	0	0
Guangdong	1	1	1	1	1	1	1	1
Guangxi	0	1	0	0	1	0	0	0
Hainan	0	1	0	0	1	0	0	0
Chongqing	1	1	0	1	1	0	1	0
Sichuan	0	1	1	1	1	1	0	1
Guizhou	1	1	0	0	0	1	0	1
Yunnan	0	1	0	0	0	1	0	0
Tibet	0	1	0	0	0	0	0	0
Shaanxi	1	1	1	1	1	1	1	1
Gansu	0	1	0	1	0	0	0	0
Qinghai	1	0	0	0	0	0	0	0
Ningxia	0	1	0	0	1	0	0	0
Xinjiang	0	1	0	1	1	0	0	1
Consistency		0.9167	0.7500	0.8333	0.8333	0.6667	0.6667	0.7500

Source. Fanrong Meng and Zitai Chen

We use fsQCA to identify other conditions that are likely to contribute to a province's decision regarding piloting vertical management. This software usually presents three possible solutions: (1) a 'complex' solution that relies only on the positive cases (i.e. only the provinces that applied to be pilots) and ignores the counterfactual cases, which generally leads to identifying all the conditions that commonly apply to the positive cases; (2) a 'parsimonious' solution that takes into account all the cases, both positive and negative, and identifies the more limited number of conditions that apply especially to the positive cases; and (3) 'intermediate' solutions that take into account the analyst's additional considerations about the plausibility of the two other solutions, including theoretical considerations.

The complex solution we identify is a combination of the other variables (vertical learning, problem severity, social development, legal development, public participation and ecological foundation). The parsimonious solution focuses only on vertical learning, legal development and public participation. While in both cases the consistency measure is high (0.8333), it is difficult to fully explain the basis of either of the two solutions. Accordingly, while we have not explicitly considered additional factors to develop some 'intermediate' solution, we have examined more specific combinations of the variables and identified two possible pathways, both of which reveal total consistency (1.0) and, when combined with horizontal competition, offer highly plausible solutions:

Table 9.4. Truth table final solutions

	Raw coverage	Unique coverage	Consistency
~VL*~PS*~SD*LD*~PP*EF	0.083333	0.083333	1.000000
~VL*PS*SD*~LD*PP*~EF	0.083333	0.083333	1.000000
Solution coverage:	0.583333		
Solution consistency:	0.875000		

* indicates positive intersection with condition, *~ indicates intersection with reverse condition

Source. Fanrong Meng and Zitai Chen

Table 9.4 lists details about the two solutions. Solution consistency measures the degree to which membership in the solution (the set of solution terms) is a subset of membership in the outcome, which is 0.875. Solution coverage measures the proportion of memberships in the outcome that is explained by the complete solution, which is 0.583. Raw coverage measures the proportion of memberships in the outcome explained by each term of the solution, and unique coverage measures the proportion of memberships in the outcome explained solely by each solution term, excluding memberships that are covered by other solution terms (Ragin 2018). Both the raw and unique coverage are low, and we discuss the implications further below.

The first path is a combination of: more horizontal competition, less vertical learning, good ecological foundation, less public participation, good legal development, poor social development and less problem severity. It is likely that such a combination presents a model driven by poor social development, where less severe environmental problems and good ecological resources cause lower levels of public pressure on environmental issues. The typical case of such a model is Guizhou, a mountainous province in south-east China with rich natural, cultural and environmental resources. Compared with other provinces, Guizhou is relatively poor and economically underdeveloped with a nominal GDP for 2015 of 1050.26 billion yuan (US$150.04 billion) and per capita GDP of RMB29,847 (US$4,264) (National Bureau of Statistics of China 2017). Demographically, it is one of China's most diverse provinces, with ethnic minorities accounting for more than 37 per cent of the population.

In such a multi-ethnic region, pursuing social stability and integration is an important task for the senior local officials. China's Constitution and laws guarantee equal rights to all ethnic groups and provide priority policies to promote ethnic minority groups' economic and cultural development. Under the pressure of a target-oriented responsibility system, which covers comprehensive performance indicators in economic, social and ecological fields, a common strategy for the local government is to develop their strong points and not exacerbate their weaknesses.

As Guizhou has good environmental resources and an ecological foundation, there is less risk politically within the party, administratively and with the general public in carrying out new attempts at environmental policymaking. There is also a greater likelihood of producing a positive outcome and reorganisation through environmental, as opposed to economic, policy innovation. Hence, the central performance evaluation system is possibly a key factor pushing local senior managers to design innovative environmental management strategies and carefully govern innovation processes; this may be regarded as a top-down model for policy adoption.

The other path leading to a local government's policy adoption is represented by a mix of more horizontal competition, less vertical learning, a poor ecological foundation, more public participation, poor legal development, good social development and greater problem severity. This depicts a different strategy of policy adoption that is largely driven by problem severity and having the resources to address it. The typical examples are Shanghai and Jiangsu provinces. Shanghai is the commercial and financial centre of China and, since 2011, its total GDP has been the highest of all Chinese cities, with per capita GDP of RMB 82,560 (US$12,784) (Dongfang Daily News 2012).

Public environmental awareness is growing fast and the city has invested in a number of environmental protection projects. On 23 January 2014, the municipal government announced that three main measures would be taken to manage air pollution in Shanghai, along with surrounding Anhui, Jiangsu and Zhejiang provinces. The measures involved delivery of the 2013 air cleaning program, a linkage mechanism with the three surrounding provinces and improvement of the emergency early warning system (CNSTOCK News 2014). The sharp contrast between poor ecological protection and rich social development leads to deeper public support for and pressure on environmental issues. In this model, good social development can provide sufficient financial resources to encourage policymakers to pursue greater policy innovation. This is more akin to a bottom-up model, given the impetus for innovation does not endogenously arise from the leaders themselves.

It is interesting to note that horizontal competition constitutes the single necessary condition for policy innovation. This suggests that pressure arising from same-level competitors is the chief driver for provinces to adopt new policy. The two multiple configurations identified are not mutually exclusive but together provide plausible bases for the decisions by most provinces.

They do not, however, provide the full answer. Despite the high 'consistency' score, the analysis reveals a low 'coverage' result (0.0833), suggesting that other factors not included in the study may be equally, or even more, important. It is common in social phenomena, which are contingent by nature, to find that additional contextual conditions influence policy decisions (Gerrits & Verweij 2013). This study mainly considers macro-level factors and does not include micro-level factors, such as individual styles of leadership and motivation. For example, the style, tenure, education and work experience of leaders may affect their policy decisions and implementation. Thus, an interesting future research avenue is to take some micro factors, such as leaders' attributes, as conditions and examine what combinations of these influence the practice of certain management strategies.

Discussion

Two general conclusions can be drawn from the above QCA of the vertical management pilot region applications of Chinese provinces. First, horizontal competition is a key factor that directly influences provincial policy adoption. Regardless of how different the internal conditions are, the provinces that had applied for the pilot reform possessed similar external conditions to neighbouring provinces that had, likewise, attempted the reform. Under external pressure, provincial leaders exhibit higher levels of motivation and tend to be more inventive in introducing new policies to win political arguments. Other jurisdictions tend to follow leading provinces that have similar preferences in terms of instruments and types of technology (Jordan & Huitema 2014). Massey et al. (2014), for instance, observed how external drivers are more prominent across Europe in the diffusion of adaptation policies on climate change issues. Biesenbender and Tosun (2014) similarly suggest that the adoption of climate policies in OECD countries is influenced by learning from international organisations, which serves as an external driver. Our study also supports these findings within the Chinese context.

Second, internal factors also influence the policy adoption process. There are two main configurations of different conditions: severe environmental problems with good social development and lagging legal development in environmental issues, or less serious environmental issues and a stronger legal foundation but with poor social development. We use the HDI to discern the degree of social development. A region scores higher HDI when the lifespan, the education level and the GDP per capita is higher. It seems that with rapid social and economic development, environmental protection has often been ignored, even with respect to legislation. The environmental Kuznets curve serves as a reminder of how economic development can initially lead to environmental degradation, but also how, after a certain level of economic growth, a society can begin to improve environmental quality, resulting in lower levels of environmental degradation (Mills & Waite 2009).

From this viewpoint, China's provinces need to adopt new methods to amend the current model of national development. As such, the pilot region applications could suggest new opportunities with regard to China's environmental governance. Stadelmann and Castro (2014) demonstrate how higher levels of GDP are positively correlated with the adoption of financial instruments, which in turn stand to motivate greater policy adoption. Conversely, for lower and middle-income provinces, local government pressure can prove to be more important than in higher income provinces. Our results also suggest, however, that there may well be other factors, not addressed in this study, that affect provincial decisions to apply to be a pilot for vertical management of environmental regulation.

Conclusion and prospects

This chapter has demonstrated how policy adoption does not depend on a single condition, but can result from a combination of internal conditions. Moreover, these configurations differ under certain case-specific or contextual circumstances. In other words, specific contexts may require, for instance, specific combinations of management and stakeholder involvement. Indeed, the patterns of policy adoption and diffusion, together with the subsequent consequences, warrant more attention. Biesenbender and Tosun (2014) have noted how the adoption of policies is dominated by learning and emulation from policy practices adopted by culturally and politically similar peer countries and that, after adoption, countries tend to modify policies again. In light of this, there is a need to further link policy content to practical circumstances, and to explore the possible (unexpected) consequences or problems associated with the emerging vertical management regions.

According to the Guidelines, the vertical management system holds the potential to transform the *kuai*-based set of authority relations to one based on centralised management, largely of personnel/budgetary allocations (*bianzhi*), cadre recruitment and allocation (nomenklatura), and revenue collection. Here, the channelling of capital happens in a more direct fashion. But, more fundamentally, local governments are ultimately accountable for environmental quality within their jurisdictions. In other words, greater accountability, clearer articulation of tasks and authority, and direct financial and policy support, contributes to reducing transaction and management costs among bureaucracies further along the line of command and, as such, improves policy efficiency. Certain risks and challenges remain, however; for instance, the fragmentation brought about by a vertical management system could undermine local governance. This challenge could very well become one of the most urgent problems in need of mitigation.

Under the vertical management system, local EPBs below provincial level have witnessed a dramatic increase in administrative subordinates within their area of direct responsibility, particularly through their ability to control personnel and budgetary flows. Local governments can no longer directly control personnel, budgetary and related arrangements. This potentially represents a significant loss of local government leverage over EPBs. Moreover, local EPBs are not created and managed by, or responsible to, the corresponding local People's Congresses. Thus, they do not need to be approved by or even report to the local People's Congress about their work.

National and local laws stipulate, however, that local People's Congresses have supervision authority over the administrative departments within a specific locality. At the very least, centrally managed units can act as 'blind spots' for the local People's Congresses. As centrally managed EPBs become more autonomous, their relations with other local administrative departments become less important, and a sense of alienation may be unavoidable. Effective implementation of environmental policies, however, requires coordination between local departments under the local EPBs' direction. In this way, a weakened relationship among government departments could give rise to obstacles to cooperation and policy enforcement.

Only through innovations to institutional, legislative and development models can China overcome these problems and achieve sustainability into the future. The case of vertical management serves as a prime example of the politics of power decentralisation and recentralisation, while also reflecting the complex principal–agent relationship between China's central and local governments. Based on China's previous experiences in enacting total control policies, the implementation and enforcement of environmental regulation has been shown to be better guaranteed by cadre evaluation and centralised data management systems (Jin et al. 2016). As a consequence, future effective implementation of vertical management depends on three considerations: a 'top design' strategy that integrates environmental protection reform, a robust evaluation system and a well-designed regional development model.

Positive examples taken from pilot areas should be encouraged and diffused. By the same token, efforts should be made to improve the 'nuts and bolts' of the country's evaluation and accountability systems. Indeed, the vertical management system could empower local party committees and governments to shoulder greater responsibility for environmental protection through the implementation of the 'one position with dual responsibilities' and lifelong accountability systems, which means that officials who fail to meet requirements and thereby contribute to environmental damage will be identified and not be appointed to other important positions or promoted; they may also be held responsible for damages even after they have left office.

As an important local organ of state power, local People's Congresses should also play stronger roles in supervising and ensuring the execution of national laws and regulations to avoid the 'blind spot' of environmental policy implementation. Among the 12 pilot regions, Chongqing and Hebei province have taken the lead in publishing documents on the vertical management framework for environmental monitoring, inspection and enforcement. They have also teased out regulations for environmental protection obligations, measures for environmental inspection and detailed rules on the accountability of leading party and government officials for ecological damage caused.

Second, centralising the data management system can be an important entry point for refining the function and responsibility of environmental protection organisations at different levels – from cities and districts to counties and townships. The accuracy of environment-related information serves as the basis for monitoring, risk assessment, policy evaluation and further adjustment. This power should be centralised to upper level government agencies to guarantee scientific validity and fairness. Some specific functions of the state environmental apparatus, such as environmental monitoring and internal inspection, should be further appropriated to city EPBs, with these functions mainly serving as a means for higher level departments to hold their subordinates accountable. District- and county-level EPBs would retain the key functions, such as the inspection of industrial facilities, that allow them to enforce environmental regulations at the local level, but these functions would be derived from national data standards and collections.

Third, a comprehensive environmental governance network, combined with a more powerful incentive structure for public participation, should also be established. Greater policy and financial support can help to encourage government units, industry, non-government organisations and volunteers to contribute more to environmental protection. Following from this, publicly accessible information platforms should be created to provide information in order to promote public participation in policy enforcement. Governance should, therefore, be pushed to be more standardised, normalised and legalised (Jin et al. 2016).

In this regard, future research should consider how institutional reform relates to other types of policy innovation and contextual factors in forming the configurations necessary for effective environmental management performance. Answering the question of whether historical institutionalism or rational choice is more correct will also require additional analysis and theoretical elaboration in this research area. Potentially, extending this topic of inquiry towards a longitudinal study could offer more insights and possible solutions.

References

Bell, S & Hindmoor, A 2009, *Rethinking Governance. The Centrality of the State in Modern Society*, Cambridge University Press, doi.org/10.1017/CBO9780511814617.

Berry, FS & Berry, WD 1999, 'Innovation and diffusion models in policy research', in PA Sabatier (ed), *Theories of the Policy Process*, Westview Press, Cambridge.

——— 2007, 'Innovation and diffusion models in policy research', in PA Sabatier (ed), *Theories of the Policy Process*, 2nd edn, Westview Press, Cambridge.

Berry, WD & Lowery, D 1987, *Understanding United States Government Growth: An Empirical Analysis of the Postwar Era*, Praeger Publishers, New York.

Biesenbender, S & Tosun, J 2014, 'Domestic politics and the diffusion of international policy innovations', *Global Environmental Change*, vol 29, 424–33, doi.org/10.1016/j.gloenvcha.2014.04.001.

Brombal, D, Wang, H, Pizzol, L, Critto, A, Giubilato, G & Guo, G 2015, 'Soil environmental management systems for contaminated sites in China and the EU: common challenges and perspectives for lesson drawing', *Land Use Policy*, vol 48, pp 286–98, doi.org/10.1016/j.landusepol.2015.05.015.

Brown, LA 1981, *Innovation Diffusion: A New Perspective*, Methuen, London.

Cao, X 2012, 'Global networks and domestic policy convergence: a network explanation of policy changes', *World Politics*, vol 64, no 30, pp 375–425, doi.org/10.1017/S0043887112000081.

CNSTOCK News 2014, 'Three main measures will be taken against Shanghai's air pollution', 24 Jan, stock.cnstock.com/stock/smk_gszbs/201401/2893760. htm [in Chinese].

Davis, C & Feiock, R 1992, 'Testing theories of state hazardous waste regulation: a reassessment of the Williams and Matheny study', *American Politics Quarterly*, vol 20, no 4, pp 501–11, doi.org/10.1177/1532673X9202000408.

Dongfang Daily News 2012, 'Shanghai per capita GDP exceeds Beijing', 20 Jan, web.archive.org/web/20120123031652/http://www.dfdaily.com/html/3/ 2012/1/20/733021.shtml [in Chinese].

Dusenbury, L & Hansen, WB 2004, 'Pursuing the course from research practice', *Prevention Science*, vol 5, no 1, pp 55–59, doi.org/10.1023/B:PREV.00000 13982.20860.19.

Dye, TR 1966, *Politics, Economics, and the Public Policy Outcomes in the American States*, American Politics Research Series, Rand McNally, Chicago.

Elkins, Z, Guzman AT & Simmons, BA 2006, 'Competing for capital: the diffusion of bilateral investment treaties, 1960–2000', *International Organization*, vol 60, no 4, pp 811–46, doi.org/10.1017/S0020818306060279.

General Offices of the CPC Central Committee & the State Council 2016, *Guidelines for the Pilot Reforms for a Vertical Management System for the Environmental Monitoring, Supervision, Inspection, and Enforcement by the Environmental Protection Branches below Provincial Level*, 22 Sep, www. gov.cn/zhengce/2016-09/22/content_5110853.htm [in Chinese].

Gerrits, LM & Verweij, S 2013, 'Critical realism as a meta-framework for understanding the relationships between complexity and qualitative comparative analysis', *Journal of Critical Realism*, vol 12, no 2, pp 166–82, doi.org/10.1179/rea.12.2.p663527490513071.

Gray, V 1973, 'Innovation in the states: a diffusion study', *American Political Science Review*, vol 67, no 4, pp 1174–85, doi.org/10.2307/1956539.

—— 1994, 'Competition, emulation, and policy innovation', in LC Dodd & C Jillson (eds), *New Perspectives on American Politics*, Congressional Quarterly Press, Washington.

Gray, V & Lowery, D 1996, *The Population Ecology of Interest Representation: Lobbying Communities in the American States*, University of Michigan Press, Ann Arbor, doi.org/10.3998/mpub.14367.

Jahiel, AR 1998, 'The organization of environmental protection in China', in RL Edmonds (ed), *Managing the Chinese Environment*, Oxford University Press, pp 33–64.

Jensen, JL 2004, 'A multi-population comparison of the diffusion of public organizations and policies across space and time', *The Policy Studies Journal*, vol 32, no 1, pp 109–27, doi.org/10.1111/j.1541-0072.2004.00055.x.

Jin, Y, Andersson, H & Zhang, S 2016, 'Air pollution control policies in China: a retrospective and prospects', *International Journal of Environmental Research and Public Health*, vol 13, p 1219, doi.org/10.3390/ijerph13121219.

Jordan, AJ & Huitema, D 2014, 'Innovations in climate policy: the politics of invention, diffusion and evaluation', *Environmental Politics*, vol 5, pp 715–34, doi.org/10.1080/09644016.2014.923614.

Li, Z 2016, 'China restructures its environmental agencies from the bottom up', 16 Apr, *Sixth Tone*, www.sixthtone.com/news/786/china-restructures-its-environmental-agencies-bottom.

Lo, CWH & Leung, SW 2000, 'Environmental agency and public opinion in Guangzhou: the limits of a popular approach to environmental governance', *China Quarterly*, no 161, pp 677–704, doi.org/10.1017/S0305741000014612.

Ma, X & Ortolano, L 2000, *Environmental Regulation in China: Institutions, Enforcement, and Compliance*, Rowman and Littlefield, Lanham, Maryland; Oxford.

Massey, E, Biesbroek, R, Huitema, D & Jordan, AJ 2014, 'Climate policy innovation: the adoption and diffusion of adaptation policies across Europe', *Global Environmental Change*, vol 29, pp 434–43, doi.org/10.1016/j.gloenvcha.2014.09.002.

Mills, JH & Waite, TA 2009, 'Economic prosperity, biodiversity conservation, and the environmental Kuznets curve', *Ecological Economics*, vol 68, no 7, pp 2087–95, doi.org/10.1016/j.ecolecon.2009.01.017.

Mintrom, M 1997, 'Policy entrepreneurs and the diffusion of innovation', *American Journal of Political Science*, vol 42, no 3, pp 738–70, doi.org/10.2307/2111674.

Mooney, CZ & Lee, M-H 1995, 'Legislating morality in the American states: the case of pre-Roe abortion regulation reform', *American Journal of Political Science*, vol 39, pp 599–627, doi.org/10.2307/2111646.

National Bureau of Statistics of China 2017, *National Data*, data.stats.gov.cn/easyquery.htm?cn=E0103.

Newman, J, Raine, J & Skelcher, C 2000, *Innovation and Best Practice in Local Government*, The Stationery Office, London.

Nice, DC 1994, *Policy Innovation in State Government*, Iowa State University Press, Ames.

Nutley, S, Downe, J, Martin, S & Grace, C 2012, 'Policy transfer and convergence within the UK: the case of local government performance improvement regimes', *Policy & Politics*, vol 40, no 2, pp 193–209, doi.org/10.1332/147084411X581880.

Ostrom, E 2005, *Understanding Institutional Diversity*, Princeton University Press.

Potoski, M 2001, 'Clean air federalism: do states race to the bottom?', *Public Administration Review*, vol 61, no 3, pp 335–43, doi.org/10.1111/0033-3352.00034.

Ragin, CC 1987, *The Comparative Method: Moving Beyond Qualitative and Quantitative Strategies*, University of California Press, Berkeley.

—— 2018, *User's Guide to Fuzzy-Set/Qualitative Comparative Analysis 3.0*, Department of Sociology, University of California.

Rihoux, B & Ragin, CC 2009, *Configurational Comparative Methods: Qualitative Comparative Analysis (QCA) and Related Techniques*, CA:SAGE, Thousand Oaks, doi.org/10.4135/9781452226569.

Ringquist, EJ 1994, 'Policy influence and policy responsiveness in state pollution control', *Policy Studies Journal*, vol 2, no 1, pp 25–43, doi.org/10.1111/j.1541-0072.1994.tb02178.x.

Rogers, EM 1995, *Diffusion of Innovations*, 4th edn, Free Press, New York.

Rose, R 2005, *Learning from Comparative Public Policy: A Practical Guide*, Routledge, New York, doi.org/10.4324/9780203585108.

Savage, R 1978, 'Policy innovativeness as a trait of the American states', *Journal of Politics*, vol 40, pp 212–19, doi.org/10.2307/2129985.

Schneider, CQ & Wagemann, C 2012, *Set-theoretic Methods for the Social Sciences: A Guide to Qualitative Comparative Analysis (QCA)*, Cambridge University Press, doi.org/10.1017/CBO9781139004244.

Sims, H 1999, 'One-fifth of the sky: China's environmental stewardship', *World Development*, vol 27, no 7, pp 1227–45, doi.org/10.1016/S0305-750X(99)00051-0.

Stadelmann, M & Castro, P 2014, 'Climate policy innovation in the south – domestic and international determinants of renewable energy policies in developing and emerging countries', *Global Environmental Change*, vol 29, pp 413–23, doi.org/10.1016/j.gloenvcha.2014.04.011.

Van, RB 2006, 'Implementation of Chinese environmental law: regular enforcement and political campaigns', *Development and Change*, vol 37, no 1, pp 57–74, doi.org/10.1111/j.0012-155X.2006.00469.x.

Walker, JL 1969, 'The diffusion of innovations among the American states', *American Political Science Review*, vol 63, pp 880–99, doi.org/10.2307/1954434.

Walker, RM, Avellaneda, CN & Berry, FS 2011, 'Exploring the diffusion of innovation among high and low innovative localities', *Public Management Review*, vol 13, no 1, pp 95–125, doi.org/10.1080/14719037.2010.501616.

Wang, A 2013, 'The search for sustainable legitimacy: environmental law and bureaucracy in China', *Harvard Environmental Law Review*, vol 365, doi.org/10.2139/ssrn.2128167.

Wang, C & Lin, Z 2010, 'Environmental policies in China over the past 10 years: progress, problems and prospects', conference paper, International Society for Environmental Information Sciences.

Wang, J 2009, 'Thirty years' rule of environmental law in China: retrospect and reassessment', *Journal of China University of Geosciences*, vol 9, pp 3–9 [in Chinese].

Williams, BA & Matheny, AR 1984, 'Testing theories of social regulation: hazardous waste regulation in the American states', *Journal of Politics*, vol 46, vol 2, pp 428–59, doi.org/10.2307/2130969.

Wright Jr, GC, Erikson, RS & McIver, JP 1987, 'Public opinion and policy liberalism in the American states', *American Journal of Political Science*, vol 31, Nov, pp 980–1001, doi.org/10.2307/2111232.

Xinhua News 2016, 'How are the environmental agencies managed vertically?', 29 Sep, www.xinhuanet.com/politics/2016-09/26/c_129298809.htm [in Chinese].

Yue, JC 2016, '14 years vertical management reform in Shaanxi Environmental System make "brother" as "stranger"', 20 Oct, www.infzm.com/content/120347 [in Chinese].

Zhang, K, Wen, Z & Peng, L 2007, 'Environmental policies in China: evolvement, features and evaluation', *Chinese Journal of Population Resources and Environment*, vol 17, no 2, pp 1–7, doi.org/10.1016/S1872-583X(07)60006-0.

Zhu, X 2014, 'Mandate versus championship: vertical government intervention and diffusion of innovation in public services in authoritarian China', *Public Management Review*, vol 16, no 1, pp 117–39, doi.org/10.1080/14719037.2013.798028.

10

MEETINGS MATTER

An exploratory case study on
informal accountability and policy
implementation in mainland China

Bo Yan and Jiannan Wu

Introduction

Over the past three decades, mainland China's pursuit of 'top-down' strategies when directing local governments to introduce new policies has encountered significant 'wicked' problems that have inhibited improvements in government performance. To address these problems, the 18th Communist Party of China (CPC) Central Committee announced an unprecedented comprehensive reform to transform governmental functions and invigorate the market, and emphasised the importance of strengthening the implementation responsibilities of city-level governments.

The difficulties of implementing policy are in part due to deficiencies in mainland China's accountability system, leading some to call for the establishment and enforcement of formal accountability (e.g. through administrative punishment or sanctions) to encourage local cadres to achieve the central government's policy objectives. In particular, some proponents advocate the benefits and necessity of formal accountability tools, which may result in the stigmatising of local cadres, with the failure to implement policy ascribed to their misconduct. The adoption of these tools could deter irresponsible behaviour and make cadres comply with CPC policy implementation.

Formal accountability is not a panacea, however, and in practice is often accompanied by specific dilemmas. The approach usually refers to ex post facto processes in governance rather than ex ante inputs (Bovens 2007), so the accountability mechanism usually means punishment or sanctions for those held accountable for their conduct and performance (Behn 2001). Punishing the bad and rewarding the good in public sector cadres may appear reasonable, but it is difficult to foster unsolicited compliance or inspire proactive behaviour ex ante. Further, the accountability paradox suggests that strengthening accountability may hinder performance improvement or even encourage failure (Chan & Gao 2009).

In fact, the formal accountability mechanism involves the CPC's centralised structure overlaying the state (the executive), the legislature and the judiciary, and operating through mainland China's five levels of decentralised government (Podger & Yan 2013). There is no strong evidence that this can prevent idle policy implementation, such as 'implementing the essence of a previous meeting by convening the next meeting'. The prevailing sluggishness of policy implementation in mainland China suggests that some public sector leaders pursue substantive action slowly, cautiously waiting for each other to make further progress on specific policy implementation.

In practice, mainland China's governments do not solely rely on the formal accountability system to implement policy. China's complex accountability system differs from the Western system in that it consists of formal and informal mechanisms. Much of the reform agenda involves addressing wicked public problems characterised by complexity and uncertainty, and depends on cross-agency collaboration.

Government leaders find it difficult to use the formal accountability system to coordinate and constrain sectors administered by peer leaders. This unsettled situation requires the blurring of formal accountability lines and taking a holistic approach across organisational boundaries (Christensen & Lægreid 2016). It also generates more space for informal accountability to affect informal behaviour, including networking through cross-agency meetings.

Government leaders often work to solve wicked problems by establishing numerous small leading teams with many meetings at various levels. The question arises, therefore, do small leading-team meetings matter for policy implementation in mainland China? If so, why do they matter and what are the underlying social dynamics behind them? Little is currently known about how policy implementation is facilitated by cross-agency meetings, or how these shape informal accountability at mainland China's local government level.

To address this gap, this study explores how regular cross-agency meetings of a local government can contribute to policy implementation under pilot reform in mainland China, from the perspective of informal accountability. We use an exploratory case study to identify the key elements and ethnographic methods to collect data, which provide the empirical evidence for developing a theoretical framework. This case offers empirical evidence from mainland China, through which we can compare local government policy implementation with the experiences of other countries. The research must also extend from a macro-level analysis of accountability structure to a micro-level analysis of the subjective experiences of the actors involved in a specific accountability relationship (Yang & Dubnick 2016). The findings will further the understanding of mainland China's administrative accountability system and its effects, and reveal the mechanism of mainland China's local policy implementation from a new perspective.

The article consists of four parts. First, we introduce the research background and clarify the research questions. The research design of the case study follows, along with a concise description of the case itself. We then take an ethnographic approach to analyse the effects of small leading-team meetings, and construct a preliminary framework to illustrate the informal accountability involved under the context of policy reform. Finally, the conclusion includes a summary of the academic contribution and presents implications for practitioners.

Research design

We use a single–case study strategy to investigate the effects of informal accountability associated with small leading-team meetings on the implementation of complex policy reforms at the local governmental level in mainland China. This strategy is particularly relevant when 'the number of variables of interest far outstrips the number of data points', and where the research questions mainly focus on 'how' and 'why'. The method is typically more explanatory than others, and can deal with operational links that must be traced over time (Yin 2003).

Despite the obvious weakness of any exploratory case study, it is still an effective method of bringing rich qualitative evidence to mainstream deductive research. The case need not be representative of a specific population (Eisenhardt & Graebner 2007), although it should aim to illustrate a broader experience. It provides a snapshot, enabling us to illuminate meaningful characteristics of complex phenomena in a real-life setting without trying to control the context. For example, Yasuda (2015) used a case of failed food safety policy implementation to illustrate China's broad 'politics of scale', including central–local conflicts and trade-offs in its scale-management framework (Yasuda 2015).

For our selected case, J City's county-level government (J Gov't) in eastern mainland China, we analysed the small leading-team meetings in which pilot reform was discussed. J City is a satellite of Q City, which is a provincial-level municipality in terms of its social and economic development planning, and thus has considerable fiscal autonomy, significantly higher official staffing authority than other municipalities, and strong fiscal conditions. Mainland China's county system has existed for two millennia and its boundaries have remained largely intact and, as the saying goes, 'good governance of the whole country depends on the counties being well governed'. Of the four levels of sub-national government, county-level governments are endowed with wide-ranging responsibilities, including comprehensive functions for implementing higher level government policies and for initiating and administering their own policies (Wu et al. 2017).

Following the guidance of the Q City government, J Gov't launched a comprehensive pilot reform program in August 2013 that covered economic, administrative and social affairs. As academic experts invited to help J Gov't implement the reform proposal, we regularly conducted field investigations and collected data for the period April 2013 to January 2014. Ethnographic methods, including participatory observations, in-depth interviews and document reviews, were also used to elicit findings on the realities of J Gov't's practice. We also used textual and social network analysis to explore the complex set of relationships and to achieve a degree of data triangulation.

Case description

Context

The pilot reforms of the J Gov't are commonly regarded as reflecting a particularly active response to the national innovation-driven development strategy of the central government. According to the State Premier Keqiang Li, 'Deeper reform is the way forward', which reveals the ambition and willingness of mainland China's government to promote structural reform and to expedite the transition to a sustainable growth model, increasingly driven by innovation and consumption rather than state-led investment. A combination of policy tools is expected to be assembled to help drive regional development, and to strike a better balance between the state and the market by offering a more enabling business environment and a leaner but effective government.

A key challenge to this ambition is how local government can make progress on this grand reform strategy. The model of 'planning and experimentation under hierarchy' (Heilmann & Melton 2013) suggests that it is common practice for higher level government in mainland China to provide local governments with both policy safeguards and policy discretion to 'go ahead of the rest and try new things out'. J Gov't was urged to launch comprehensive reform in the name of transforming government functions, mainly by focusing on streamlining administration and delegating power, strengthening regulation and ensuring better provision of public goods and services.

The reform covers 10 policy domains, 41 policy categories and 74 policy tasks in total,[1] so all of the township-level governments and almost all of the principal bureaus in J Gov't were involved in this policy experiment. The leadership team consists of the mayor, one first deputy mayor (FDM), and five deputy mayors (DMs). The FDM and DMs are peers and each has different duties in assisting the mayor in directing and steering subordinates. They are each in charge of managing a number

---

1   The 10 policy domains are: removing administrative approval, removing administrative charge, removing certification, centralising administrative approval, centralising law enforcement, centralising trading, centralising payment, streamlining business registration, normalising management of NGOs, and trade and investment facilitation. Corresponding policy tools reconcile the demands from National Structural Reform on '*Streamlining* administration and *delegating* power, *strengthening* regulation, *facilitating* public goods provision'.

of the principal bureaus, and coordinating the vertical administrative institutions (VAIs). A VAI is a type of bureau directly managed by and accountable to the respective central or provincial government bureaus rather than city-level government.

For example, J Gov't has no power to appoint or remove the leadership of the Bureau of Quality and Technology Supervision (BQTS) as it is a provincial VAI, whereas most of the other bureaus (e.g. the Administrative Service Center (ASC) and the Bureau of Human Resources and Social Security) are jurisdictional administrative institutions and their personnel and fiscal or other vital resources are dependent on J Gov't. Thus, the complex formal accountability structure makes it difficult for the FDM or DMs to coordinate each other's subordinate sectors (whether or not they are VAI) as they each have different 'turf' to maintain.

The local cadres, however, recognised the considerable complexity, uncertainty and risk associated with the reform and informally expressed unwillingness and a lack of ability to promote the reform locally. The leaders of J Gov't were squeezed from above and below in that they not only had to conduct the pilot reform in response to the direction from Q City, but also had to address the serious concerns and lobbying of their subordinates. They feared that, at the beginning of the process, 'the more active the reform is, the more passive the individual is'. Many of the bureau leaders are middle-level cadres responsible for implementing aspects of the reform and reporting progress to the J Gov't, and they were concerned that their leaders were ignoring their bureaus' tight budgets and heavy ongoing duties, along with other obstacles to implementation.

Even frontline workers who were grassroots cadres in bureaus and township-level governments were fearful that the reform was too burdensome for them, and some complained that 'we are incapable of getting things done in this timeframe'. They also believed that they would be trapped if they made and implemented new policies faster than superior agencies ('The more aggressive the junior staff member is, the more embarrassing it will be if their changes are not first endorsed by the higher-up' ---下动上不动越动越被动). Thus, many local cadres were reluctant to implement the reform at the beginning and responded slowly to the directive.

Conduct of reform

To promote and manage the implementation of the pilot policy reform, J Gov't established a small leading team and set up a series of regular meetings. The team's regular weekly or bi-weekly meetings were led by the FDM, with chief leaders from 13 selected bureaus constituting the core ongoing membership. Representatives of other relevant bureaus were invited to these meetings as necessary. In some cases, the CPC party secretary of J City, the mayor, the other DMs, and even deputy leaders of Q City in charge of corresponding projects, were also invited to attend. The FDM was always the de facto moderator of the meetings, delegated by the CPC's standing committee in J City to coordinate almost all bureaus involved in the pilot reform.

The meetings were organised to follow a series of steps for each explicit reform topic. First, the moderator revealed the problems and opportunities associated with policy implementation. Next, the bureau in charge of solving a specific problem was required to report on progress, provide relevant information and describe analytical investigations. The moderator facilitated subsequent dialogue among the meeting members who would then make or adjust decisions jointly, or agree to a means of conflict resolution for the topic addressed.

Meetings of this sort generate a policy-mandated network where an administrative superordinate actor can impose coordination and collaboration on other actors (Saz-Carranza et al. 2016). In this instance the FDM, as the meeting moderator, is the superordinate actor who sets the rules of the game, and has the unique authority to ask each actor to be responsible for their own performance. Moreover, they are obliged to follow up on previous decisions and commitments. Unlike meetings in private organisations, which usually serve as a venue for accomplishing work-related goals (Odermatt et al. 2017), this kind of meeting provides the means for displaying each actor's performance to others and involves image-building and other political behaviours. It requires a focus on the systematic progress of policy implementation, while also emphasising a shared approach to performance improvement through interaction within the network.

Consequences

The meetings have resulted in an obvious structural change from hierarchical management to flattening and networking. J Gov't's previous formal hierarchical leadership structure has been transformed into a network associated with many mutual relationships. Although the small leading team is a temporary organisation and the network is ad hoc and additional to the formal structure, this change is meaningful. It engenders a blurring of lines of accountability, however, and some interactions in practice are different from the pre-reform formal line of accountability. For example, bureaus such as the ASC and BQTS have clearly become core actors within the policy-mandated network rather than of equal importance to other peripheral bureaus, as they were before the reform. They are now required to be directly accountable to the FDM regardless of their original domain or duties.

Consequently, almost all of the tasks required for policy implementation were completed by means of this network. The concerns of the local cadres before the reform were unfounded, and Q City government and higher level agencies admired the pilot reform of J Gov't. The party secretary of J Gov't was promoted to be one of the main leaders of the Q Gov't soon after the success of the J Gov't pilot reform. He is regarded as representative of how successful policy entrepreneurship can promote the transformation of governmental functions.

Discussion

According to this case analysis, the regular meetings of the small leading team have played a vital role in promoting policy implementation under the reform launched by J Gov't. The effects of this kind of management action, particularly in the Chinese context, have not been fully explained. The informal accountability resulting from the meetings has influenced local actors' behaviour through a combination of mechanisms that support the accomplishment of the policy reform's targets and objectives. In the following sections, we elaborate on this informal accountability and the corresponding effects on policy implementation, and draw on additional insights to further understand the informal accountability dynamics.

As we observed, the bureaus involved in the small leading-team meetings were held accountable to the FDM, who was authorised to coordinate them regardless of the formal hierarchical structure that applied before the pilot reform. There was little formal agreement, however, on how each of the actors was to implement the policies or be held accountable. The objectives and the responsibilities of each actor were largely implicit and were subject to constant change and refinement, and the dialogue and agreement among the meeting members was mainly dependent on the moderator's improvisation and discretion. In addition, the rewards and sanctions for success or failure were ambiguous and neither ex ante or ex post formal monetary incentives or punishments have been applied so far. The interactions across meetings do not only rely on formalised rules, but also on being reproduced via informal *guanxi* such as patron–client relations and interpersonal relationships.

Informal accountability can be distinguished from formal accountability in several aspects such as facilitative behaviour, norms, and informal rewards and sanctions. First, the meetings exhibited explicit facilitative behaviour through relationship building, frequent and ongoing communication, information sharing, and recognising and acknowledging responsibility for mistakes. This gave public officials a nudge to achieve compliance by frequent scrutiny in the meetings. Second, norms refer to the shared values or the informal code of conduct among network actors, by which they can distinguish between appropriate and inappropriate behaviour in specific settings (Romzek et al. 2012), such as weekly meetings. An obvious norm derives from the fact that the local cadres involved in pilot reform were concerned about the legitimacy of their conduct. Finally, informal rewards and sanctions were key components of informal accountability in this study, along with the meetings. Instead of additional bonuses, career promotions or punishments, informal rewards and sanctions were revealed and concealed through the subtle and intricate gestures of meeting members.

As described, uncertainty and risk aversion made local officials reluctant to pursue policy implementation before the pilot reform. In essence, these officials exhibit two types of behavioural characteristics. First, they worried about the additional workload associated with the reform. In China's centralised institutional system, it is difficult to avoid this lack of sustainable incentives and to achieve the corresponding commitment. Through the series of meetings, however, these rational actors decided to collaborate and proceed with the policy implementation. As noted, evidence shows that informal accountability, incorporated in the small leading team meetings and supported by interpersonal ties, has contributed to the success of J Gov't pilot reform during the policy implementation process. This innovative approach ensured the success of their endeavour.

Compared with the subsequent comprehensive reform across mainland China that took place one year later, the pilot reform enacted by J Gov't displayed proactive and exploratory initiatives, which demonstrate the feasibility of and the possible barriers to conducting reform. This exploratory case study provides a unique insight into the institutional logic behind the actions of Chinese local government in response to the ongoing reform directed from the top down. Our analysis shows that informal accountability, consisting of informal facilitative behaviour, norms, and sanctions and rewards, can contribute significantly to reinforce motivation and build capacity in local actors. Regular cross-sectoral meetings play a key role through informal accountability and encourage local cadres to meet their reform responsibilities in the local political arena.

Conclusion

This study extends previous research on policy implementation by focusing on a distinct organisational phenomenon: the meetings of a small leading team to promote pilot reform. We derive preliminary findings from an exploratory case study in mainland China. First, this reveals that local government leadership can successfully utilise informal accountability generated by regular meetings authorised to promote the policy implementation. This type of meeting cultivates a networking and holistic approach among multiple bureaus, involving interaction and joint decision-making, where the broad reform goals have been specified and implemented by local government mandate.

The case of J Gov't's pilot reform provides a specific example of comprehensive administrative reform in mainland China today. As a pioneer of this round of reform, J Gov't provides a positive example for other local governments to implement reform. J Gov't was prudent and smart to comply with directions from superior agencies while making the policy implementation feasible in practice. The example offers two lessons when finding a solution to difficult-to-implement problems. First, it is essential to select leaders with qualities of perseverance and political wisdom, who can reinforce the motivations of subordinates and build up organisational capacity to complete tasks adroitly. Second, effective meetings provide a political arena for designing, implementing and evaluating several policy issues before scaling-up the local experiment. These lessons contribute to the understanding of how to promote ongoing comprehensive reform.

Inevitably, this study has significant limitations. While the case study approach is an effective strategy for developing a theory, this method does not allow the theory to be tested for more general application. This exploratory study, however, demonstrates a local government behavioural pattern when responding to the advocacy and requirements of the 3rd Plenary Session of the 18th CPC Central Committee. Alternative patterns for promoting policy implementation under the reform may be applicable, and thus further comparative and quantitative studies are required.

References

Behn, RD 2001, *Rethinking Democratic Accountability*, Brookings Institution Press, Washington, DC.

Bovens, M 2007, 'Analyzing and assessing public accountability: a conceptual framework', *European Law Journal*, vol 13, pp 447–68, doi.org/10.1111/j.1468-0386.2007.00378.x.

Chan, HS & Gao, J 2009, 'Putting the cart before the horse: accountability or performance?', *The Australian Journal of Public Administration*, vol 68, pp S51–S61, doi.org/10.1111/j.1467-8500.2009.00621.x.

Christensen, T & Lægreid, P 2016, 'Accountability relations in unsettled situations: administrative reform and crises', working paper, Stein Rokkan Centre for Social Studies.

Eisenhardt, KM & Graebner, ME 2007, 'Theory building from cases: opportunities and challenges', *Academy of Management Journal*, vol 50, pp 25–32, doi.org/10.5465/amj.2007.24160888.

Heilmann, S & Melton, O 2013, 'The reinvention of development planning in China, 1993–2012', *Modern China*, vol 39, pp 580–628, doi.org/10.1177/0097700413497551.

Odermatt, I, König, CJ, Kleinmann, M, Nussbaumer, R, Rosenbaum, A, Olien, JL & Rogelberg, SG 2017, 'On leading meetings: linking meeting outcomes to leadership styles', *Journal of Leadership & Organizational Studies*, vol 24, pp 189–200, doi.org/10.1177/1548051816655992.

Podger, A & Yan, B 2013, 'Public administration in China and Australia: different worlds but similar challenges', *Australian Journal of Public Administration*, vol 72, pp 201–19, doi.org/10.1111/1467-8500.12023.

Romzek, B, LeRoux, K & Blackmar, JM 2012, 'A preliminary theory of informal accountability among network organizational actors', *Public Administration Review*, vol 72, pp 442–53, doi.org/10.1111/j.1540-6210.2011.02547.x.

Saz-Carranza, A, Salvador Iborra, S & Albareda, A 2016, 'The power dynamics of mandated network administrative organizations', *Public Administration Review*, vol 76, pp 449–63, doi.org/10.1111/puar.12445.

Wu, X, Ramesh, M & Yu, J 2017, 'Autonomy and performance: decentralization reforms in Zhejiang Province, China', *Public Administration and Development*, vol 37, no 2, pp 94–109, doi.org/10.1002/pad.1786.

Yang, K & Dubnick, M 2016, 'Introduction: accountability study moving to the next level', *Public Performance & Management Review*, vol 40, pp 201–07, doi.org/10.1080/15309576.2016.1266880.

Yasuda, JK Kojiro 2015, 'Why food safety fails in China: the politics of scale', *The China Quarterly*, vol 223, pp 745–69, doi.org/10.1017/S030574101500079X.

Yin, RK 2003, *Case Study Research: Design and Methods*, Sage, Los Angeles.

11

THE PERFORMANCE REGIME OF PUBLIC GOVERNANCE IN TAIWAN

From enhancing implementation to improving bureaucratic responsiveness[1]

Bennis Wai Yip So

Introduction

This chapter provides an overview of the developmental stages that have led to the application of performance-related management to government and examines performance movements in Taiwan through a critical review of the evolution of its performance regime as an institution of public governance, moving from the authoritarian era to the democratic one. This experience is compared to that of Anglophone countries. Taking advantage of and expanding on the insight from the performance regime framework offered by Colin Talbot (2008, 2010), this chapter explores the institutional context of performance movements in Taiwan and thereby identifies how various performance interventions were developed to steer public sector performance.

1   This study is sponsored by the Ministry of Science and Technology of Taiwan (NSC 102-2410-H004-163-MY2).

Taiwan's performance movements have their roots in the Kuomintang's rule of mainland China and paralleled those of Anglophone countries; however, Taiwan's path, agenda and institutions were unique, despite being influenced by the concurrent Anglophone development trend. The author argues that Taiwan experienced three waves of performance development, where the emphasis was initially on enhancing the capacity to implement development programs before gradually moving to building up bureaucratic responsiveness to the citizenry in public service delivery. The institutional context and its implications for the performance regime should be viewed in light of its developmentalism and paternalism. Democratisation then multiplied accountability holders and reshaped and complicated the original institutional context.

Although Western performance management models, including new public management (NPM), have diffused into Taiwan, this represents an instrumental learning intended to help the country realise its own purpose rather than simply a convergence with the Western path. Three specific shifting techniques of performance interventions, which combine local and foreign wisdom, have been identified: tracked monitoring, achievement/performance evaluation, and for-the-people service/quality management. These interventions were adopted to varying degrees in response to the aforementioned shifting emphasis on bureaucratic responsiveness.

These points are illustrated in this chapter through a historical review of the development of the Research, Development and Evaluation Commission (RDEC) – a ministry-level agency in charge of performance-related management – and a snapshot of the performance evaluation of social welfare programs. In the following sections, a modified version of Talbot's performance regime will be first presented as an analytical framework and, subsequently, the institutional context and the performance interventions adopted in Taiwan will be examined to facilitate a comparison with the experience of Anglophone countries.

A modified version of the performance regime framework

Studies of public sector performance are weakened if the focus is exclusively on the measurement and reporting of the performance of public organisations without considering the complicated public governance domain in which they operate. Talbot (2008, 2010) suggests that the unit of analysis should be expanded beyond the organisational level to encompass factors outside and around an organisation that may influence its performance. A performance regime, as an umbrella concept, has been raised to realise such a macro perspective.

Talbot's 'performance regime', as a framework, is composed of two elements: institutional context and performance interventions. Institutional context refers to the 'institutional environment' of individual public organisations, but Talbot uses the term in reference to institutional actors that steer the performance of these organisations. In the United Kingdom, apart from state institutions such as central and line ministries, the legislature and judicial bodies, these actors also consist of professional associations and user organisations (Talbot 2010: 92–96). This forms a web of principal–agent relations with accountability arrangements between the actors and the public organisations, wherein the organisations must, to varying degrees and in varying ways, respond to these actors.

'Performance interventions' refers to any means and action taken by institutional actors to influence performance, including performance contracts, targets and standards. Further, taking the UK Government's approach as an example, its model of interventions contains not only top-down performance management but also market-incentive mechanisms, the participation of users, and the capability and capacity building of public organisations. These four functions are officially claimed to spur 'better public services for all' (Talbot 2010: 102).

This chapter follows this framework to examine the case in Taiwan, but the author utilises the 'institutional environment' definition of 'institutional context', which not only focuses on institutional actors and the complexity of accountability arrangements but also takes into account the state–society relationship, as well as the ideas and purposes behind performance steering. This definition is especially relevant to countries with non-democratic and non-Western settings. For instance, when the aim of performance steering for the United Kingdom is claimed to promote 'better public services for all', this is not necessarily the case for other countries, even when they have adopted the same instrument. Moreover, the performance movements of Anglophone countries should not be considered as a wholly static process (van Dooren et al. 2015).

Institutional context: A comparison with Anglophone countries

Performance movements in Anglophone countries

According to a historical review by van Dooren et al. (2015),[2] Anglophone countries have witnessed eight performance movements since the 20th century. These movements can be clustered into three periods: 1) three between 1900 and the 1940s; 2) two in the 1950s to 1970s; 3) three in the 1980s to 2010s. They can also be grouped into two orientations: policy and management.

The emergence of the social survey movement (policy), scientific management and the science of administration (management), and cost accounting (management) in the early 20th century are identified as the earliest attempts at informing, understanding and standardising public performance. The rise of performance budgeting (management) in the postwar era further indicated the state's intention to build a mechanism of financial accountability.

The parallel effort of collecting social data for evaluating the development impact on society generated the social indicators movement (policy) in the 1960s. Fiscal hardship in the 1980s generated the well-known NPM movement (management) that subsequently spurred the evidence-based policy movement (policy) in the 1990s, which prescribes that facts and figures on outcomes rather than ideologies or opinions should inform policymaking. The latest movement was revisionism (management). It witnessed the revision of the financial and performance framework in the 2010s that further emphasised the use of performance information and tried to integrate it into accountability, budgeting and management processes.

---

2   An earlier version of the review can be found in van Dooren (2008).

Despite Anglophone countries experiencing more than 100 years of development, van Dooren et al. (2015) argue that the basic ideas of performance management are stable. This point is exemplified by the case of the New York Bureau of Municipal Research (NYBMR), which was already engaged in performance measurement in the early 20th century, with many features consistent with the contemporary version (see Williams 2003). What has changed is the technological advancement that helped materialise ideas and improve measurement, as well as the increase in institutionalisation and professionalisation of performance information usage.

Another aspect of stability noted by van Dooren et al. (2015) is that the policy and management orientations coexisted rather than rotated during each period. The process of the movements, however, reflected a pendulum swing between the strategies of depoliticisation and politicisation. The first wave of the movements was to separate politics from administration (e.g. scientific management), while the movements concerning budgetary reforms demonstrated the intention of political executives to exercise control over administration. The promotion of an evidence-based policy movement appears to depoliticise policymaking (van Dooren 2008). The increasing significance of enhanced fiscal accountability as a core aim of the performance movements in Anglophone countries should also be noted.

Background of Taiwan's performance movements

Taiwan has its own storyline of performance movements, albeit under the shadow of Anglophone countries. This story can be traced back to the Kuomintang's rule in mainland China during the Second Sino-Japanese War (1937–45), when the idea of performance management was initiated and experimented with. We can see its continuance in Taiwan, where all government agencies dedicate a unit (or at least a staff member for street-level agencies) to address tasks concerning performance management. Since the establishment of the RDEC under the Executive Yuan (the highest authority of the state's executive branch) in 1969 (reshuffled into the National Development Council (NDC) in 2014), this function has been known as 'research and evaluation' (R&E). Local governments duplicate this setting and all special municipalities have an RDEC for R&E tasks. Without an RDEC, a county-level government assigns R&E tasks to a staff agency, usually a planning bureau.

The establishment of R&E agencies/units and functions in Taiwan's governments arose from an administrative reform to enforce the idea of the administrative trinity system (ATS), coined by Chiang Kai-shek, the then supreme leader of Kuomintang and China, in 1940. This can be considered the first modern reform in China to focus on the topic of 'administration'. Why 'administration'? Because Chiang was discontented with the poor enforcement of national policies at the time. In his seminal address to present the ATS concept, titled 'Principles of administration: an outline of the administrative trinity system', on 1 December 1940, Chiang defined the principles of administration as implementing political orders (Chiang 1954: 1).

He further noted that the most serious defect in China's politics at the time was a shortage of talent to conscientiously enforce these orders (Chiang 1954: 2). In another address to a cadre training class on 6 December 1940, Chiang attributed poor performance to 'the absence of a well-established supervision system and the failure to develop precise and practical evaluation methods'. In addition, the problem also lay in the 'disconnection between implementation and planning'. Overall, his diagnosis was that planning, implementation and evaluation (supervision) were not well linked. The ATS aimed to effectively connect these three parts (RDEC 1989a: 5). In this regard, the ATS was policy-oriented, especially concerning the enforcement of policy or implementability that was supposed to be enhanced by using evaluation or monitoring tools. The evaluation in turn provided feedback for planning purposes.

Chiang's initiative can be considered a Chinese version of Woodrow Wilson's *Study of Administration* (1887). This Chinese version did not, however, call for developing a field of administration that '[lay] outside the proper sphere of politics' (Wilson 1887: 210), which later evolved into the notion of a politics–administration dichotomy. What Chiang contributed, rather, was his identification of distinct functions between politics and administration and his calling for the development of the talent of administration.

This initiative was not followed by the establishment of a politically neutral civil service. Interestingly, the then prevailing scientific management movement also appealed to Chiang, but it was promoted not only to enhance administrative efficiency but also to serve in building the nation and to establish an 'omnipotent government' (RDEC 1989a: 10, 35, 90).

In this sense, for Chiang, an administration equipped with scientific management was only an extension of politics for the state-led purpose of development.

During the period from 1941 to 1947, two institutions were established to realise the concept of the ATS. One was the Central Planning Bureau (CPB) and the other was the Party–Government Work Evaluation Commission (PWEC). The CPB took charge of the state's general policy planning and examination of political and economic development plans of party–government agencies; the PWEC took charge of the evaluation of the performance of party–government agencies. The new institutions had a limited impact during the wartime era.

Despite the failure of the reform, prototypes for many R&E practices advocated by Chiang in his ATS address were already sprouting and were later transplanted into Taiwan. *The Rules of Evaluation of Party–Government Works*, promulgated in June 1941, stipulated how an evaluation exercise for government agencies should be conducted. The evaluation involved reviewing written work reports and an annual site visit. The rules already required work reports to present statistical data that would help project the work's progress. An agency's evaluation report was expected to compare its performance with that of the previous year.

Cross-agency performance comparison was expected to be conducted for subsequent sanctions and rewards (PWEC 1941). To further realise the ATS, in 1943, all party–government agencies were required to establish a Planning and Evaluation Committee for performance management. Moreover, to enhance work efficiency and skill, agencies were encouraged to organise various job competitions (Li 1953: 202–04). The aforementioned practices appear surprisingly similar to the concept of a 'competitive government', which was advocated in one of the major NPM works, *Reinventing Government* (Osborne & Gaebler 1992).

During the war, the ATS had already embraced the principles of contemporary performance management, such as in the case of the NYBMR. Its lack of impact was due to the absence of techniques and practical skills to fulfil the given principles. However, learning and transfer of knowledge was not undertaken until the Kuomintang's rule in Taiwan.

The R&E system in Taiwan

The CPB and the PWEC were abolished after the enforcement of the constitution of the Republic of China in 1947. The fall of the Kuomintang's rule on the mainland in 1949 further suspended the development of the ATS. The émigré regime in Taiwan relaunched the evaluation exercise in the name of 'achievement evaluation' as early as 1951, but administrative reforms were not salient in the first years of its rule on the island. Indeed, an across-the-board administrative re-engineering was not launched until the end of 1966, when Chiang ordered the Executive Yuan to carry out a thorough administrative overhaul. He further suggested that each party–government organ should establish a research unit to study methods of improving their management operations and of utilising monitoring and evaluation for improvement (RDEC 1989a: 179–80). Chiang's idea was later crystallised into the founding of the RDEC in March 1969 and subsequently into other R&E agencies or units in central and local government agencies.

The founding of this staff agency marked a new attempt to realise the ATS. The RDEC, to a large extent, combined the functions of the CPB and the PWEC. From the perspective of its institutional context, in addition to the basic principal–agent relationship between levels in the administrative hierarchy, from June 1969 the RDEC, together with the Council for Economic Planning and Development (CEPD) and the National Science Council (NSC) (both being ministry-level agencies under the Executive Yuan), formed a systemic monitoring mechanism to respectively oversee performance in three functional areas: administration, economic development, and science and technology development. The RDEC played the role of coordinator among the three oversight institutions. Moreover, the RDEC was the government's think tank, conducting research on administrative reforms and taking charge of various reforms concerning the overall performance improvement of government agencies.

The RDEC, as well as other R&E units affiliated with various agencies, formed nodes for coordination with external accountability holders, including the Legislative Yuan (the national legislature) and the Control Yuan (the state supervision organ). The R&E agencies/units at various levels of government were assigned to help follow up on the concerns and issues raised by state organs and to issue timely responses (see Figure 11.1). In this regard, tracked monitoring became the first important instrument for exercising top-down implementation control. (Further details are provided in the next section.)

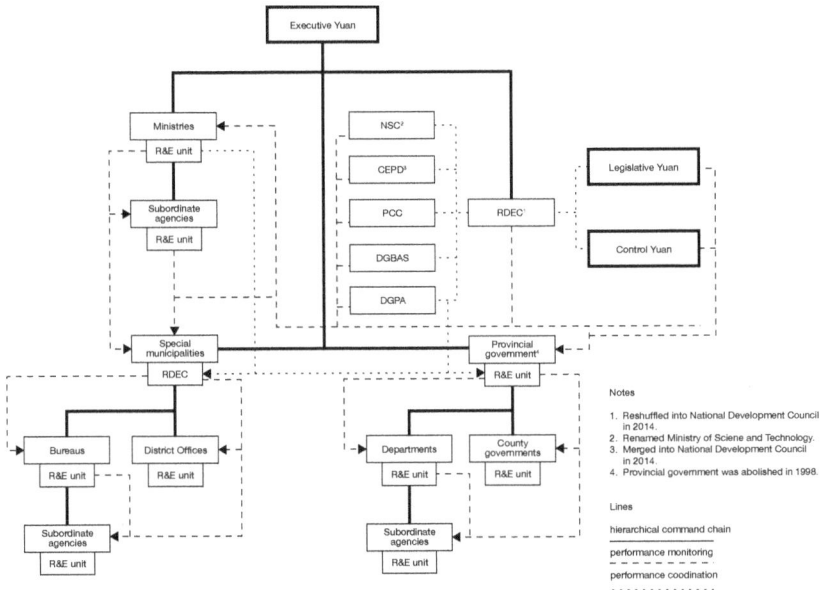

Figure 11.1. Performance regime of Taiwan

Source. Bennis Wai Yip So

With Wei Yung, a US-trained professor of political science, assuming the role of minister of the RDEC in 1976, the function of the RDEC further expanded, especially in terms of capacity building of the government. This included strengthening comprehensive and long-term policy planning and introducing computer and office automation technology to government offices. Foreign impact became increasingly manifest during his 12-year ministership. US public administration and policy science and its state-of-the-art policy research techniques (e.g. the use of opinion polls) were transferred to Taiwan. This second wave of performance movements remained policy-oriented (Wei 2004); for instance, policy implementation remained a focus point for the RDEC's research up to the early 1990s (RDEC 1994). Furthermore, under the authoritarian setting, the learning was instrumental in strengthening the state's capacity and the rationale of policymaking, even though the for-the-people service had been instigated at this stage. (Further details are provided in the next section.)

The RDEC was a powerful arm of the Executive Yuan before democratisation, directly monitoring and shaping the performance of government agencies nationwide. The Executive Yuan also assigned the RDEC ad hoc tasks to settle various public policy issues and bureaucratic conflicts, exemplified by its effort to help integrate scattered health insurance systems, which had been developed or overseen by various government departments, into a uniform system in the early 1990s (RDEC 1996). However, the RDEC has never extended into the financial domain to become a super ministry. Hence, its authority is somewhat different from the Office of Management and Budget (OMB) in the United States.

In general, the role of the RDEC can be compared to a 'technostructure' of the 'machine bureaucracy' under the structural configurations of Henry Mintzberg (1979). The technostructure is located between the 'strategic apex' at the top and the 'operating core' at the bottom, but it is not part of 'middle line' management and lies outside the basic flow of operating work. The technostructure serves as an analytical unit to standardise the work of other units and to apply analytical techniques that help organisations adapt to their environment.

During the democratisation process of the 1990s, in the third wave of performance movements, the RDEC's power gradually declined in parallel with ebbing authoritarianism. Workload pressures on the RDEC also entailed the concentration of its functions on key missions. The rise of local autonomy made local governments more accountable to the local people than to the central government. The RDEC thus repositioned itself as a facilitator of administrative reforms. Government agencies were required to monitor their performance with pre-existing management tools, except for those issues and policies spotlighted by the central government.

The RDEC/NDC only provided incentives to improve performance (such as offering government service awards) and started promoting the use of performance information for indicator setting. A former minister of the RDEC told the author that the RDEC/NDC is now engaged in 'coordination rather than control, service rather than tracking'. The machine bureaucracy has been transformed into a 'divisionalised form' of structure whereby the central government only designs the overall performance control system and local governments have their own technostructure to steer the performance of their agencies (Mintzberg 1979: 390).

Furthermore, the concept of NPM diffused into Taiwan and the performance movement appeared more management-oriented. The notion of direct responsiveness to the public was introduced. The RDEC promoted a customer-oriented total quality management approach that required frontline agencies to develop diverse, tailor-made services for their communities. After the Democratic Progressive Party's (DPP) assumption of power in 2000, the government further revamped the outmoded year-end achievement evaluation into a performance evaluation by imitating the *Government Performance and Results Act 1993* of the United States, associating the ex post facto evaluation with performance indicators set under an ex ante strategic plan. Performance evaluations outside the domain of the RDEC now also adopt a similar model. Despite the imitation, this wave of performance movements was less driven by fiscal restraint in Taiwan than was the case in the United States, even though performance-based budgeting was adopted (Lee & Wang 2009).[3] This can be partially explained by the fact that the RDEC/NDC has never taken charge of or overseen a budget and finances, unlike the OMB. After two ruling-party turnovers in 2008 and 2016 and the restructuring of the Executive Yuan in the early 2010s, the basic structure of the performance regime has, to date, remained intact.

Shifting techniques of performance interventions

The emergence of the performance regime can be reviewed by considering the transformation of performance interventions. The following does not describe all the tools adopted but examines a selection of those major tools that illustrate the shifting focuses of accountability relationships and the impact of foreign developments.

Tracked monitoring

As noted earlier, tracked monitoring was the first instrument used for performance management. It contains self-developed procedures to ensure the implementation of policy programs or orders and can be compared to a form of 'process evaluation' (Weiss 1998). Any policy

---

3   The evaluation of budgetary performance in Taiwan mainly measures the spending ratio; it does not have any practices for cutback management or savings.

program, public issue, official resolution (including the ruling party's during the authoritarian era) and assignment by higher up authorities, can be identified as a target for tracked monitoring. Priorities are set for various targets. Higher level R&E agencies track key targets, while the agency-in-charge self-monitors the non-key targets and regularly reports on progress. The attainment of these targets under tracked monitoring are counted in the year-end achievement/performance evaluation. Since 2001, targets have been classified into three levels in accordance with their significance: Executive Yuan, ministry and sub-ministry. Those classified into the Executive Yuan level are tracked by the RDEC. The R&E units affiliated with the respective ministries or the agencies-in-charge track the remainder.

Tracked monitoring is not simply a control function and was originally considered a method to facilitate the implementation of development projects. In its earliest practice, the RDEC transplanted some US enterprise management techniques, such as management by objective and program evaluation and review techniques, into the executive agencies during the process of tracked monitoring (Wei 1986: 2–3). This contributed to the Ten Major Construction Projects in the 1970s (RDEC 1980: 73–88). In addition, once a program or project encountered a bottleneck, the RDEC would be directly engaged in problem-solving and sending officers to the site to help settle problems. It was especially effective for resolving issues involving inter-agency coordination and excessive red tape. Chiang's ATS address promoted such site visits for monitoring work progress (Chiang 1954: 40).

The procedures of tracked monitoring remain in use even now; however, its positive effects and impacts have been challenged and questioned in the democratisation era due to a growing formalism that does not adequately report actual performance (Tsao 1999). Recently, frontline officials reportedly condemned the procedures as time-wasting paperwork (Yu Kai 2016).

From achievement to performance evaluation

If tracked monitoring is a process evaluation, then the achievement/performance evaluation is an outcome evaluation. It is a year-end organisation-based evaluation that assesses the overall performance of government agencies. Its origin can be traced back to the evaluation exercise promoted during the Kuomintang's rule on the mainland.

The version in Taiwan, originally called 'achievement evaluation', was launched in 1951 and managed by the secretariat of the Executive Yuan. The RDEC took over the exercise from its launch and conducted it in collaboration with the CEPD; the NSC; the Directorate-General of Budget, Accounting and Statistics (DGBAS) (the state organ for fiscal control); and the Directorate-General of Personnel Administration (DGPA) (the state personnel agency).

The performance scrutiny originally involved a written report and a site visit, but the site visit was only carried out once because of the time and resources that it consumed. From 1971, the evaluation exercise mainly focused on the targets of tracked monitoring (RDEC 1999a: 101–02), and a site investigation was conducted if necessary. In this early period, the assessment was descriptive and subjective. Agencies received comments on their performance but were not privy to their rating grade (Ho 1993).

In the 1990s decentralisation promoted self-monitoring of performance and the evaluation exercise only focused on the targets prioritised by the Executive Yuan. Personnel and fiscal performances were separately and respectively assessed by the DGBAS and the DGPA (RDEC 1999a). During this stage, an incentive system was introduced in which the evaluation result would incur a reward or penalty imposed on the officials-in-charge (Ho 1993).

Since the accession to power of the DPP in 2000, the evaluation has been renamed a 'performance evaluation' and it is linked with key performance indicators set by agencies, with common targets shared by all agencies, such as achieving at least the cost cutting of a service, service-standard promotion or customer satisfaction (Chang 2004). The evaluation is more quantitative and result-oriented and involves independent scholars and experts, and the evaluation report and result is disclosed to the public. This laid down a foundation of 'accountability for performance'; however, the performance information has not attracted much attention from the Legislative Yuan. Legislators do not take it into account in their budget review because the budget allocation remains a consequence of political bargaining rather than rational analysis (Chang 2013).

Despite the poor use of performance information arising from the RDEC's evaluation exercise, the practices of evaluation have diffused into other domains and have had a substantial effect. For instance, the performance evaluation of social welfare programs since 2001 has been conducted with a similar model and helps project a complicated institutional context under democratisation. This annual exercise to assess the performance of social welfare programs run by local governments involves a written report and a site visit. In light of the burden involved, however, since 2005, the site visit has only been carried out in alternate years.

Various central government agencies manage this evaluation, including the Ministry of Health and Welfare, DGBAS and the National Treasury Administration. For the site visit, evaluation teams are sent to each local government for one day to scrutinise their self-evaluation reports and, if necessary, to question the officer in charge. The evaluation teams are composed of officials from the central government agencies in charge of the relevant policy, as well as scholars and delegates from social welfare organisations. They examine the self-evaluation report and rate every item in accordance with given performance rating criteria. At the end of the process, the performance grades of all local governments are publicly released. Those local governments whose aggregate scores are less than 80 (full score: 100) suffer a cut in their general grant allocated by the central government.

The setting of performance indicators is not solely determined by the central government agencies. Review committees are formed for formulating the indicators for different dimensions of social welfare. All committees are composed of delegates from central government agencies, social welfare organisations and local governments, and scholars. They make adjustments to indicator settings for each exercise based on majority rule. The formulation of performance indicators resembles a participatory process, with all players able to shape the mechanism used. This results in a complicated stakeholder evaluation model that multiplies those to whom local governments are held accountable. Although local implementers can participate in the formulation of indicators, they are held accountable not only to the central government (vertically) but also to other stakeholders (horizontally).

From for-the-people service to quality management

If the ex post facto performance evaluation continues, to a large extent, responding to higher up authorities, a complementary approach to introducing the 'for-the-people service' was supposed to enhance responsiveness to the general public. The idea of for-the-people service was put forward by the then newly appointed premier Chiang Ching-kuo (son and successor of Chiang Kai-shek) in 1972, and it was enacted by the RDEC during the ministership of Wei Yung. A special taskforce under the RDEC was formed to hasten the service improvement of frontline agencies, especially in terms of streamlining administrative procedures (RDEC 1999b: 23–26). Note that there was no causality between the idea of for-the-people service and democracy. What Chiang wanted to promote was an ideal attitude of public servants towards the public that, he thought, should be 'like parents treating their own children with a benevolent heart' (Ministry of Civil Service 1986: 56). In this vein, we should consider it a sort of 'Chinese-style paternalism'.

Wei realised Chiang's new order by accounting for public opinion (collected from an opinion poll) through an instrument of 'system analysis', but he defined for-the-people service as 'government making use of its resources, manpower and policies to maximise the welfare for [the] majority of the people … [through] enhancing administrative efficiency, streamlining legal and administrative procedures' (Wei 1987: 56). This seems an elite-driven 'welfare economics approach' to judging what the people's wellbeing should be.

The idea of total quality management diffused into Taiwan in the mid-1990s, transforming for-the-people service into a 'program for enhancing total service quality' in 1996. The notion of customer orientation was thus introduced. Subsequently, the Service Quality Award of the Executive Yuan (1998–2007), Government Service Quality Award (2008–16), and Government Service Award (2017–) were organised by the RDEC/NDC to encourage government agencies to actively improve their services. This practice is, to a certain extent, similar to the Beacon Scheme for local governments in the United Kingdom (Radnor 2009), which aims to disseminate best practices by encouraging applications for the award.

Different from for-the-people service, quality management now requires the participation of frontline officials in devising innovative services and directly responding to the public, whereas for-the-people services were devised by external experts, with recommendations subsequently forwarded to the agencies for adoption (RDEC 1989b: 23).

Discussion and conclusion

At first glance, the performance movements of Anglophone countries and Taiwan are similar, especially in recent NPM-styled reforms and Taiwan's performance interventions have not gone beyond the UK Government's approach. This is not, however, simply a diffusion of the Anglophone experience into Taiwan, albeit with explicit instrumental learning and sharing of similar rhetoric. Both have worked in tandem with each other, and Taiwan has its own path, agenda and institutions.

First, the root of the movements was locally generated, and some fundamental notions behind the performance regime and means of performance interventions stem from the Kuomintang's rule in Mainland China, such as the policy-oriented ATS and the practice of performance evaluation exercises. Interestingly, certain basic ideas resemble the contemporary performance movement. This coincidence may reflect some universal principles of performance interventions.

Despite this coincidence, Taiwan's performance movements have proceeded in a unique context, in terms of a transition from an authoritarian regime to a democracy. This demonstrates the different demands of performance management that led to an alternative path to that of Anglophone countries, which sheds light on the performance regime of other transitional states, especially Communist China.

Taiwan has experienced three waves of performance movements since the founding of the RDEC. These movements gradually shifted from a policy to a management orientation. Implementation was the first concern and it underscored the state's intention to build up the function of vertical accountability through process controls during the authoritarian era. Incessant renovations of ex post facto evaluation during the first two waves of movements, albeit less significant, realised the same function as outcome evaluation, but its transformation into an NPM-styled performance evaluation after 2000 has turned it into a function of public accountability. The rise of for-the-people service during the second wave of movements marked the first attempt at building public accountability during the late authoritarian era. The third wave's encouragement of innovation in frontline service through quality management further hastened direct bureaucratic responsiveness to the public.

In terms of the agenda, however, the movements were less fiscally driven and did not serve any purpose of depoliticisation, unlike in the Anglosphere counterparts and some Western European countries where professionalisation, in terms of developing neutral competence and professional autonomy, was a critical element (Kearney & Sinha 1988; Farazmand 1997; Peters & Pierre 2004). Taiwan's movements only expanded the bureaucrats' political responsiveness, with the ruling party responding directly to the public. It seems that the performance movements during the transition from authoritarianism to democracy have not passed through a process of depoliticisation.

Furthermore, Taiwan started its performance movement with the purpose of establishing an 'omnipotent government', which is a catch-up form of developmentalism engaged in by a developing country, but also a sort of state paternalism. This legacy is apparent today, even though Taiwan's democratic governments have never resurrected this symbol or slogan. State interventionism sponsored by developmentalism and paternalism has been sustained and further upheld under the enhanced legitimacy of democracy, especially as Taiwan has experienced an economic recession since the beginning of the 21st century.[4]

Lastly, Taiwan established a unique performance regime, in terms of the R&E system that sprang from the authoritarian regime and continued to evolve during democratisation. The RDEC/NDC and other R&E units have been playing the role of performance coordinators between executive agencies, decision-making bodies and other oversight institutions. Their powerful role in monitoring and directing performance in the authoritarian era, however, has faded. Now, the R&E system offers instruments and incentives to agencies to improve performance.

The system remains the key engine that triggers administrative reforms, even though it is less connected with the fiscal aspect. To be sure, democratisation has complicated the institutional context of the performance regime, especially with the increased engagement of various stakeholders in performance management. This phenomenon is still evolving. Further research is warranted for inquiring into its consequences.

---

4   Taiwan is considered to be one of East Asia's 'developmental states' in which a high degree of state interventionism spurred its economic takeoff during the authoritarian era (Wade 1990; Vartiainen 1999). Despite the growth of neoliberalism since democratisation, the state attempted to maintain the statist approach to development, despite its lack of success (Chu 2002; Wong 2006). When the thesis of illiberal democracy is applied to East Asia, some scholars argue that democratisation would not lead to the decline of state interventionism (Bell et al. 1995).

References

Bell, DA et al. (eds) 1995, *Towards Illiberal Democracy in Pacific Asia*, St Martin Press, New York, doi.org/10.1057/9780230376410.

Chang, B-S 2004, 'Current situation of implementing performance evaluation of administrative agencies', in RDEC (ed), *Government Performance Evaluation*, Taipei, pp 175–90.

Chang, S-M 2013, *A Review and Renovation of Government Performance Management System in Taiwan*, RDEC-RES-101-003, Taipei.

Chiang, K-S 1954 (1940), *Outline of Administrative Trinity System*, Central Material Supply Center, Taipei.

Chu, Y-H 2002, 'Re-engineering the developmental state in an age of globalization: Taiwan in defiance of neo-liberalism', *The China Review*, vol 2, no 1, pp 29–59.

Farazmand, A 1997, 'Professionalism, bureaucracy, and modern governance: a comparative analysis', in *Modern Systems of Government: Explaining the Role of Bureaucrats and Politicians*, Sage, Thousand Oaks, California, pp 48–73, doi.org/10.4135/9781483327938.n2.

Ho, S-L 1993, 'Operational ideas and practices of the current achievement evaluation of administrative agencies', in RDEC (ed), *Selective Collection of Administrative Performance Evaluation No. 1*, Taipei, pp 1–41.

Kearney, R & Sinha, C 1988, 'Professionalism and bureaucratic responsiveness: conflict or compatibility?', *Public Administration Review*, vol 48, no 1, pp 571–79, doi.org/10.2307/975521.

Lee, JY-J & Wang, X 2009, 'Assessing the impact of performance-based budgeting: a comparative analysis across the United States, Taiwan, and China', *Public Administration Review*, vol 69, no s1, pp S60–S66, doi.org/10.1111/j.1540-6210.2009.02090.x.

Li, CH 1953, *Administration Trinity System*, China Local Self-Governance Association, Taipei.

Ministry of Civil Service 1986, *Selective Collection of Administrative Management Essays*, Ministry of Civil Service, Taipei.

Mintzberg, H 1979, *The Structuring of Organizations*, Prentice-Hall Inc, Englewood Cliffs, New Jersey.

Osborne, D & Gaebler, T 1992, *Reinventing Government: How the Entrepreneurial Spirit is Transforming the Public Sector*, Addison-Wesley, Reading.

Peters, BG & Pierre, J (eds) 2004, *Politicization of the Civil Service in Comparative Perspective: the Quest for Control*, Routledge, London, doi.org/10.4324/9780203799857.

PWEC (Party–Government Work Evaluation Commission) 1941, *Rules of Evaluation of Party–Government Works*, Party–Government Work Evaluation Commission, Taipei.

Radnor, Z 2009, 'Understanding the relationship between a national award scheme and performance', *International Review of Administrative Sciences*, vol 75, no 3 pp 437–57, doi.org/10.1177/0020852309337689.

RDEC (Research, Development and Evaluation Commission) 1980, *Establishment and Development of Research and Evaluation System*, Taipei.

—— 1989a, *Selected Collection of Speeches on Administrative Management of Late President Chiang Kai-shek*, Taipei.

—— 1989b, *The 20th Anniversaries of RDEC: A Special Issue*, Taipei.

—— 1994, *Theory Building of Strengthening Policy Implementability*, Taipei.

—— 1996, *Case Collection of Putting Forward the Tracked Monitoring for Exercising Control (1993–96)*, Taipei.

—— 1999a, *30 Years of Research and Evaluation System: The 30th Anniversaries of RDEC*, Taipei.

—— 1999b, *Establishment and Development of the R&E System in the Government of Republic of China*, Taipei.

Talbot, C 2008, 'Performance regimes – context of performance policies', *International Journal of Public Administration*, vol 31, pp 1569–91, doi.org/10.1080/01900690802199437.

—— 2010, *Theories of Performance: Organizational and Service Improvement in the Public Domain*, Oxford University Press.

Tsao, J-H 1999, *A Study of Functional Integration of Staff Agencies under the Executive Yuan*, Taipei.

van Dooren, W 2008, 'Nothing new under the sun? Change and continuity in the twentieth-century performance movements', in W van Dooren & S van de Walle (ed), *Performance Information in the Public Sector: How It is Used*, Palgrave Macmillan, London, pp 11–23, doi.org/10.1007/978-1-137-10541-7_2.

van Dooren, W, Bouckaert, G & Halligan, J 2015, *Performance Management in the Public Sector*, 2nd edn, Routledge, London.

Vartiainen, J 1999, 'The economics of successful state intervention in industrial transformation', in M Woo-Cumings (ed), *The Developmental State*, Cornell University Press, Ithaca, pp 200–34.

Wade, R 1990, *Governing the Market: Economic Theory and the Role of Government in East Asian Industrialization*, Princeton University Press, doi.org/10.1515/9780691187181.

Wei, Y 1986, 'The current situation and the key issues of future effort of "control" and "evaluation" operation', in RDEC (ed), *Collection Works of Evaluation and Assessment*, Taipei, pp 1–13.

—— 1987, 'Essential ideas and key points for promoting the for-the-people service', *R&E Monthly*, vol 11, no 6, pp 3–9.

—— 2004, *Introduction to Public Policy*, Wunan, Taipei.

Weiss, CH 1998, *Evaluation: Methods for Studying Programs and Policies*, 2nd edn, Prentice Hall, Upper Saddle River, New Jersey.

Williams, DW 2003, 'Measuring government in the early twentieth century', *Public Administration Review*, vol 63, no 6, pp 643–59, doi.org/10.1111/1540-6210.00329.

Wilson, W 1887, 'The study of administration', *Political Science Quarterly*, vol 2, no 2, pp 197–222, doi.org/10.2307/2139277.

Wong, J 2006, 'Technovation in Taiwan: implications for industrial governance', *Governance*, vol 19, no 4, pp 651–72, doi.org/10.1111/j.1468-0491.2006.00332.x.

Yu Kai 2016, *Take-Off of Rookies in the Public Sector*, Locus Publishing, Taipei.

CONCLUSION

Lessons and continuing challenges for greater China and Australia

Andrew Podger

The different social and economic contexts that prevail in one nation compared to another, and their different histories and institutional arrangements, limit the transfer of experience across nations including the applicability of governance structures. According to Rudolf Klein, to 'learn from' you must first 'learn about' (Klein 2009). Moreover, international pressure for 'policy learning' and 'policy transfer' can have deleterious effects. The differences between the People's Republic of China (PRC) and Australia make this advice particularly apposite.

Notwithstanding its much longer history and the richness of its past experience in government administration, China is in the midst of an extraordinary transition in which it is actively considering lessons from elsewhere that it might adapt to its institutional framework. The transition is not just from a developing country to a more advanced economy but also from a political command economy to a more market-oriented approach in which government plays a different role and is subject to new forms of social accountability for performance (Ma 2009). The emerging concepts of accountability and performance have yet to be fully institutionalised, and are most unlikely even in the longer term to reflect a democratic system of government such as Australia's (Podger & Chan forthcoming).

Of course, even in Australia, the concepts of accountability and performance continue to evolve. This is evidenced by new public management's (NPM) shift to management for results (or 'outputs and outcomes') as distinct from a focus on conformance with rules and processes (or 'inputs'), and by new public governance's (NPG) encouragement of 'outwards' accountability direct to clients and citizens in conjunction with standard 'upwards' accountability through the democratic parliamentary process. Sadly, Australia is now shifting to a narrower focus on implementation of politically determined policies and priorities and away from consideration of the overall impact of both policy and management.

Despite the remarkable developments in China over the last 40 years, its outstanding reform agenda remains substantial and it is important to recognise that the country is still in transition. Unlike many Western nations in which systemic 'checks and balances' act as forms of institutional controls, China's system of government is based primarily on hierarchic control, but within a highly devolved regional and local context. At the highest political level is the legislature (the People's Congress), the executive (the State Council) and the judiciary, and their relationship with the Communist Party of China (CPC); also the respective roles and responsibilities of China's five levels of government. For the most part, these constitutional structures are *not* the focus of this book, though undoubtedly they must shape other institutional structures.

The continuing reform agenda that is relevant to the focus of this book concerns the institutional framework within the executive arm of government. This includes the structure of 'core' ministries and their coordination arrangements; the structures for 'non-core' organisations including public service delivery agencies (and arrangements for non-government organisations (NGOs) engaged to assist in service delivery), regulatory agencies, various 'integrity' agencies that oversee other parts of government, and state-owned enterprises; and frameworks for horizontal management.

This description of the elements of the continuing reform agenda reflects the cascading classification of government functions commonly used in Australia and other democracies, and may not be relevant to China's more organic institutional framework today or into the future.

For example, central to the discussion in several of the chapters in this book that focus on circumstances in Australia is consideration of the appropriate level of administrative independence from politics for performing different functions. That is not the Chinese approach, where the fusion of politics and administration is seen as 'a positive step to stable, adaptable, highly competent, rule-based and legitimacy-enhancing administration' (Chan 2016). Yet this idea of a degree of independence, or relative autonomy, may have more relevance than is formally recognised in China at present, as it may still be appropriate to vary the balance between conformity and flexibility, and between political control and professional independence, with different functions. Moreover, the forces that led to some separation of politics from administration in Western democracies in the 19th century (and the forces that led to concepts such as the separation of powers in the 18th and 19th centuries, and the more recent neoliberal measures expanding market forces including within government) are affecting China today. These include the importance of professional expertise, the need to contain corruption and to promote efficiency, administrative and budgetary reform agendas, the need to apply regulation fairly and consistently, the importance of serving all citizens equitably and justly and, at the international level, the need to apply agreed standards on free trade and other aspects of international interaction.

Modern Chinese ideas such as 'social accountability' rely upon increased transparency and professionalism, which in turn require standards of integrity that are not just set politically, but often by bureaucratic edicts, reflecting society norms set more widely – including by professions and internationally. As discussed in *Value for Money* (Podger et al. 2018), which was compiled from the 2015 workshop of the Greater China Australia Dialogue on Public Administration, China has been pursuing an ambitious agenda of financial management and budgetary reform drawing heavily on the experience of Organisation for Economic Co-operation and Development (OECD) countries, including Australia. Increasingly implicit in these reforms are similar (if evolving) concepts of performance and accountability explored in this book on institutional structures.

Despite the apparent slowing down of reforms over the last few years under President Xi Jinping, which are referred to in Chapter 1, further administrative and organisational reform is very likely to be required to maintain China's economic growth and to meet the growing expectations of its people. Institutional reform will be a key part of this agenda. My view is that this will need to include:

- further strengthening of the policy and coordination capacity of the core ministries, building on the modernising measures already undertaken via umbrella agencies and coordinating bodies

- reviewing the governance of non-core agencies including:
  - public service institutions such as schools, hospitals and universities to strengthen their professional competence and performance in terms of outputs and impact, and to clarify good practice in the outsourcing of service delivery to non-government organisations
  - greater alignment between levels of government, especially over the central government's mandates and the capacities of provincial and lower level governments to meet central expectations
  - regulatory bodies to strengthen their competence and consistency and reliability, so as to improve their effectiveness
  - 'integrity' agencies, clarifying what functions should be categorised as such, ensuring their capacity to 'speak truth to power' and reviewing their relationship with the legislature as well as the executive
  - the development of more transparent reporting of performance to citizens and the community by jurisdictions and public sector organisations on matters of targets, milestones, service delivery standards and satisfaction levels
  - state-owned enterprises, building on the major reforms already implemented, and addressing outstanding issues arising from WTO obligations and wider international concerns about competitive neutrality (recognising that there is no single approach even across the OECD to ownership of public enterprises)
- clarifying good practice in horizontal as well as vertical management, including by drawing on the lessons from studies such as those in chapters 8 and 9.

Much of this reform to improve accountability, capability and performance could be advanced notwithstanding the firmer CPC control evident under Xi; aspects, however, would require allowing more flexibility and autonomy subject to open performance scrutiny. As Chapter 1 concludes, the appropriate degree of autonomy should vary with the function of the organisation.

The chapters that focus on Australia demonstrate that institutional reform is an ongoing challenge including for countries with mature systems of civil service administration within well-established political systems. For example, there is clearly room to improve Australia's utilisation of NGOs in the delivery of services and to achieve the aim of citizen-centred services.

Those chapters also identify the risks from slowing or backsliding reform. Australia has got the balance between political control and autonomy wrong in some fields in recent years, thereby undermining civil service capability and performance (this is a reversal of the concerns over excessive independence expressed widely in the 1970s and 1980s) (Podger 2019).

Australia could also learn from China without compromising its firm attachment to democratic principles and to the separation of politics from administration. Lessons may be drawn in particular from China's management of reform – its systematic use of experimentation before finalising national policies and promoting implementation across the country. These experiments may be initiated locally or be pilots established by the national government in cooperation with selected local governments. China's unitary system also ensures close vertical links within ministries that could be worth closer examination in Australia without compromising Australia's federal approach. China's arrangements support more shared learning between tiers of government, and provides opportunities for the national government to articulate minimum standards to be achieved (such as in health care, poverty alleviation, air pollution and crime prevention) and to promote particular national priorities (such as infrastructure investment). One downside to Australia's approach to the separation of politics from administration is the risk of politics being immersed in immediate issues and becoming stridently populist. The resulting chopping and changing of policy in an atmosphere of hyper-partisanship and diminished appreciation of expertise and the importance of longer term strategic reform, are increasingly apparent in Western democracies (Wanna 2016). While China's structural arrangements have avoided this in a way that will remain inapplicable in Australia, aspects of Chinese practice are worth reflecting upon.

China's challenge is not only to continue with its multilayered reform agenda to clarify institutional roles and responsibilities and governance arrangements, but also to address new pressures resembling those emerging in many developed countries, such as Australia, to provide more responsive citizen-centred services, to ensure high-quality and effective regulation and to sustain capability and productivity.

References

Chan, H 2016, 'The making of Chinese civil service law: ideals, technicalities and realities', *American Review of Public Administration*, vol 46, no 4, pp 379–98.

Klein, R 2009, 'Learning from others and learning from mistakes: reflections on health policy making', in T Marmor, R Freeman & K Okma (eds), *Comparative Studies and the Politics of Modern Medical Care*, Yale University.

Ma, J 2009, 'The dilemma of developing financial accountability without election', *Australian Journal of Public Administration*, vol 68, no 1, pp 62–72.

Podger, A 2019, 'Protecting and nurturing the Australian Public Service', Australian Parliamentary Library Lecture, 11 Sep.

Podger, A & Chan, H (forthcoming), 'The challenge of comparing public administration in China and Australia: developments and prospects for China', in A De Percy & A Podger (eds), *Public Administration in Practice: Essays in honour of John Wanna*.

Podger, A & Su, T, Wanna, J, Chan, H & Niu, M (eds) 2018, *Value for Money: Budget and Financial Management Reform in the People's Republic of China, Taiwan and Australia*, ANU Press, Canberra. doi.org/10.22459/VM.01.2018.

Wanna, J 2016, 'Pro-activism in the face of systematic trends to hyper-government', in Australia and New Zealand School of Government, *Hyper-Government: Managing and Thriving in Turbulent Times, Conference Highlights*, www.anzsog.edu.au/documents/14-annual-conference-2016-highlights-report/file.